A Development Strategy for Iran through the 1980s

Robert E. Looney

The Praeger Special Studies program—utilizing the most modern and efficient book production techniques and a selective worldwide distribution network—makes available to the academic, government, and business communities significant, timely research in U.S. and international economic, social, and political development.

A Development Strategy for Iran through the 1980s

PRAEGER SPECIAL STUDIES IN INTERNATIONAL ECONOMICS AND DEVELOPMENT

Praeger Publishers   New York   London

Library of Congress Cataloging in Publication Data

Looney, Robert E
   A development strategy for Iran through the 1980s.

   (Praeger special studies in international economics and development)
      Bibliography: p. 191
      Includes index.
      1. Iran—Economic conditions—1945-
2. Iran—Economic policy. I. Title.
HC475.L635 1977   338.955   75-44936
ISBN 0-03-021956-6

PRAEGER SPECIAL STUDIES
200 Park Avenue, New York, N.Y., 10017, U.S.A.

Published in the United States of America in 1977
by Praeger Publishers,
A Division of Holt, Rinehart and Winston, CBS, Inc.

789   038   987654321

© 1977 by Praeger Publishers

All rights reserved

Printed in the United States of America

PREFACE

This volume is intended to bring up to date, and indeed to extend, some of the principal findings of the author's earlier book, The Economic Development of Iran: A Recent Survey with Projections to 1981.[1] That book, written in late 1972 and early 1973, took into account several oil agreements signed by Iran in 1971 and 1972 that greatly increased the government's revenues. The increase in revenues was in turn used to evaluate the country's development potential during the country's Fifth (1973-77) and Sixth (1978-82) Five-Year Plans.

Since the publication of my earlier book, the well-publicized increases in oil revenues brought about by the OPEC price increases of late 1973 and early 1974,[2] and also a fundamental change in Iran's development strategy, have occurred. The nation's development priorities have been reformulated in a revised Fifth Plan[3] and implemented through a sweeping reorganization of the Iranian bureaucracy. These dramatic changes warrant a new examination of the Iranian economy, one intended: to analyze the impact of the increased oil revenues on the economy of Iran; to assess the implications of the revised Fifth Plan's allocations as they pertain to the country's development through the 1980s; to determine the effectiveness of the government in managing the economy in light of such problems as increased inflationary pressures; and, on the basis of the first three considerations, to outline a feasible development strategy for the sixth and seventh development plans, that is, for the period from 1978-88.

While my earlier study was made without considering the policies, either domestic and foreign of other countries, this approach is no longer realistic. To a large extent, what will happen in Iran during the remaining years of the 1970s and 1980s will be determined not only by the actions of the other members of OPEC, but also by the major consuming countries.[4] Thus, a number of reasons call for a reconsideration of the methodology used and of the projections made in the initial study.

The book is directed primarily toward development officials, scholars, and businessmen outside of Iran, but I am hopeful that my Iranian friends will also find it informative. It is certainly immodest for an outsider to presume to tell Iranians about themselves. Yet, sometimes an outside observer who is familiar with other countries at a similar stage of development can see certain parallels that may be missed by an overworked planner or government official in Iran. In addition, sometimes an outside observer familiar with, but not a regular participant in, the hectic pace of the Iranian development effort is able to identify trends, forces, and implications that are not easily perceived by those who are involved on a day-to-day basis with the country's development process.

NOTES

1. Robert Looney, The Economic Development of Iran: A Recent Survey with Projections to 1981 (New York: Praeger, 1973).

2. An excellent account of this period, and an evaluation of the prospects for oil prices, is given in Dankwart A. Rustow and John F. Mungo, OPEC: Success and Prospects (New York: New York University Press, 1976).

3. Iran, Plan and Budget Organization, Iran's Fifth Development Plan 1973-1978, Revised—A Summary (Tehran: Plan and Budget Organization, 1975).

4. A number of options are given in Edward R. Fried and Charles L. Schultze, eds., Higher Oil Prices and the World Economy—The Adjustment Problem (Washington, D.C.: Brookings Institution, 1975). See also Khodadad Farmanfarmaian, et al., "How Can the World Afford OPEC Oil?" Foreign Affairs 53, no. 2 (January 1975): 201-22.

ACKNOWLEDGMENTS

The individuals in Iran who assisted me are so numerous that I cannot mention all of them. During my field work many former and present government officials were kind enough to make time for me in their crowded schedules. Among these were Ahmad Ashraf, director, Division of Planning for Social Development, National University; Reza Doroudian, undersecretary for economic affairs, Ministry of Cooperatives and Rural Affairs; Hormaz Farhat, vice-chancellor, University of Farabi; Ahmed Kooros, deputy, Bank Markazi Iran; A. S. Schaheen, Ministry of Economy; Guido Schanerocheen, Iranian Ministry of Economy Export Promotion Trade Center; Amhad Sabouchi, director, Research Arya Shipping Lines; Constantin Mejloumian, deputy director, Plan and Budget Organization; Firouz Tofigh, deputy minister of state and director of Iran's Statistical Office; Mahmood Tajdar, director general in charge of statistics affairs, Central Bank of Iran; and Firouz Vakil, director, Planometrics and Central Economy Bureau, Plan and Budget Organization.

I am also indebted to many people for their assistance, comments, and suggestions; to Drs. Robert Davenport and Daniel Dick of Stanford Research Institute; and to Dr. Mario Belotti of the University of Santa Clara. But I should make it clear that I assume full responsibility for the final results of this effort.

Finally, I must give special recognition to Christine Tapley, who used her editorial skills to provide highly professional assistance on my manuscript; to my wife, Anne, who reviewed several drafts of the study and made valuable suggestions from her own perspective on Iran; and to Mrs. Judy Thompson and Mrs. Marlene Plumb, who processed the many versions of my draft manuscript with patience, efficiency, and good cheer.

CONTENTS

	Page
PREFACE	v
ACKNOWLEDGMENTS	vii
LIST OF TABLES	xii

Chapter

1 INTRODUCTION 1

    Introduction 1
    The Importance of the Iranian Experience . . . 1
    Scope of the Study 2
    Notes 3

2 THE IRANIAN DEVELOPMENT PROBLEM . . . 4

    Introduction 4
    Recent Developments 5
    Problems Ahead 8
    Constraints on Policy 9
    Conclusions 12
    Notes 13

3 SOURCES OF ECONOMIC GROWTH 14

    Introduction 14
    Sources of Growth 15
    The Role of Oil 18
    Economic Planning 20
    Objectives of the Fifth Plan 23
    Overall Social and Economic Policies and
      Courses 23
    The Revised Fifth Plan 24
    The Dynamic Role of Government 27
    Conclusions 34
    Notes 35

Chapter		Page
4	CONSEQUENCES OF GROWTH	37
	Introduction	37
	Employment	38
	Wages	45
	Income Distribution	46
	Social Security and Social Legislation	51
	Conclusions	52
	Notes	52
5	THE ECONOMY: FOREIGN TRADE	54
	Introduction	54
	Commodity Composition of Imports	54
	Commodity Composition of Exports	59
	Oil and Foreign Trade	60
	Future Developments	65
	Conclusions	67
	Notes	69
6	ALLOCATION OF OIL REVENUES– AGRICULTURE AND AGRARIAN REFORM	70
	Introduction	70
	Characteristics of the Agricultural Sector	73
	Progress in Land Reform	73
	Growth in Production	75
	Current Problems	76
	The Failure of Commercial Farming	78
	Future Trends in Policy	80
	Conclusions	81
	Notes	81
7	THE USE OF OIL REVENUES FOR NATIONAL DEVELOPMENT	83
	Introduction	83
	Domestic Consumption and Investment	84
	Discretionary Spending	86
	Foreign Aid	87
	Defense Expenditures	87
	Domestic Versus Foreign Investment	89
	Oil Revenues and Inflation	92

Chapter		Page
	Conclusions	94
	Notes	95
8	INFLATION	97
	Introduction	97
	Increases in Import Prices	97
	Demand Pull Inflation	99
	The Government's Stabilization Program	106
	A Suggested Income Policy	111
	Conclusions	114
	Notes	115
9	THE EXPERIENCES OF IRAQ, ALGERIA, ECUADOR, AND VENEZUELA	117
	Introduction	117
	Iraq	118
	Algeria	125
	Venezuela	130
	Ecuador	136
	Similarities in Development	140
	Conclusions	141
	Notes	143
10	A DEVELOPMENT STRATEGY FOR IRAN	147
	Introduction	147
	Problems and Policy	148
	Oil Revenues	148
	Forecasts	149
	Future Domestic Economic Challenges	155
	Conclusions	159
	Notes	159

Appendix

A	IRAN IN THE ADELMAN-MORRIS STUDY	161
B	PATTERNS OF INCOME DISTRIBUTION	164
C	INDEXATION OF CRUDE OIL PRICES	166

Appendix		Page
D	STABILITY OF THE IRANIAN ECONOMY	169
E	PROBLEMS OF MONETARY CONTROL	173
F	A MACROECONOMIC MODEL OF IRAN	177
BIBLIOGRAPHY		191
INDEX		203
ABOUT THE AUTHOR		208

LIST OF TABLES

Table		Page
2.1	Major Characteristics of the OPEC Producers	10
3.1	National Income Accounts, 1959-74	16
3.2	Performance During the Third and Fourth Plan Periods	22
3.3	Sectoral Revisions in the Fifth Five-Year Plan	25
3.4	Sectoral Output, 1959-74	29
4.1	Sectoral Distribution of Employment, 1956-72	39
4.2	Occupational Pattern of Employment, 1956-72	40
4.3	Decile Distribution of Household Expenditures, Urban Areas	47
4.4	Decile Distribution of Household Expenditures, 1971	48
4.5	Measures of Inequality of Expenditure in Urban Areas	49
5.1	Composition of Imported Goods, 1959-68	55
5.2	Composition of Imported Goods, 1969-74	57
7.1	Variation in GNP Deflator and Oil Revenues	93
7.2	Rate of Inflation, First Half of 1975 Compared to First Half of 1974	95
8.1	Imports from Iran's Leading Trading Partners	99
8.2	Consolidated Balance Sheet of the Banking System—Liabilities, 1968-74	101
8.3	Factors Responsible for Changes in Money Supply, 1962-73	102

Table		Page
8.4	Credits of the Banking System	103
8.5	Measures of Inflation	107
8.6	Credit Requirements for Ten Percent Real GNP Growth, 1975-82	112
8.7	Credit Requirements for Ten Percent Real GNP Growth, 1983-90	113
9.1	Iraq: Major Economic Trends, 1955-75	120
9.2	Algeria: Major Economic Trends, 1965-75	126
9.3	Venezuela: Major Economic Trends, 1955-75	134
9.4	Ecuador: Major Economic Trends, 1955-75	138
10.1	Forecast of Oil and Gas Revenues	150
10.2	Domestic and Internal Gaps, 1975-82	152
10.3	Domestic and Internal Gaps, 1983-90	153
10.4	External Gaps, 1975-90—Medium Oil Revenues	154
10.5	Financial Surplus, 1975-90	156
E.1	Factors Responsible for Changes in the Money Supply, 1972-75	174
E.2	Foreign Exchange Receipts and Payments, 1972-75	175
F.1	Macroeconomic Model, 1962-74	178
F.2	Impact-Multiplier Matrix Derived from the Macroeconomic Model, 1974	181
F.3	Domestic and External Gaps, 1975-82	182
F.4	Domestic and External Gaps, 1983-90	183

Table		Page
F.5	Domestic and External Gaps, 1975–82	184
F.6	Domestic and External Gaps, 1983–90	185
F.7	External Gap, 1975–90—High Oil Revenues	186
F.8	External Gap, 1975–90—Low Oil Revenues	187
F.9	Financial Surplus, 1975–90	188
F.10	Financial Surplus, 1975–90	189

CHAPTER 1

INTRODUCTION

INTRODUCTION

Iran's extraordinary economic performance has attracted much attention. Over the seven year period from 1970 to 1976, Iran increased its national output by an amount equal to its total cumulative economic growth over all the previous centuries of its history. (This is, of course, a rough approximation.)[1] Such a performance has been matched by relatively few countries, even among the advanced industrial economies.

The Iranian achievement is even more impressive when one considers that the country's growth was achieved concurrently with (until recently) little domestic inflation. The international inflation and the world recession of the mid-1970s have, however, created serious problems, and it appears that Iran will not be able to continue its development drive at the pace maintained in the early 1970s.[2] Iran is now entering a development phase in which a number of consolidations of domestic achievements, and adjustments to the new external environment, must be made before long-run rates of growth can be maintained.

THE IMPORTANCE OF THE IRANIAN EXPERIENCE

Not surprisingly, the attention of U.S., Japanese, Canadian, and European multinational companies seeking opportunities for business expansion has been attracted to Iran. Many officials of other developing countries have been scrutinizing the Iranian experience, seeking policies and practices that might be adapted to their own efforts to accelerate economic growth. Academic scholars, also, have begun focusing attention on Iran in order to obtain new insights into the process of political, social, and economic development.

The Iranian economy has even broader international importance. In a world where the supply of natural resources is becoming scarce relative to growing demand, Iran stands out as one of the few areas with vast potential for increasing the supply of a number of strategic minerals, in addition to oil. The country also possesses a diversity of renewable natural resources.[3] It has only begun to tap its large mineral deposits. It can also significantly expand agricultural output by increasing the amount of land under irrigation and the productivity of those areas currently under cultivation. The country can therefore be counted on, under the right circumstances, to add large amounts of a number of raw materials to world supplies.

The rather recent occurrence of the Iranian economic miracle has meant that the press has been, for most foreigners, the principal source of information on Iran.[4] Iran has received both glowing eulogies and bitter criticism in the foreign press. Business journals by and large have accentuated the economy's positive features, emphasizing the business opportunities created by rapid growth and the political stability maintained by an authoritarian government.[5] Other journalists, frequently joined by scholars, question the ethics of economic development that allegedly has taken place in an environment that has curtailed civil liberties and has permitted the torture of political prisoners. The critics generally point out that, while the economy as a whole is doing well, the great majority of its citizens see little of Iran's newly found wealth.[6]

The Iranian experience is sufficiently significant to warrant a comprehensive analysis that allows the observer to evaluate the nation's recent economic achievement in light of the political and social costs associated with accelerated growth. Iran's development progress gives the nation a chance of becoming one of the first major countries to cross the wide chasm separating the less developed and the developed countries. If it achieves this distinction, while at the same time improving the economic, political, and social quality of life for the majority of its people, Iran will be a source of encouragement and hope for billions of the world's people still in poverty.

SCOPE OF THE STUDY

To contribute toward a better understanding of Iran's medium-term prospects, this book attempts: to provide a long-term overview of Iran's development efforts and accomplishments; to examine in

INTRODUCTION

greater depth the evolutionary patterns in key economic, social, and political sectors; to explain the motive forces and sources of growth; to identify the major problems Iran faces in the future; and to suggest the lessons that might be learned from other countries—namely Iraq, Venezuela, Algeria, and Ecuador—that, in various ways, have had to deal with development problems similar to those facing Iran.

NOTES

1. See Julian Bharier, Economic Development in Iran, 1900-1970 (London: Oxford University Press, 1971). Data on national income for earlier periods, particularly before 1959, is very unreliable.

2. Speculation on how long countries can maintain rates of real growth over 10 percent abounds in the literature. For a recent summary, see Prem Laumas, "A Note of Friedman's Law of Economic Growth," Weltwirtschaftliches Archiv (1975), pp. 116-20.

3. A detailed examination of Iran's resources is given in Marion Clawson, et al., The Agricultural Potential of the Middle East (New York: Elsevier, 1971).

4. One of the better surveys is "A Survey of Iran," The Economist (August 28, 1976), pp. 1-44.

5. See "Trading with OPEC," Financial Times (April 29, 1976), pp. 15-19.

6. Frances Fitzgerald, "Giving the Shah Everything He Wants," Harpers 249, no. 1494 (November 1974): 77.

CHAPTER 2

THE IRANIAN DEVELOPMENT PROBLEM

INTRODUCTION

Despite recent attempts at diversification, the Iranian economy is still dominated by the petroleum sector. Iran is the fourth largest producer, and the second largest exporter, of oil in the world (the largest, of course, being Saudi Arabia). Total oil exports in the last few years (through a consortium of multinational oil companies and via joint ventures between the National Iranian Oil Company and its foreign partners) increased from about 1.3 billion barrels in 1969-70 to about 21 billion barrels (nearly 300 million tons) in 1974-75.[1]

During Iran's fourth development plan (1968-72) oil incomes increased at an annual rate of about 22 percent per annum, and averaged about 75 percent of total foreign exchange receipts earned from the export of goods and services. Eighty percent of these revenues were allocated for development projects. Nonetheless, until the four-fold increase in the posted price of oil under the Kuwait and Tehran agreements, and finally the series of price rises beginning in December 1973 and early 1974, the increase in annual petroleum revenues was not sufficient to pay for the accelerating growth of imported goods and services. The country's balance-of-payments deficits were mainly financed by the public sector; that is, World Bank loans and Eurocurrency bonds, official borrowing by the public sector, and suppliers' credits granted by foreign companies to the private sector.

In the first year of the oil boom (1974), not only did the country's external account show a sizable surplus, thus obviating any need for external borrowing, but a large part of the nation's outstanding loans were repaid prior to their maturity. More specifically, in 1974

THE IRANIAN DEVELOPMENT PROBLEM   5

Iran's current account showed a marked reversal from the net inflow of $590 million in 1972 and $740 million in 1973 to a net estimated outflow of $4,300 million.*

RECENT DEVELOPMENTS

Circumstances in Iran, however, have changed fast, much faster than anyone could have forecast. Few would have imagined that as late as January 1975 the government would be forced to undertake a major stabilization program, that budgets of all the major ministries would be tightened, that Iran, having lent money to Britain and France in 1974, would by mid-1975 be looking to the international market for funds, or that the rial (the nation's currency), which was pegged to the international monetary fund's SDRs (special drawing rights) in February 1975 to ensure against the decline of the value of the dollar,[2] would itself be devalued against the dollar by 1.6 percent.†

Just as the rise in oil prices in 1973-74 showed the strength of an oil-based economy, so the slack international demand for petroleum products between the summers of 1975 and 1976 has exposed its weaknesses. The exceptionally high growth rates in Iran followed the oil price increases, and the resulting escalation of economic activity, could not have been sustained indefinitely without severe distortions of the economy. This became quite clear by the latter part of 1974, as bottlenecks arose from manpower shortages, port congestion, and shortages of a number of essential items, including building materials. The result was inflation, which reached unacceptably high levels. These problems were made more severe when oil revenues fell short of their projected levels.

Indeed, the extent to which oil production and revenues declined has been much greater than anticipated. As a result, the authorities lost much flexibility in their implementation of the necessary domestic stabilization policies. The expanded version of the five-year plan of 1973-78 had allowed virtually no room for maneuver in the event of an oil revenue short fall. The plan has therefore been reduced in many instances to a mere articulation of the government's development intent.

As an indication of the rapid changes in Iran's fortunes, the Fifth Plan (drawn up in early 1973) envisaged the country as having

---

*Unless otherwise stated, currency is in U.S. dollars.
†Iran has decided to define the value of the rial in terms of SDRs rather than dollars. (See "Snags of Indexing Oil Prices," Financial Times [February 14, 1975], p. 4.)

to borrow $6.5 billion from the World Bank and other official lending agencies, in addition to floating bonds in the Euromarket, to finance the plan. After the December 1973 price rises, the planners estimated that the country would actually run a budget surplus of $17.7 billion during the plan period. Following a surplus of $5.2 billion in 1974 (after liquidation of $1.3 billion of its debt) Iran had a deficit of nearly $2.0 billion in fiscal 1975-76 with a similar deficit expected for fiscal 1976-77; the country's oil production in 1975 was down 11.2 percent, particularly because of the lack of demand for its overpriced heavy crude.

Similarly, the gap between foreign exchange receipts and payments has narrowed. While current receipts rose in 1975 by only 4 percent, current payments were up 53 percent, and the balance on current account fell below $3 billion from $8.5 billion the previous year. Worse, the balance on capital account began to deteriorate as a result of increased public and private investment abroad. In the year ending March 20, 1975, the overall balance of payments surplus was $5 billion. But a year later, Iran had an overall deficit of almost $1 billion, despite the fact that imports at $11 billion were lower than most official forecasts.

The balance of payments deficit on current account for 1976 was approximately $3.5 billion and would have been considerably higher if the demand for Iranian oil had not strengthened in the latter part of the year. After a poor first half of 1976 when oil production increased by only 1 percent over the same period in 1975, Iranian crude output showed a substantial increase. Production in August was 5 percent over July and by September had risen to 6.4 million barrels per day, an all time high and nearly 9 percent over the August level.

By the end of 1976 however, Iran's fortunes were again on the down-swing. At the OPEC meeting in Doha Iran, together with the majority of OPEC countries decided to increase oil prices by 10 percent. Because Saudi Arabia and the United Arab Emirates were determined to restrain the price for their oil to 5 percent, Iran's crude quickly became over priced. Output fell by 38 percent in January 1977.

In large part, the government's fiscal difficulties stem from its inability to control expenditure. During the first quarter of the fiscal year that began on April 1, 1975, government spending was up 208 percent over the same period in 1974. During the first three months of the year, 40 percent of the increase in credit to the private sector authorized by the authorities had been utilized.[3] In past years never more than 19 percent had been extended by the central bank during such a period. Some banks, in fact, had utilized their entire allocations for the year and were faced with the prospect of relying solely upon repaid loans as a source of local finance. To secure extra funds they turned to foreign lenders for short-term borrowing. As a result of these developments the domestic money supply was increasing at a rate of almost 60 percent. Much of this credit was used to finance imports, which began averaging $1.2 billion per month—almost 100 percent up in value over the same period in 1974.

Given this increase in credit and expenditures, the drop in world demand for oil had a dramatic effect on the economy. With the drop in foreign receipts in the last quarter of the fiscal year (ending March 21, 1976) to a rate of 2.8 percent, imports, because of back orders, expanded at a rate of 48 percent. Foreign exchange earnings should rise again as the West moves out of recession, but as a trend, receipts are likely to level off while import demand continues to grow. It is clear that the authorities cannot continue to indulge in spending at the unprecedented levels of 1974 and 1975. Moreover, by seeking to develop at such an accelerated pace, the cost of development has risen through demurrage (payments to ships waiting in congested ports), distribution, delays, higher wages, and simple waste.

Iranians are understandably upset at the inefficient manner in which much of the oil windfall has been squandered. In particular they resent the way their economic problems have been presented in the international press. There is a deep sense of hurt at the change from laudatory articles on the Iranian "miracle" to descriptions of economic shambles with allegations of political torture and increasing urban terrorism thrown in for good measure. However, the Shah has set very high standards for Iran, and by these standards the country has been judged. While Iran's development plans have been full of sound aims, they have also been characterized by a number of impractical prestige projects, such as some of the agribusiness ventures in the Khuzestan. In addition, military expenditures have not been cut back,[4] thus leaving the government's development program and the private sector to absorb the entire shortfall in oil revenues.

The doubling of expenditures for the Fifth Plan has, in retrospect, become more a wish fulfillment than a realistic exercise. Now it appears that many of the projects and programs included in the revised Fifth Plan will take at least an extra one or two years to complete. Iran's hope of being able to replace, by the 1990s, its dependence upon oil with a wide manufacturing base capable of sustained growth and substantial export earnings is receding into the distance.

Iran is not alone. Venezuela, Iraq, Ecuador, Algeria, and several other members of the Organization of Petroleum Exporting Countries (OPEC) are also going through a painful period of cutbacks in expenditures as the oil boom begins to subside. While a handful of smaller countries are continuing to generate surpluses far beyond their immediate demands, Iran and the larger oil-producing countries have deficits and are either borrowing on the international markets or cutting back their development programs.* The wilder expectations aroused in these countries in early 1974 have subsided to more reasonable and sober proportions.

PROBLEMS AHEAD

The sharp rise in domestic inflation and the need, by late 1975, to supplement oil revenues by borrowing in international capital markets are only two instances of the Iranian economic crisis that began in mid-1975. There are many others. The basic truth being brought home to the nation is that it is impossible to undertake a massive increase in government investment and heavy private spending in a country with a semiliterate population and an underdeveloped infrastructure without causing inflation. Inflation, in turn, is likely to have side effects that in the long run may inhibit growth.[5]

Despite the fall in oil production below anticipated levels and the prospect of renewed borrowing, the first sentence of the revised Fifth Plan remains valid for reasonable rates of economic growth: "The quadrupling of revenues anticipated from oil during the Fifth Plan from the original $26.8 billion to an estimated $98.2 billion has removed financial constraints on development spending."[6] Iran's current problems may be seen as a temporary phenomenon stemming from attempting to achieve too much too soon. From the beginning of the oil boom, Iranian planners have known that sooner or later their ambitious development plans would be constricted by bottlenecks in transportation and skilled manpower[7]—the real question was, when? Around the summer of 1975 this point was reached, at a time when development spending was just building up the momentum required for full development disbursement during the Fifth Plan period.

The major elements that must be examined in any estimate of future Iranian economic potential are those that will influence the country's response to a significant reduction in the demand for its oil. These include such factors as the country's domestic needs for oil revenues, the Shah's ambition in foreign affairs, the country's perceived obligations to the oil consuming world, domestic needs

---

*Iran is certainly not the only oil exporting country to turn to international borrowing in 1975-76. By the end of 1975, Algeria had contracted up to $5 billion in foreign loans. (Francis Ghiles, "Bankers Have Reasons that Algeria Will Ignore at Its Peril," Euromoney [August 1976], p. 49.)

for oil, and pressures from other oil exporters attempting to increase their share of the market. Since Venezuela, Algeria, Iraq, and Ecuador face a number of similar problems, useful insights into Iran's best course of action through the 1980s can be gained from their experience.

CONSTRAINTS ON POLICY

A number of productive measures can undoubtedly be implemented in Iran on the basis of their success in the countries mentioned above, but the country still must face the fact that it will not have a free hand in determining many of the factors crucial to the success of its long-run development goals. If Iran is to succeed in achieving its long-range plans of economic development it must resolve two central issues with respect to the oil sector—pricing and production levels in the sector, and the time phasing of the total flow of national income from the sector. The former is unlikely to be an urgent issue in the next several years because a series of recent agreements will be in effect during this period.[8] In any case, the country has little room for independent action in this area. As a member of OPEC, Iran has committed itself, more or less, to a unified position with other exporting countries. While the country has maintained that OPEC should increase oil prices, it has had little support from the other members in that regard.[9]

The second issue is more complex and the government has much more discretion in its policies. It can increase future income accruing to the economy at the expense of current income either by limiting the rate of extraction, or by acquiring equity shares in the producing companies of other international firms; that is, it has a certain degree of freedom concerning the time phasing of national income flows from its reserves of oil. To a large extent the total range of government action will be determined by its relative resource position vis-a-vis other OPEC countries. The country's resource position will impose a significant constraint on its production and price policies, and in this sense Iran faces problems similar to those of several other leading OPEC countries.

For purposes of analysis, the 11 principal oil exporters can be put in three major groups, although this classification is obviously somewhat arbitrary[10] (see Table 2.1). Each group has the following characteristics:

Group I (Saudi Arabia, Kuwait, Libya, United Arab Emirates, and Qatar) has 66.4 percent of proven reserves and 48.2 percent of current output, but only 11 million population and limited levels of

TABLE 2.1

Major Characteristics of the OPEC Producers

Countries	Population (millions)	Oil Reserves[a] (billions of barrels)	Oil Reserves/Population (billions of barrels per capita)	1974 Average Production (millions of barrels per day)	Estimated Production Capacity (millions of barrels per day)	Reserve Life[b] Capacity (years)
Group I						
Kuwait[c]	0.9	81.0	9000	2.9	3.8	58
Libya	2.1	27.0	12857	1.5	3.0	29
Quatar	0.1	6.0	60000	0.5	0.7	23
Saudi Arabia[c]	7.6	173.0	22763	8.5	10.5	45
United Arab Emirates	0.3	34.0	113333	1.7	2.2	42
Subtotal	11.0 (4.0)	321.0 (66.4)	298953 (97.3)	14.7 (48.2)	20.2 (53.3)	
Group II						
Algeria	14.2	7.7	542	1.0	1.1	19
Ecuador	6.5	2.5	385	0.2	0.2	29
Iran	30.6	66.0	2157	6.0	6.5	38
Iraq	10.1	35.0	3465	1.9	2.6	37
Venezuela	11.0	15.0	1364	3.0	3.3	12
Subtotal	72.4 (26.1)	126.2 (26.1)	7913 (2.6)	12.1 (39.7)	13.7 (36.1)	
Group III						
Indonesia	122.0	15.0	123	1.4	1.5	27
Nigeria	72.0	21.0	292	2.3	2.5	23
Subtotal	194.0 (69.9)	36.0 (7.4)	415 (0.1)	3.7 (12.1)	4.0 (10.6)	
Total	277.4	483.2	307281	30.5	37.9	

[a]As of January 1975.
[b]Assumes no new reserve discoveries and production at present capacity rates.
[c]Includes half of the neutral zone.

Note: ( ) indicates percent of total.

Sources: World Bank, World Bank Atlas, various issues; Oil and Gas Journal, various issues; Petroleum Intelligence Weekly, various issues; Middle East Economic Digest, various issues.

absorption for economic development. The five countries in this group will most likely take a long-term view of petroleum policy. Their reserves at current pumping rates have a potential life of 50 years or more, and they have few other resources.

Group II contains five countries—Iran, Venezuela, Algeria, Ecuador, and Iraq—that have already achieved considerable economic development, and are depleting their petroleum reserves at higher rates than the countries in Group I. They have a combined population of 72.4 million, and are in a position to make effective use of most of their increased oil revenues for internal development, if not now, at least within the next decade. This group is more likely than is Group I to attempt to secure maximum revenues, either through increased production, higher prices, or both, over the next few years because of the opportunities for production investment within their own economies.

Group III consists of two large countries, Indonesia and Nigeria, that have only a limited share of OPEC resources and will have little trouble absorbing all their oil revenues in the near future. They will not accumulate significant financial surpluses.

A major constraint on oil price increases is the fact that Saudi Arabia, by far the largest producer, is concerned that a high price set by OPEC (say, $10 per barrel) may induce the major consuming countries—the United States, Western Europe, and Japan—to develop alternative sources of energy on a significant scale. Given the demand for oil, this would cause a sharp decline in revenues for OPEC as a whole. On the other hand, if prices are lowered somewhat (to $7-8) a rather stable flow of revenues may develop through till the early 1990s, over time building up the ability of these countries to absorb efficiently the increased revenues in domestic investment. In this situation the OPEC countries are faced with the classical monopolist's dilemma of trying to estimate the speed with which alternative supplies will be developed, and whether the gains of maximizing short-run profits will exceed the losses from lower volumes (and perhaps lower prices) in the future.[11] Unless they are able to find relatively profitable investments in their domestic economies in the near future, the OPEC countries—particularly the Group I countries with large reserves—would benefit in the long run from reducing the price of oil (because of the possibility of the consuming countries searching for substitutes at high prices, and the inability of Group I countries to absorb the revenues domestically).

Saudi Arabia rather than Iran, therefore, is the key country in implementing a petroleum policy for OPEC. The Saudis command nearly a third of OPEC's total present production capacity, and they do not actually need to sell their oil as much as do the Group II countries, because the Saudis already have more foreign exchange accumulated than could be efficiently spent in the next several years.

When forecasting future oil prices and revenues for Iran, therefore, there are probably two quite different periods to consider. The first has already taken place, a period of stability with a small decline in price. The second period began in 1975, with an increasing rate of price reductions resulting from overproduction (due to slackening world demand caused by higher prices) and the Saudi position of preferring lower prices.

These developments in the international petroleum markets are likely to have four major implications for Iran: declining oil revenues; the need to drop a number of marginal projects from the development budget; high domestic inflation; and the erosion of the country's balance of payments, brought about by increased prices for imports.

At the heart of the nation's problems is the fact that no effective mechanism has been devised or implemented in the country whereby the new wealth can efficiently penetrate into the rural areas[12]—Azerbaijan in the northwest, the villages around the central desert, and Baluchistan in the southeast. Despite stepped up government expenditures in the rural areas, at least 2 million Iranian farmers still produce at subsistence levels.[13] Worse off are the landless poor without education and productive work. Seventy percent of Iran's personal wealth is concentrated in Tehran. The result of the country's strategy of high growth has been the creation of a very unequal income distribution, both by region and among households.

CONCLUSIONS

A number of possible adjustments and alternative strategies are available to help solve the Iranian economy's current problems in adjusting to the changing markets for oil. A number of these have already been implemented by the other Group II oil exporters—Iraq, Venezuela, Algeria, and Ecuador. These countries, like Iran, must continue to rely on petroleum as the principal source of their foreign exchange earnings and as the key to their future development. They differ greatly, however, in their development strategy, ideology, allocation of oil revenues (both domestic and foreign), and policies to curb domestic inflation and the deterioration in their balances of payments. Obviously these countries have not been more successful than Iran in all aspects of development policy. Still, from their experiences, both positive and negative, it is possible to establish a new set of policies and a new development strategy for Iran. This new approach to development will be the basis for a series of projections of the country's growth and pattern of production. These projections will be compared with a series of forecasts, assuming that Iran makes no fundamental changes in its utilization of oil revenues or its development policies.

NOTES

1. Data on oil production, exports, and prices, unless otherwise specified, is taken from Oil and Gas Journal, various issues.
2. See International Monetary Fund, International Financial Statistics (October 1976) for the various exchange rates of the Iranian rial vis-a-vis the dollar and the SDR.
3. Data are taken from Bank Markazi Iran, Bulletin, various issues.
4. Robert Looney, "Iran: Rise of a World Power," Countermeasures, no. 2 (May 1975), p. 16.
5. For an analysis of this situation, see E. M. Croonk, "Inflation and Growth: The Case of Developed Countries," in V. V. Bhanoji Rao, ed., Inflation and Growth (Singapore: Stamford College Press, 1974), pp. 133-55.
6. Iran, Plan and Budget Organization, Iran's Fifth Development Plan, 1973-1978, Revised—A Summary (Tehran: Plan and Budget Organization, 1975), p. ii.
7. Forecasts were given in International Labor Office, Employment and Income Policies for Iran (Geneva: International Labor Office, 1973), ch. 6.
8. For an excellent presentation and summary of these agreements see Fereidun Fesharaki, Development of the Iranian Oil Industry: International and Domestic Aspects (New York: Praeger, 1976), ch. 5.
9. Adrian Hamilton, "End of Old Assumptions on Oil Prices," Financial Times (September 29, 1975), p. 25.
10. For a discussion of this type of grouping, see C. A. Gebelein, "Effect of Conservation on Oil Prices: Analysis of Misconceptions," Journal of Energy and Development, no. 1 (Autumn 1975), pp. 53-69.
11. An interesting model along these lines is given by Paul Leo Eckbo, The Future of World Oil (Cambridge, Mass.: Ballinger, 1976), ch. 4.
12. Robert Looney, Income Distribution Policies and Economic Growth in Semi-industrialized Countries (New York: Praeger, 1975), ch. 6.
13. International Labor Office, Employment and Income Policies, p. 26.

CHAPTER 3

SOURCES OF ECONOMIC GROWTH

INTRODUCTION

The easiest task in examining the growth of any country is to describe what has happened in terms of its overall macroeconomic trends and growth rates in the key sectors. A more difficult task, particularly in the case of Iran, is to explain why certain events happened, and how specific goals set for the economy by the authorities were or were not achieved. It may be trite—but still true—to state that the process of development in Iran is complex and poorly understood.* Growth in Iran is the result of a number of intangibles, such as the nation's cultural patterns and social values (see Appendix A). The country's development, therefore, has political and human, as well as economic, dimensions. It depends both on external factors, which to a large extent are uncontrollable, and on internal forces, which are more susceptible to government control. Because of its multidimensional aspects any explanation of the "why" and the "how" of Iran's recent growth must involve some speculation, must be influenced by the experience and perspective of the analyst, and is certain to evoke differing views.

---

*As Firouz Vakil notes, "Indeed one of the major obstacles to proper planning (in Iran) is obtaining a tableau of the economy with all its interrelationships. Because economic entities such as Iran are very complex, it is quite impossible to build models capable of reflecting all the interactions of the social and economic matrix." (See Firouz Vakil, <u>Determining Iran's Financial Surplus—1352-1371</u> [Tehran: The Institute for International, Political, and Economic Studies, 1975], p. 21.)

SOURCES OF ECONOMIC GROWTH 15

Further, it is impossible to expect widespread agreement as to whether certain features of the Iranian experience are "good" or "bad." There are no universally accepted standards against which such an evaluation can be made. Few, however, would question the fact that the growth trend in Iran since 1964 has been outstanding. The increase in national income has accelerated during this entire period. From 1962 to 1967, GNP increased at an average rate of 9.65 percent annually with constant prices (see Table 3.1). During the years of the Fourth Plan—1967-72—growth averaged 11.8 percent annually, against the plan target of 9.4 percent. The rate of growth between 1972 and 1974 was 37.7 percent in real terms, rising under the impact of the oil boom to 41.6 percent in 1974. In the wake of the fall in demand for oil in world markets and the resulting shortfall in revenues, growth decelerated in 1975 to approximately 15 percent in real terms*—a rate still the envy of nearly every country in the world.

SOURCES OF GROWTH

A number of factors, both economic and noneconomic, underlie Iran's recent development success. These include: the country's abundant natural resource endowment on which to build a development effort; an imaginative and far-reaching role played by the government through economic planning, development policies and strategies adopted and implemented, massive infrastructure investments, and direct participation in business activities via state enterprises; and the vigorous response of both domestic and foreign private enterprise to development opportunities and incentives.

One basic ingredient that has nurtured Iran's development efforts has been the emergence of a national concensus for accelerated growth and development, stimulated by the initiation, in 1963, of the Shah's White Revolution.[1] Today the vast majority of Iranians agree that the government should take deliberate and affirmative planning action to assure that a firm foundation for long-run sustained growth will be established.

A second basic ingredient that has supported Iran's development drive is its physical setting. Rich natural resources, however, are neither a necessary condition—as shown by the spectacular success of resource-poor Japan—nor a sufficient condition—as suggested by the long-delayed economic expansion of oil-rich Indonesia—for development success.

---

*All national income figures for 1975 are obtained from the Bank Markazi Iran and are preliminary estimates unless otherwise specified.

TABLE 3.1

National Income Accounts, 1959-74

	Billion Rials Constant Prices							Average Annual Rate of Growth (percent)		
	1959	1962	1967	1968	1971	1972	1974	1962-67	1968-71	1972-74
Gross national product	283.9	324.2	513.8	569.4	778.4	1183.1	2243.4	9.65	10.98	37.70
Private consumption	209.2	233.4	330.6	370.3	451.4	663.7	862.0	7.21	6.82	13.96
Government consumption	30.3	31.9	73.6	86.7	159.3	252.6	410.4	18.20	22.48	27.46
Total consumption	239.5	265.3	404.2	457.0	610.7	916.3	1272.4	8.79	10.15	17.84
Investment in machinery	21.3	13.9	26.4	45.0	66.0	112.9	177.4	13.69	13.62	25.35
Investment in construction	31.4	35.5	71.9	81.3	113.3	174.5	228.7	15.16	11.70	14.48
Total investment	52.7	49.4	113.1	126.3	179.3	287.4	40.61	18.02	12.39	18.87
Savings	44.4	58.9	109.6	112.4	167.7	266.8	971.0	13.22	14.27	90.77
Savings-investment	-8.3	9.5	-3.5	-13.9	-11.6	-20.6	564.9	—	—	—
Imports	48.2	40.8	90.0	107.9	164.5	n.a.	n.a.	17.14	15.09	—
Net factor income	-19.8	-30.3	-52.4	-65.0	-96.7	n.a.	n.a.	—	—	—
Exports	59.7	80.6	138.9	159.0	249.6	n.a.	n.a.	11.50	16.22	—
Imports-exports	8.3	-9.5	3.5	13.9	11.6	20.6	-564.9	—	—	—
Gross domestic product	307.3	354.5	566.2	634.4	875.1	1239.5	1581.7	9.82	11.32	12.96

Note: Constant 1959 prices, 1959-71. Constant 1972 prices, 1972-74.
Source: Computed from Bank Markazi Iran, Annual Report and Balance Sheet, various issues.

SOURCES OF ECONOMIC GROWTH

Another supporting element has been Iran's human resources, especially the role played by the country's top government administrators and entrepreneurs. As a result of the critical need for trained people and of the nation's traditional social values that placed education in an elite category, Iran has long given high status and positions of public responsibility to a small corps of highly trained people.[2] In addition, a younger group of highly educated technocrats, many of whom were trained under the military education system initiated by the White Revolution, has played a dominant role in Iran's recent development success.

Iran's human resource endowment has been rich in entrepreneurial talents. Unlike a number of other developing countries, however, the new entrepreneurial class has not been built up by immigrants. Instead, this vigorous class has developed in such traditional centers as the old imperial capital of Isfahan, in the ancient city of Tabriz, and, of course, in Tehran itself.[3] An increasingly flexible social structure has permitted great upward economic and social mobility for Iranians who were not members of the oligarchy or landed aristocracy as educational and occupational opportunities have expanded with economic growth.

Thus, when the national concensus for growth and development emerged in Iran in the early 1960s, the country had a favorable mix of several basic ingredients that could support that drive. In contrast to other Middle Eastern countries that were steeped in doctrinaire ideologies, the country adopted a pragmatic approach toward its development.[4] This approach again follows from the tenets of the Shah's White Revolution. Unlike many other countries that have been committed to some ideology such as private capitalism, free enterprise, or socialism, Iran has never placed itself in an ideological straitjacket. Admittedly, at certain times and in relation to specific events, such ideologies as nationalism, socialism, and communism have attracted some popular support. Yet, adherence to ideology or doctrine has rarely obstructed Iran's development drive.

Pragmatism has permeated the development drive in virtually all its dimensions. It has resulted in a nondoctrinaire approach to reliance on private versus government enterprise. It has encouraged periodic reexamination of and changes in economic planning approaches and strategies, and it has characterized the evolution of policies both to fight inflation and to resolve the full range of development-induced problems. The government's pragmatic approach to economic policy has resulted in a substantial number of failures but, more importantly, in an impressive series of imaginative innovations.

In terms of the major indicators of economic development, the country's development effort can be measured by the rapid improvement in:

1. the number and sophistication of the country's financial institutions, as measured by the growth in private savings flowing through the banking system and the growth in bank lending on medium and long terms to the private sector
2. physical overhead capital, as measured by the improvement in transport systems
3. agricultural productivity achieved through the application of modern inputs and techniques
4. the degree of modernization of outlook measured in part by the extent to which development programs have gained the support of both the rural and urban populations
5. the degree of commitment by the leadership to promoting economic development, as measured: by the existence of concerted efforts by the heads of agencies involved in central guidance of the economy to promote economic growth; by whether the planning effort included serious attempts to alter institutional arrangements that clearly blocked the achievement of planning goals; and by the existence of a national plan or planning agency

THE ROLE OF OIL

The country's development has resulted from the interaction of three sectors: oil; the modern sector (manufacturing and services); and the indigenous (or traditional agricultural) sector.[5] These distinct sectors interact in several ways.

The oil sector provides the capital needed for the growth of the other two sectors, but does not receive any substantial return flow of resources from either the modern or the indigenous sector. By contributing a large share of the capital needed for the growth of the rest of the economy, however, the oil sector obviates the most pressing constraint on growth faced by developing countries—foreign exchange.

The modern sector draws on the oil sector for funds needed for its expansion, and on the indigenous sector for labor and raw materials. Its output is sold mostly to the indigenous sector. If Iran is to become an advanced country, no longer dependent on oil revenues, the modern sector must ultimately be capable of generating its own capital requirements. At that time the economy must be in a position to look to the oil sector not so much for its capital requirements, but as a source of inexpensive raw materials and energy. The oil sector, therefore, must become an appendage of the rest of the economy if the country is ultimately to achieve self-sustained growth. By the time oil revenues begin to decline, perhaps in 20 years, the modern and traditional sectors must have structures flexible enough to provide not only for their own capital needs but also to utilize effectively the low-cost energy supplied by the oil sector.

The indigenous sector currently uses the products originating in the oil sector and the modern sector. Because of limited employment opportunities in the oil sector, however, labor leaving the agricultural sector must find work in the modern sector. As the country's development continues, this loss of labor will inevitably lead to the shrinkage of the indigenous sector relative to the other sectors. For the country to sustain growth, the transfer of workers out of agriculture must be accompanied by increases in productivity so that the increasing demand for food and other rural products can be met without increased prices or imports.

The major mechanism of growth in the country involves the manner in which oil revenues are channeled into the economy. Initially, revenues reach the modern and agricultural sectors through the government budget, which is itself composed of two basic components: current expenditures for the running of government agencies and the meeting of expenditures arising out of public services (for example, defense, justice, health, education, and welfare); and development expenditures used for implementation of the nation's public investment allocation, as outlined in the five-year plans. Once allocated and expended, these oil-financed development expenditures contribute greatly to the expansion of the economy's productive capacity. Indeed, many of the current bright spots in the agricultural, industrial, and services sectors are a direct result of the transfer of resources to them from the oil sector. Oil revenues thus represent an easy source of savings and of foreign exchange, readily convertible to capital formation via imports of machinery and equipment. Because of its oil revenues the country has not had to use fiscal and monetary policies so necessary in other developing countries for increasing the share of investment in GNP. Oil revenues on the scale currently received by Iran actually allow for the attainment of increased growth and consumption. In effect, oil revenues soften the conflict that any country must resolve between meeting the needs of the present and future generations.

While the numerous benefits of oil to the country are clear, the authorities must deal with a number of risks inherent in the reliance on oil revenues for development. Currently, there are three particularly pressing development problems facing the country. The nation's growth process has begun to require an ever-increasing level of oil revenues in order to sustain its growth momentum. Measures must therefore be undertaken to develop the modern sector in a manner that will enable it to pick up the slack in demand when the trend in the growth of oil revenues begins to taper off and decline. The dependence of the authorities on oil as an easily accessible source of revenue has also tended to retard the development of a tax base sufficiently broad to be closely interwoven with the mainstream of domestic economic activity. In addition, an easy supply of foreign exchange, as provided by the oil sector, has encouraged newly established industrial firms in the private sector to orient their production towards the rapidly growing modern sector rather than towards the more competitive external markets. The long-term development of the Iranian economy, as in the case of all oil-exporting countries, will ultimately depend on the building of a nonoil export sector capable of meeting the future import requirements. The government is aware of these problems and has not let the present availabilities of foreign exchange divert its attention from the country's long-range growth requirements. A number of measures have been introduced into the country's development plans to enable the economy to adjust to the eventual decline in oil revenues.[6]

ECONOMIC PLANNING

Economic planning in Iran has made a continuing contribution to the country's growth through improving both private and government decision processes. Although planning results have fallen short of the high technical standards for planning set by economic and public administration specialists in more developed countries, the government's planning strategy has recognized the technical, personnel, and institutional limits that have prevailed in Iran.[7] Iranian planners have focused on upgrading development performance rather than on trying to prepare a perfect plan. In this way they have been able to maintain a position of influence and political effectiveness throughout most of the postwar years.

The First Seven-Year Plan (1949-55) resulted in total investments of 14,100 million rials, while the Second Seven-Year Plan achieved greater success with investments totaling 83,200 million rials. The Third Plan was designed to increase national income by 6 percent annually.[8] Although the early years of the plan were disappointing in terms of results, extremely rapid growth was attained toward the end of the plan period. Actual expenditures during the entire Third Plan period (1963-67) totaled 204,600 million rials, representing 88.9 percent of the original allocations to the Plan Organization (the official governmental agency in charge of allocating oil revenues for development purposes).

The Third Plan was more successful than the first two plans because of its emphasis on smaller projects that were capable of yielding a high rate of return; its emphasis on the utilization of local resources (for example, in agriculture, small irrigation projects, financial aid to farmers, rural feeder roads to link farmers to the main trunk road systems) and industrial enterprises that used local raw materials; its inclusion of the private sector as an integral part of the country's development effort; and the increasing share of oil revenues allocated by the government during this period to the country's development effort[9] (see Table 3.2).

In the Fourth Plan (1968-72) a large proportion of public sector funds was directed towards infrastructure such as transport and communications. During this period, rapidly rising oil income allowed the original allocations to the Plan Organization to be greatly increased. The final expenditure of the Plan Organization was 577,000 million rials, 20.5 percent above the original Fourth Plan allocations. The performance of the economy during the Fourth Plan was generally above expectations. The rate of economic growth at constant prices was 11.8 percent, enabling GNP to increase from 556 billion to 1,186 billion rials during the plan period. This represented an average growth of 16.3 percent. Both the oil and industrial sectors showed strongest progress during this period. Agriculture, with an average rate of growth of 3.9 percent, was the only sector failing to achieve its original target growth rate.[10]

By the end of the Fourth Plan, Iran's GNP per capita was $550 per annum, roughly equal to that of Turkey and above that of all other Middle Eastern countries except Israel, Lebanon, and Kuwait. The country's high rate of economic growth during the Fourth Plan was the result of the rising proportion of GNP devoted to capital formation, and returns from directly productive investment, following the government's massive investment in infrastructure during previous plan periods.

In contrast to Iran, other countries have attempted to begin with sophisticated and comprehensive planning when the necessary preconditions were not present. In some instances the planning activity in these countries lost its influence over the political decision process because usable plans were not available when decisions had to be made (Iraq).[11] In other cases the plans broke down in implementation because the institutional framework had not been prepared (Ecuador).[12]

Iran's planning strategy has involved recognition of the country's prevailing limitations. It has allocated relatively large amounts of resources to developing more and better statistical information and to the advanced training of elite personnel. To this end, the expansion and modernization of university education, particularly in economics and administration, received higher priority than did primary and secondary education. One consequence of this has been that many foreign universities have established special programs in Iran for training students in economic analysis and administration.

TABLE 3.2

Performance During the Third and Fourth
Plan Periods
(percentage)

	Third Plan (1963-67)	Fourth Plan (1968-72)
Gross domestic fixed capital formation	22 of nonoil GDP	27 of nonoil GDP
Allocation of investment	22 industries 25 transport and communications	33 industries 21 transport and communications
Public sector's share in capital formation	44	58
Public sector savings to meet financial requirements	27	26
Public sector non-investment expenditures	22	22
Net external borrowing	4.2 of total financing for capital formation	8.6

Source: Computed from Bank Markazi Iran, Annual Report and Balance Sheet, 1349, pp. 116-17 and Bank Markazi Iran, Annual Report and Balance Sheet, 1353, pp. 141-43.

Further, large numbers of Iranian students are currently studying in the world's leading universities.

The results of the country's drive to upgrade the quality of its high-level administrators has been impressive. For example, the number of trained economists in Iran at the master's level or above increased from about a dozen in the early 1950s to several thousand in 1976.

The great merit of Iran's evolutionary approach to economic planning was its de facto, though not explicit, recognition that the country was not prepared in terms of technical, personnel, and institutional resources to run before it could walk.

While the Fourth Plan went a long way towards establishing the basis for further growth, it also revealed some of the constraints that continue to plague the Iranian economy, and that are likely to handicap its rapid expansion and absorptive capacity in the future. To overcome these constraints (mainly the country's shortage of

SOURCES OF ECONOMIC GROWTH 23

technically trained personnel and the economy's inability to provide productive employment for a rapidly growing labor force), the Fifth Plan (1973-77) marked a sharp change in the country's orientation towards development.

OBJECTIVES OF THE FIFTH PLAN

The basic aims of the original Fifth Plan were established in the following order of priority:

1. to raise as much as possible the level of knowledge, culture, health, and welfare of the society
2. to attain a more equitable distribution of national income, with special attention to the rapidly increasing rise in the living standard and welfare of the underprivileged groups
3. to maintain the rapid and sustained rate of economic growth parallel to relative price stability and balance of payments
4. to provide productive employment in all regions of the country at a level that would absorb all the new manpower joining the labor market and substantially reduce concealed or seasonal unemployment
5. to operate fully the established production capacities built under the previous development plans, and to raise productivity and efficiency in the supply of goods and services in the public and private sectors
6. to improve the administrative order, in keeping with the lofty national aims and objectives, and to strengthen the country's defense capacity
7. to protect, improve, and revitalize the living environment
8. to increase Iran's share in international trade, particularly in manufactured goods [13]

OVERALL SOCIAL AND ECONOMIC POLICIES AND COURSES

To attain the general objectives of the plan the projected investment was set at $24.5 billion (76.5 rials = $1). Given this sum, the planners anticipated that Iran's per capita income would increase to $2,000 by 1978 (from $550 in 1972). A major aim in this direction was to reduce the annual rate of population growth by about half the 1972 level (31 per thousand) by the end of 1991. In the shorter run the Fifth Plan's goal was to reduce the rate of population increase from the 31 per thousand figure to 26 per thousand by the end of the plan, in 1977. It was anticipated that such a reduction would result in higher incomes and in improved living standards for the low-income classes in the urban centers.

This plan placed special emphasis on agriculture, with a target of attaining an annual increase in agricultural output of 5.5 percent and self-sufficiency in basic food items by the end of the plan period. Accordingly, it gave agriculture a large share of government investment—102.6 billion rials (see Table 3.3)—intended to raise yields. Also, it gave incentives such as guaranteed minimum farm income prices for some products; increased agricultural credit; and lowered the prices of seeds, chemical fertilizers, and other basic requirements, to stimulate private sector investment in agriculture. These policies were expected not only to achieve greater efficiency in this sector but also to lessen the increasingly inequitable income distribution (since most of the lower-income households are in the rural areas).

THE REVISED FIFTH PLAN

The Fifth Plan was originally approved by the Majiles (Iranian parliament) and the Senate early in 1973. But the subsequent sharp increases in oil prices and government revenues during 1973 and 1974 radically altered the plan's financial projections, enabling the government to undertake a wholesale revision upward of the plan's targets. The revised plan was submitted to Parliament in the winter of 1974 and called for a total fixed capital investment of Rls. 4,699 billion (nearly $70 billion) between 1972 and 1977; it thus doubled the scope of the original 1973 version and increased seven-fold the Fourth Plan (1968-72).

In revising the Fifth Plan four basic considerations were of paramount significance to the planners. First, the shortage of domestic and foreign revenues, which had limited the size of previous development plans and influenced their order of priorities, was no longer a constraint. With the nearly certain prospects of continually rising oil revenues, the planners chose to aim at the maximum attainable growth in all sectors of the economy. Second, in setting the new priorities and growth targets, the planners remained mindful of such constraints as the country's inadequate supply of skilled manpower and technical personnel. The size of the plan was therefore intended to be commensurable with the country's domestic absorptive capacity, and allowances were made for potential new foreign investments. Third, for the first time an attempt was made to coordinate the process of five-year planning with the annual budget: in theory the revised Fifth Plan's expenditures were to parallel annual

TABLE 3.3

Sectoral Revisions in the Fifth Five-Year Plan
(value added in billions of 1972 rials)

	Original Fifth Plan Targets			Revised Fifth Plan Targets		
	1972	1977	Average Annual Growth Rate	1972	1977	Average Annual Growth Rate
Agriculture	203.0	265.0	5.5	201.1	282.1	7.0
	(16.6)	(12.6)		(18.1)	(8.0)	
Oil	317.0	554.0	11.8	216.5	1712.0	51.5
	(25.9)	(26.3)		(19.5)	(48.7)	
Industry and mining	240.5	489.0	15.0	274.4	566.0	18.0
	(19.6)	(23.2)		(24.7)	(16.1)	
Manufacturing and mining	165.0	336.0	15.3	—	—	—
	(13.5)	(15.0)				
Construction	56.0	103.0	13.0	—	—	—
	(45.7)	(48.8)				
Water	2.7	4.7	12.0	—	—	—
	(0.2)	(0.2)				
Power	16.8	45.3	22.0	—	—	—
	(13.7)	(21.5)				
Services	465.5	802.0	15.5	445.8	953.9	16.4
	(38.0)	(38.0)		(40.1)	(27.1)	
Gross domestic product	1226.0	2110.0	11.4	1110.8	3514.0	25.9

Notes: ( ) indicates percent of GNP. Between 1973 and 1975, the 1972 national income accounts for 1972 were revised. Between 1973 and 1975, the treatment of oil's contribution to GNP was changed so that the 1972 figures for oil are not comparable.

Source: Iran Trade and Industry Supplement No. 200, The Fifth Plan (Tehran, March, 1973), p. 7; Kayhan Research Associates, A Guide to Iran's Fifth Plan (Tehran, 1975), p. 11.

budgetary allocations closely. Finally, the new plan was to be set up in the context of a long-term, twenty-year perspective linking it to the as yet undrafted and unstructured sixth and seventh plans.

Qualitative Objectives of the Revised Fifth Plan

Some revision was made in priorities in the revised version of the Fifth Plan, but basically the priorities were similar to those of the original version. In order of importance these objectives were:

1. to raise living standards of all social strata in the economy, and to enhance social justice by providing equal economic, political, and cultural opportunities for all individuals and groups
2. to maintain a high and sustained rate of economic growth, consistent with relative price stability and a more equitable distribution of national income and welfare
3. to improve the quality and size of the country's active labor force, to increase productivity
4. to preserve, rehabilitate, and improve the environment, especially in overpopulated areas
5. to upgrade the level of science, technology, and creativity
6. to preserve the country's cultural heritage and enhance the quality of life

Quantitative Allocations and Priorities

In allocating investment funds among the various sectors of the economy, the planners were motivated by three basic criteria. They assigned highest priority to industries involved with the nation's relatively abundant resources. Thus, the oil, gas, and petrochemical industries were singled out for the largest share of funds. Steel and machine tool manufacturing and copper mining activities were among the other industries receiving relatively large sums. The planners also gave top priority to interior development, particularly of ports, roads, and communications systems. These investments were undertaken by the planners with the goal of overcoming existing, and in some cases anticipated, physical bottlenecks. Agriculture received relatively high allocations, with the intention of allowing the country to achieve more and higher quality foodstuffs, as well as greater raw material output for growing industries.

Social investments—housing, education, health, regional development, and environmental protection—were also given high priority by the government. In addition public affairs allocations were geared toward giving the provinces a greater voice in how public expenditures for urban and rural development, free education, a nationwide preventive health program, family planning, and expanded subsidies for the essential needs of the lower income groups should be disbursed.

THE DYNAMIC ROLE OF GOVERNMENT

As the goals of the Fifth Plan indicate, the government has assumed broad responsibility for macroeconomic management of the economy and its development. Although Iran is often classified as having a capitalistic economy, the label is misleading. Iran's pragmatic policy has made use of whatever oil revenues and technological or entrepreneurial inputs were available. Depending on the specific situation it has been receptive to foreign business firms, it has encouraged private domestic companies, and it has created large government enterprises in critical production areas, particularly in steel, aluminum, and power.

Although planning is becoming increasingly important in influencing economic development of the country, Iranians are keenly aware of the limited capability of government institutions for successful economic management. They believe that the government can, however, make use of a number of tools in addition to its massive expenditures. For example, the government has played a dominant role in guiding, inventing, and shaping decisions in the marketplace. It has done this through controls, numerous incentives, and its fiscal and monetary policies.[14] The central tenet of Iran's drive to modernize has been expansion of the industrial base as fast as possible in order to generate a solid manufacturing capacity, which would eventually produce the necessary export earnings when oil resources are depleted.

The reasons for a development strategy based on diversification are clear. If Iran continued to specialize in oil exports without the development of industry, growth would ultimately come to an end because of the well-known tendency (Engel's Law) of consumers to decrease the share of rising incomes spent on food while increasing the demand for manufactures. In short, to make sure development in Iran becomes an on-going process, the authorities have developed another sector, industry, to complement the dynamic impetus given by oil revenues. Iran's entry into an intensive phase of industrialization constitutes an imperative of its economic reality.

The pattern of industrialization has begun to change in Iran as the government has increased its direct involvement in the economy. Until the mid-1960s, and even into the early 1970s, industry in Iran developed somewhat independently of the oil sector. While such a pattern was valid in the past because of the predominant number of small-scale, privately owned firms, it is now evident that petroleum may be one of the best fields for industrial expansion in the country, since it can be a major source of fuel and feedstocks. Although most petroleum-oriented enterprises are highly capital intensive, the government's strategy in developing related industries has a twofold purpose: generating capital, and moving the country into more complex types of activities such as petrochemicals, thus moving the economy away from one of a simple crude oil producer.

The move toward industrialization has inevitably resulted in a first phase with focus on internal development.[15] Orientation toward the domestic market has been necessary because the country's limited infrastructural support hinders the success of firms competing in foreign markets. While the internal development emphasis has, together with oil revenues, not completely freed Iran from foreign exchange constraints, it has managed to keep the development momentum going through import replacement and excessive importation of foreign technology and technicians. The faster the country has expanded, however, the greater its reliance on imports to set up and maintain its new industries has become.

Despite the growth of industrial output in the country (reaching an average annual rise of 10.8 percent during the 1960s), however, manufacturing contributed only modestly to national income (see Table 3.4) and employment. A major problem still to be faced is how to improve the international competitiveness of Iranian industrial products. Here, raising per capita productivity is essential, whether incentives or training are used.[16] Equally important is the need to resist the lure of self-sufficiency, where the drive for independence overshadows cost factors, efficiency, and, ultimately, consumer interests. Efficiency in Iranian industry can be improved by specialization in industries that require low cost inputs and in areas with adequate labor supply. The debates of the 1950s and 1960s about whether or not to industrialize are no longer relevant; it is now a matter of deciding what specific industries are to be established and expanded.

Future development of industry in Iran has been and will be affected by the availability of capital, the availability of cheap energy, and the ability to diversify as a means of offsetting the rapid loss of its most important asset, oil.

TABLE 3.4

Sectoral Output, 1959-74
(billions of rials)

	1959	1962	1967	1968	1971	1974
Agriculture	85.4	96.9	128.4	119.7	124.4	304.8
	(27.9)	(27.7)	(22.8)	(20.0)	(15.0)	(9.4)
Oil	47.1	64.4	112.7	145.4	221.9	1634.5
	(16.5)	(18.4)	(20.0)	(24.4)	(26.8)	(50.6)
Manufacturing and mining	30.9	41.8	76.0	82.8	118.1	312.7
	(13.3)	(13.8)	(28.4)	(26.2)	(33.0)	(125.9)
Water and electricity	1.1	2.5	7.4	10.8	19.5	25.7
	(0.4)	(0.7)	(1.3)	(1.8)	(2.4)	(0.8)
Transportation and communication	27.5	29.9	33.3	37.5	46.7	92.4
	(9.6)	(8.6)	(5.9)	(6.3)	(5.6)	(2.9)
Banking and insurance	5.6	8.3	16.6	18.3	35.4	152.7
	(2.0)	(2.4)	(2.9)	(3.1)	(4.3)	(4.7)
Domestic trade	22.8	27.2	47.6	43.1	56.2	151.7
	(8.0)	(7.8)	(8.4)	(7.2)	(6.8)	(4.7)
Housing rent	15.5	21.1	29.9	29.9	36.7	72.4
	(5.4)	(6.0)	(5.3)	(5.0)	(4.4)	(2.2)
Public services	23.3	27.9	58.9	57.1	97.1	273.1
	(8.2)	(8.0)	(10.4)	(9.6)	(11.7)	(8.5)
Private services	13.0	15.5	25.2	26.1	38.5	83.3
	(4.6)	(4.4)	(4.5)	(4.4)	(4.7)	(8.5)
Gross domestic product (at factor cost)	285.5	349.3	564.4	596.9	827.5	3229.2
Nonoil income (at factor cost)	238.5	284.9	451.7	451.5	605.6	1594.7

Note: ( ) indicates percent of GDP.
Source: Computed from Bank Markazi Iran, Annual Report and Balance Sheet, various issues.

Infrastructure Investments

A second major development role of government has been in providing infrastructure to support Iran's development drive. Much of the economic development literature has treated infrastructure investments as a prerequisite and necessary stimulant of economic growth. A contrary view, identified with Albert O. Hirschman,[17] sees infrastructure investments as following and being induced by shortages resulting from the expansion of "directly productive activities" such as manufacturing. Iran has been a prime example of the Hirschman view. Throughout the postwar period Iran's development progress has occurred in spite of persistent shortages of building materials, transport, and communications, all of which have required massive and continuing infrastructure investments. Although infrastructure investments have followed a lag rather than a lead pattern, they have made a significant contribution to Iran's development drive by virtue of the scale of investment and the support thereby given to the directly productive activities.

The total expenditures of the public sector increased about five times in real terms between 1959 and 1974. As a share of the GNP, total government expenditures expanded from 17 percent in 1959 to about 30 percent in the early 1970s. This ratio has been high by international standards, and a large share of these large government expenditures has gone for economic and social infrastructure investment.

Inadequate transportation facilities in Iran have been a serious problem for centuries. Lack of an extensive river system has meant that movement by land was the only mode of transport connecting the northern and southern parts of the country until the relatively recent construction of modern airports. Railroads were originally built in the 1930s to connect Tehran with the ports on the Persian Gulf, but in recent years they have not been able to handle the vastly increased volume of imports. The large size of the country and the concentration of population around Tehran and a few other urban centers in the interior have prevented the establishment of a nationwide transport network except for aviation, which by its nature is largely confined to passenger traffic and high-value cargo. The development of inland waterways has been limited to the Dez River because most of the other rivers either do not flow directly to the coast or have rapids that prevent navigation.

Iran has seven principal commercial ports, of which all the important ones are on the gulf. These gulf ports handle 91 percent of all seaborne trade; two of them—Bandar Shahpur and Khorramshahr—handle 77 percent of total trade. The only Caspian port of any significance is Bandar Pahlavi, which handles about 7 percent of the total trade. The main emphasis has been, and will continue to be, on the gulf, since shipping to Caspian ports depends upon the Volga-Don Canal, which is only open for four months in the summer.

The aim of the government is to increase nominal port capacity by 1978 to 28 million tons, which the authorities estimate could give a total capacity in the region of 60 million tons per annum (on a 24-hour basis)—currently the ports are handling one million tons a month. The cost of this expansion program is expected to be over $1,250 million. This will be coupled with improved warehousing and nationwide coordination of distribution through expanded railways and better roads.

Modern communications made their debut in Iran in 1965 with the CENTO (Central Treaty Organization, comprised of Iran, Pakistan, and Turkey) system, which permitted direct dialing between Tehran, Karachi, and Ankara; it now forms the backbone of a newly completed satellite network that brings Iran into the modern telecommunications age. Prior to the completion of the country's new communications system, many private companies and government agencies operated their own extensive and viable networks. The long-term objective, now rapidly being achieved, is for the whole of the Iranian telecommunications system to be completely integrated.

The building of a modern telecommunications system essentially from scratch means that the country will not have to incur the costs of scrapping an existing system in order to incorporate new technical developments, a problem facing several European countries. Because of rapidly changing technologies inherent in the electronics industry, however, the present shortfall of engineers and technicians must be overcome. Iranian planners have recognized the problem, and the technical colleges and schools now being built should provide an adequate stream of graduates for the growing industry.

Government Enterprises in Key Business Sectors

The direct participation by federal and state governments in business operations that provide infrastructure support and that have increased the profitability of directly productive activities has been one of the most powerful sources of growth in Iran. As industrialization has made headway, the traditional responsibilities of government have been steadily augmented by the tasks of providing development financing, increasing the electric power supply, managing the transport sector, and undertaking the domestic production of certain basic products, notably steel.

In most nations, particularly the industrialized countries of Western Europe, public utility industries have long been government owned and operated. In Iran, in the public utility and other areas, the steadily expanding, direct participation of government was not the result of a carefully conceived plan or of a pervasive ideological commitment, except possibly regarding the petroleum and steel industries, but a matter of adopting solutions imposed by objective conditions of economic change. In some cases, such as with the transport network, the government assumed ownership when existing companies ceased to be profitable. In other instances, producer functions were forced upon the government by the private sector's inability or unwillingness to undertake activities vital to development.

One of the most interesting questions concerning the Iranian experience is how a number of public enterprises have been able to become efficiently managed businesses when the conventional wisdom held throughout so much of the world is that government enterprises are generally inefficient and riddled with politics. The probable explanation in the case of Iran involves the form of organization used, the success of the companies in attracting highly qualified personnel, and the willingness of political leaders to rely on professional managers and technicians to direct these companies, because of the possible political consequences of failure in such large and complex ventures.

The ability of government enterprises to recruit excellent managers and technical staff is not simply related to salaries. In terms of opportunities for professional advancement and for assuming challenging responsibilities, the state enterprises have long been attractive to young people with high potential. Until the last decade or so the private sector, consisting of small- and medium-sized companies, was dominated by family enterprises in which managerial and other key positions were reserved for the owners and members of their families. In the past, opportunities in foreign companies were also limited because the high posts were traditionally reserved for non-Iranians. Iranians are now assuming more of those high positions as many foreign companies locate their regional headquarters in the country and delegate responsibility and authority to local managers.

Other reasons for the success of Iran's pioneer state enterprises were the use they made of personnel trained by foreign companies, their extensive investments in the training of their own personnel, and their willingness to contract for foreign technical assistance when needed. The Iranian steel industry has had marked success and illustrates a number of these points.

Iran's ambition to become a major steel producer goes back to the period before World War II. Originally Reza Shah had contracted a German firm to build the country's first blast furnace. Work was halted by World War II before completion. In the 1950s a number of Western countries, including the United States, refused for one reason or another to aid Iran in developing the industry.[18] Finally, in 1966 the Soviet Union agreed, in exchange for natural gas, to supply and construct the Ayramehr steel mills at Isfahan. The project was a major undertaking involving the development of iron deposits at Bafq and coal deposits at Kerman, as well as the construction of both a railway from Isfahan to the new mines and a new town to house the steel workers.

Since the autumn of 1973, when the $380 million plant began operation, it has run at more or less the full rated capacity, with the Soviet-supplied blast furnaces performing well and capable of producing at a rate of up to 700,000 tons per annum. The mill is operated by the state agency, the National Iranian Steel Industries Company (NISCO). NISCO is, in effect, a holding company that controls five mining companies in addition to the Ayramehr Steel Company.

Since the development of the mill at Isfahan, the government has decided to expand the industry using the gas reduction method. Despite the high technology involved with this process, it fits in with the government's long-run strategy of industrializing by exploiting the country's abundant supply of readily available and cheap gas. Three additional steel plants, based on gas reduction, are either planned or under construction. Total investment in the three plants, and related infrastructure, is likely to be over $5 billion in the next five years. Iran is spending larger sums only on nuclear power installation and the oil industry.

The gas reduction plants are all to be owned and controlled by NISCO. State involvement is to be limited to the production of steel, while the private sector has been encouraged to enter the industry with less capital intensive ventures, such as the pipe rolling mill at Ahwaz. With these mills the government aims to raise capacity from the 1976 level of nearly one million to 15 million tons by the end of the Sixth Plan period in 1983, and to 20 million tons in 1986. If the target is fulfilled, this would make the country a significant net exporter despite the very rapid growth, of some 20 to 25 percent annually, in anticipated domestic demand.

The Shah's target of a 15 million ton steel output by 1983 may not be met, but it is a goal that NISCO and NISIC (State National Iranian Steel Industries Company), in a healthy rivalry, are vigorously pursuing. At least Iran can look forward fairly confidently to being a net exporter of steel in the second half of the 1980s, and one of the more significant producers in the developing world.

Government Policies, Strategies, and Incentive Programs

The indirect contributions of the Iranian government, through a series of policies, strategies, and incentive programs, have also been a major source of economic growth. They are characterized by pragmatism, flexibility, innovation, and an emphasis on using the incentive pull of the carrot more than the coercive threat of the stick. They have been especially important in stimulating and facilitating the involvement of Iranian and foreign private enterprises in contributing to the rapid expansion of productive activities.

Iran's generally flexible and self-confident policy has encouraged crucial contributions of foreign capital to the country's development effort. Foreign activity in the economy has taken place in the form of inflows of external capital, transfers of technology, increased opportunities for training Iranians in management skills, and a greatly enlarged access to foreign markets via the export capabilities of international firms. With some discontinuities and divergences, Iran has yet maintained a steady course in welcoming types of foreign investment that had priority in her development strategy, and over the years has generated a high level of competence and sophistication in making use of foreign investment to achieve such goals as expanding exports. It has followed a policy of defusing latent antagonism towards foreign ownership by encouraging joint ventures with Iranian private and public enterprises in sensitive fields, and by achieving a mix of foreign nationalities in many fields, so that foreign investment, as in the form of anti-Americanism, is now less likely to become a political issue.

Pervading Iran's policies towards foreign investment has been a continuing awareness that a sovereign state has substantial leverage in dealing with foreign firms, that rapid growth of the economy has increased Iran's bargaining power, and that in its relations with multinational enterprises Iran must have highly competent government officials in charge of maximizing national development goals. A second key area of policy making relates to financial institutions. Particularly since the early 1960s, the government has provided leadership for extensive innovations in developing financial markets and institutions.[19]

CONCLUSIONS

The government's ambition is to transform Iran within a comparatively short time—20 years—into an industrialized society, a society free from dependence upon oil revenues, substituting a strong manufacturing base capable of sustained growth and sizable export earnings. Through a series of imaginative government policies and institutions, Iran is acquiring an impressive industrial base. The country is, however, a long way from being a major economic power. The policies undertaken by the authorities during the next decade will undoubtedly go a long way towards determining whether or not Iran will join the elite group of developed countries before its oil revenues run out.

NOTES

1. An excellent discussion of the White Revolution and the events leading up to its initiation is given by Gregory Lima, et al., The Revolutionizing of Iran (Tehran: International Communicators Iran, 1973).

2. See Marvin Zonis, The Political Elite of Iran (Princeton: Princeton University Press, 1971).

3. W. B. Fisher, ed., The Cambridge History of Iran, Vol. I, The Land of Iran (Cambridge: Cambridge University Press, 1968), p. 546.

4. Summarized in Jahangir Amuzegar, "Ideology and Economic Growth in the Middle East," Middle East Journal (winter 1974), pp. 1-9.

5. This classification is based on M. Ali Fekrat, "Economic Growth and Development in Iran," in Jane Jacqz, ed., Iran: Past, Present and Future—The Persepolis Symposium (New York: Aspin Institute for Humanistic Studies, 1976), pp. 73-80.

6. See Jahangir Amuzegar and M. Ali Fekrat, Iran: Economic Development Under Dualistic Conditions (Chicago: University of Chicago Press, 1971), ch. 3.

7. Reza Doroudian Shoja, "Econometric Models for the Fourth Plan," Tahqiqat-e Eqtesadi (1968), pp. 432-51.

8. For an excellent survey and analysis of these early plans, see Ahmed Saboonchi Ispahani, "The Optimization of Economic Resources for Economic Growth in Iran" (Ph.D. dissertation, University of Southern California, 1966).

9. Jahangir Amuzegar, "Capital Formation and Development Finance," in Ehsan Yar-Shater, ed., Iran Faces the Seventies (New York: Praeger, 1971), pp. 66-87.

10. Oddvar Aresvik, The Agricultural Development of Iran (New York: Praeger, 1976), p. 55.

11. E. Kanovsky, Economic Development of Iraq (Tel Aviv: Tel Aviv University, The David Horowitz Institute for the Research of Developing Countries, 1974), p. 59. See also A. Alnasrawi,

Financing Economic Development in Iraq (New York: Praeger, 1967), for a similar interpretation of Iraqi planning.

12. R. Echeverria et al., Current Economic Position and Prospects of Ecuador (Washington, D.C.: IBRD, 1973), p. 61.

13. Iran, Plan and Budget Organization, Iran's Fifth Development Plan, 1973-1978, Revised—A Summary (Tehran: Plan and Budget Organization, 1975), ch. 1.

14. M. H. Pesaran, "Banking and Credit Control in Iran," Euromoney (May 1975), p. 51.

15. Dragoslav Avramovic, "Industrialization of Iran: The Records, the Problems and the Prospects," Tahqiqat-e Eqtesidi (spring 1970), pp. 1-13.

16. William Bartsch, "The Industrial Labor Force of Iran: Problems of Recruitment, Training and Productivity," Middle East Journal (winter 1971), pp. 15-30.

17. Albert O. Hirschman, The Strategy of Economic Development (New Haven: Yale University Press, 1961), ch. 3. For a critique of Hirschman's views relating to labor productivity, see J. Gouverneur, "Hirschman on Labor Productivity Differentials: An Empirical Analysis," Bulletin of the Oxford University Institute of Economics and Statistics (November 1970), pp. 259-65.

18. An interesting account of the events leading up to the establishment of Iran's steel industry is given in George Baldwin, Planning and Development in Iran (Baltimore: Johns Hopkins University Press, 1967), pp. 105-10.

19. See the articles contained in the special issue of Euromoney (May 1975) on the development of Tehran as a financial center.

CHAPTER 4

CONSEQUENCES OF GROWTH

INTRODUCTION

In evaluating Iran's rapid growth, concern must ultimately lie with the manner in which the economic and social welfare of the country's citizens has increased in recent years. A number of nations, including Iran, have begun to accept the philosophy that economic growth is not an end in itself; instead, increases in national income are seen as a means to facilitate improvement in the quality of life.[1]

Iran and the other oil countries are attempting to achieve economic and social development on a self-sustaining basis. This is not an easy task. Unlike other developing countries, oil economies encounter a number of unique circumstances. They are something of an enigma, in that their oil wealth may be having an unfavorable impact on their political and social evolution, on their government's decision-making processes, and on the nature of their economic planning: oil income is largely generated and sustained by forces and change outside these countries and not by the organization of their domestic economies and their productive effort. Perhaps because growth in terms of GNP increases has been so effortless, leaders in several of the oil-producing countries have not attached the same priorities to investments in such areas as education, public health, and social welfare—undoubtedly because they have seen rapid growth take place without improvements in these areas. The development of vocational schools, for example, may in fact have been impeded by the accumulation of oil revenues. These countries are impatient for growth, yet investments in areas such as education often take generations to bear fruit. Oil revenues have enabled the oil exporting countries to overcome their manpower deficiencies by simply hiring foreign technicians.

Among the difficulties present in evaluating trends in a nation's social welfare, not least is the question as to the standards to be used for measuring improvements in the general well-being. One measure of improvement considers whether the economic and social situation of an individual is currently better than it was in the recent or more distant past; another analyzes the rate of improvement among different social classes or income groups; and a third assesses the current status of individuals and their families in relation to some hypothetical minimum welfare standard.[2] The first measure assumes that the absolute gains of individuals and families are the most relevant measures of improvement. The second assumes that absolute gains are less important, given the fact that some groups may have gained at a faster rate than have others. The third evaluates the welfare levels of individuals and their families against a standard, rather than in terms of any gains that have or have not been made. Because of the general lack of consensus on what measure to use in evaluating the consequences of Iran's growth, the same trends in welfare have sometimes been judged good by some observers and bad by others.

Rather than becoming embroiled in the debate over the best measure to be used in evaluating Iran's recent growth, a more productive approach is to examine a number of trends in such areas as employment, wages, social security, distribution of income, and education. The data for these variables are often less comprehensive than for GNP and its components, but they still provide considerable information on the benefits obtained by the population from the country's economic growth. The justification for putting together such incomplete information is that major changes are impending not only in Iran but in the other oil countries as well—changes which cannot but cast their shadows ahead.

EMPLOYMENT

The extent to which economic growth in Iran has created new job opportunities is crucial to any evaluation of the country's growth and ability to utilize oil revenues for the betterment of the people. This is a key issue, because Iran's high rate of population increase has meant that larger numbers of new workers are joining the labor force each year, and unless they can be absorbed in the labor force the country will suffer. Most forecasts indicate that the country's labor force will increase by approximately 1.5 million during the Fifth Plan (1973-77), 1.8 million during the Sixth Plan (1978-82), and 2.2 million during the Seventh Plan (1983-87). In addition, many new job opportunities will be needed in nonagricultural employment for those farm workers who have already lost or are likely to lose their jobs because of technological innovations and improved agricultural productivity; other jobs will be required to reduce, and eventually eliminate, the high numbers of workers who are considered to be underemployed.

Iran's efforts at reducing unemployment have, in the last decade or so, been fairly successful. A large surplus of workers existed in 1956, during which time the size of the labor force was 6,066,000, with a 2.6 percent rate of unemployment. By 1966 this figure had increased to 7,584,000, with 9.6 percent unemployment. By 1972, however only 1.15 percent (88,000 workers) of the labor force was unemployed.[3]

While the overall rate of unemployment has been reduced to a minimal level, underemployment has continued to be an important problem, particularly in the rural sector. In 1966, 11 percent of the employed population were working 28 hours per week or less. By 1972 this rate had been reduced to 2.2 percent, but the proportion of the labor force working less than 36 hours per week was approximately the same as in 1966.

The distribution of employment by broad sectors of economic activity has shown a number of distinctive trends. A steady decline has taken place in the agricultural sector (see Table 4.1). Between 1956 and 1966 most of the workers leaving agriculture were absorbed by the industrial sector, but in the subsequent period (1966-72) a higher proportion of workers began to be absorbed by the service sector. The observed shifts in the country's employment pattern can therefore be largely attributed to the rapid pace of industrialization and urbanization.

The trend towards industrialization and urbanization in Iran has made great demands on technical, managerial, and other workers.

TABLE 4.1

Sectoral Distribution of Employment, 1956-72
(percentage)

Sector	1956	1966	1972
Agriculture	56.3	46.2	39.8
Industry	20.1	27.1	29.4
Services	23.6	26.7	30.8

Source: F. Amin Zadeh, "Human Resources Development: Problems and Prospects," in ed. Jane W. Jacqz, Iran: Past, Present and Future (New York: Aspen Institute of Humanistic Studies, 1976), p. 190.

TABLE 4.2

Occupational Pattern of Employment, 1956-72
(percentage)

Occupation	1956	1966	1972
Professional, technical, and related	1.6	2.9	3.5
Administrative, managerial, and clerical	3.1	3.0	4.3
Sales	5.8	7.1	8.5
Service	7.7	7.2	6.3
Agricultural	55.6	47.1	48.5
Production	22.6	29.0	28.7
Other	3.6	3.7	0.2

Source: F. Amin Zadeh, "Human Resource Development: Problems and Prospects," in ed. Jane W. Jacqz, Iran: Past, Present and Future (New York: Aspen Institute of Humanistic Studies, 1976), p. 190.

These groups have increased at a very rapid rate (see Table 4.2), but not sufficiently to fill all the positions created by the country's rapid expansion, particularly since 1973.

An interesting change has occurred in the oil industry, which, in spite of its impact on national income and the supply of foreign exchange, has never absorbed a high proportion of the labor force. The number of employees in this industry rose only slightly and, in several countries, decreased all through the 1960s and into the 1970s. Employment in the Iranian oil sector stabilized at about 27,000 by the mid-1970s.

Manpower

Official Iranian censuses have indicated that 30-35 percent of the population is economically active. This figure, however, clearly underestimates the participation of women. Even though Iran has remained one of the world's most patriarchial societies, with an extremely low participation of women in the economically active population, The Institute for Social Studies and Research of Tehran University has estimated the country's economically active women at about 40 percent of the labor force. Other studies place the figure at around 30 percent.[4]

However, the issue of adequate and modern national manpower is more complicated than these numerical ratios indicate. The ability of Iran's manpower to utilize effectively the country's oil revenues depends upon the numbers of literate workers, skilled craftsmen, scientists and engineers, administrators and managers, and competent teaching staff for training the future generation. Obviously, physical fitness, mental health, and the age structure of the work force are important factors in determining the adequacy of manpower.

Iran and the other oil countries have belatedly discovered that modern manpower is a prerequisite of growth, and its imperfection constitutes one of the most critical bottlenecks in their economic development. Since 1973, underutilization of available capital has arisen in most of the countries owing to shortages in qualified and skilled workers.

On the whole, very few serious attempts have been made toward comprehensive manpower planning in the oil countries. Some development plans, such as the Iranian Fifth Five-Year Plan, have established employment as a prime goal. That plan's goal is not only the absorption of all new entrants into the labor force, but also the reduction of open or disguised unemployment. Other current development plans, such as Iraq's, however, simply state that only a part of the new entrants to the labor force can be employed.[5] These plans usually argue that the industries necessary for the economy's development are those that can utilize the country's cheap sources of energy. These include petrochemicals, steel, and aluminium, which are highly capital intensive and thus incapable of employing many workers, especially unskilled laborers. On the other hand, Iraq has started an important program for the improvement of the nation's educational, vocational, and health standards, though the results in these sectors can be expected only after considerable time. In Iran, the skilled labor force has increased by only 2 percent on an annual average; that is, much below agricultural and industrial requirements as envisaged by that country's development plans.

In Iraq, manpower shortages have been a constraint on both agricultural and industrial development for some time. Until very recently, the country's agricultural extension services had a staff of less than 500 workers, of whom only about one-fifth were college graduates. Industrial efficiency has been seriously affected by the lack of adequately trained manpower at all levels. Thus,

> experienced managers are not available in the required numbers and the government has resorted to the use of expatriate managers, but more are needed. Equally difficult are problems arising out of the scarcity of middle level and workbench manpower.[6]

Iraq's manpower problems have arisen from an imbalance in the nation's educational system. While primary, intermediate, and preparatory (general upper-secondary) education increased rapidly during the 1960s (primary by 200 percent, intermediate by 300 percent), enrollment in technical secondary education (industrial, agricultural, commercial, and home economics) actually declined during the decade. At the end of the 1960s only 10,000 students, or 20 percent, of the 50,000 students in preparatory schools were in technical schools. Such numbers are far below the country's requirements. Educational planning has been practically nonexistent until the current plan.

The lack of management and skilled labor has also resulted in the underdevelopment of health services. For example, the number of hospitals remained constant over the 1965-69 period.[7]

Future Manpower Requirements

Iran's revised Fifth Plan set as one of its main targets the creation of 2.1 million new jobs, including a large number of jobs in the teaching and medical professions. But realistic estimates now indicate that Iranians are likely to be able to fill only two-thirds of that number—a shortfall of 720,000 jobs. Initially the Ministry of Labor announced that 90,000 of these jobs would be offered to foreigners and that the remainder would have to be filled by Iranians, as training programs were established.

By mid-1975, however, shortages of skilled manpower in most industries and occupations were beginning to pose a serious constraint on growth. Both private company executives and ministry officials were complaining that projects were being delayed by months or even being postponed indefinitely because sufficient manpower—chiefly middle-level technical staff—was impossible to obtain. A number of industrialists have put great pressure on the government to fill all 720,000 vacancies with foreigners, but this is not likely to happen.

The country is becoming increasingly aware of the potential dangers to the nation's culture and long-term economic growth by importing so many foreigners. With this in mind, the Ministry of Labor has decided to exclude all requests for semi-skilled and skilled labor from the country's foreign recruitment drive. Still, by the end of 1975 the total number of working expatriates in Iran was over 36,000.

Many of the newcomers have assumed immediate positions in the medical field (where 22,600 jobs were available), or have joined

Iran's hard-pressed education sector, where Fifth Plan projections indicate a shortfall in teaching staff of 57,400.

The country's manpower shortage seems to affect every sector and profession, but the construction sector seems to have suffered the most. The country is not only obviously short of building materials—such as cement, steel, and bricks—but builders are unable to fill 50,000 vacancies unsuitable for foreign labor because of the high cost of importing this type of worker, and the government's reluctance to allow workers of this skill level into the country.

Meanwhile the government is preparing plans for enabling the country to replace the foreigners with equally competent Iranians. The Ministry of Labor's Vocational Training Board is now responsible for graduating 15,000 trained Iranians each year.

On the basis of guidelines drawn up in 1973 by the International Labor Organization (ILO), Iran has launched a massive training program, with a goal of establishing 500 vocational and training schools and a sophisticated network of 200 mobile training centers by the end of the Fifth Plan.[8]

One of the biggest difficulties in implementing this goal is the lack of qualified teachers. To alleviate the problem the government has contracted the ILO to train 600 Iranian instructors a year at the ILO's industrial training center in Turin, Italy. In addition, the ILO is setting up a training center in Karaj, just outside of Tehran, that will be able to graduate 4,000 Iranians a year when completed by the end of 1977.

By the end of the Fifth Plan Iran hopes to have trained more than 72,000 first-class technicians, 132,000 second-class technicians, and at least 656,000 semi-skilled and skilled workers.[9] The costs of these programs are high: a crash four-month course at one of the Industrial Training Board's centers, for example, costs about Rls. 45,000 or $650, per student.

While Iran's manpower shortages are currently hindering growth, in the long run the country should have no problem in finding additional workers, although these workers must learn new skills before they can be effectively assimilated into the work force. For example, seasonal agricultural workers currently constitute one-third of the rural work force. These workers have been classified by the Ministry of Labor as "redundant"; that is, they can be taken out of agriculture with no real decline in output. Between 4 and 5 million such workers are to be retrained for jobs in industries that will be located in new rural communities. This is part of a larger rural restoration plan aimed at consolidating rural villages into efficiently sized market centers.

This brief overview of the country's manpower situation conceals many complexities. Suffice it to say that the notorious lack of any sort of manpower planning (and its implementation) in Iran until the last few years has led to the contradiction of unemployment of unskilled labor, both open and disguised, on the one hand, and a scarcity of skilled and high-level domestic manpower, on the other.

The job of manning Iran's industrial expansion will be very difficult, at least until the end of the Sixth Plan in 1982, when, according to the Ministry of Labor, there will be enough skilled Iranians to replace the remaining foreign technicians.[10]

In the meantime there are more than 20,000 Iranian students studying abroad for advanced degrees. Until recently many students stayed abroad because of better job opportunities.[11] Several thousand professional Iranian personnel are also working abroad. The knowledge and experience of these personnel could prove to be invaluable in the country's development if they could be attracted back to Iran. Several efforts have been made by the government to this end, with some success. There is a clear need to widen this effort and initiate a comprehensive program for attracting back technical, professional, and scientifically trained Iranians studying and working in other countries.

While in the short term the use of foreign labor is unavoidable, there are several aspects of this means of filling the country's manpower gaps that should be considered. First, the decision to permit foreign workers to take employment in the country presupposes a full knowledge of the employment market for the particular skill as well as the availabilities of domestic laborers in the region of the country where work is to be performed. This involves continuous effort by the government at investigation, inspection, and decision making. Second, the social aspects of importing large numbers of foreign workers from different countries and in different categories are important. Third, the organizational arrangements required for this purpose should be adequate in view of the magnitude and nature of work involved. Fortunately, much experience has been gained in this regard over the last few years. It now seems appropriate to review the situation from time to time and adjust the various policy elements in accordance with changing needs. It is important to emphasize that in the course of time the manpower shortage should be filled by locally available personnel. The basic manpower policy of the country seeks to ensure this. It is therefore necessary for the authorities to be selective in approach and to identify priority sectors and categories in which employment of foreign workers needs to be encouraged.

The Shah has linked Iran's educational problem to the issue of income distribution. He has given heavy emphasis to the relationship of low incomes to low levels of educational attainment, and supports a strategy of improving the distribution of income by raising the educational levels of the low income groups. In the long run this will create a more equitable income distribution than that achieved by short-term increases in minimum wages, or the imposition of sharply progressive income taxes.

The need for continued improvement in education is only too apparent. Illiteracy and the lack of education account for a major share of the lag in agricultural areas in adopting new technology and in achieving higher rates of productivity. The educational deficiencies of potential industrial workers have required employers to make large expenditures on basic worker training. In addition, the shortage of managers and engineers has made Iran highly dependent upon foreign enterprise for transfers of technology. Until recently the virtual absence of a research and development capacity in both the private and public sectors also added to the dependence of the Iranian economy on foreign transfers of scientific and production know-how.

WAGES

Another key economic and social welfare measure is wages. The important question here is the degree to which the real income of Iranian workers has increased. Although the limitations of the data make it difficult to offer a comprehensive and well-supported answer to this crucial issue, it seems that in the period up to 1972 only a slight number of workers had substantial gains in real wages.

On the basis of an examination of minimum wages, it is evident that up to 1971 most workers' wages had barely kept up with inflation. In any case, until that time the minimum wage was only a lower limit set by the government, and was not rigorously enforced. Even more important, it was not a measure of the actual wages received by a worker or of the wages being paid for a specific job category. In 1971 the minimum daily wage was about 100 rials (about $1.30), and in many cases actual wages were barely equal to, if not lower than, that minimum (for instance, in the hand-weaving of carpets and in construction).

Ministry of Labor figures indicate that the average daily wage in 1971 for skilled and semi-skilled workers in manufacturing in Tehran (where wages are highest) was about 170 rials, plus 19 percent in overtime pay, and 17 rials representing any profit sharing. This amounts to 220 rials a day, or 66,000 rials a year ($870).[12] In executive positions in large private firms and in the upper ranges of the government service, annual salaries of over one million rials ($12,000) a year were not uncommon.

Since then, wages have increased dramatically—by 17 percent in 1974 and over 20 percent in 1975. Secretaries can now make $900 per month, and truck drivers up to $180 per week. These dramatic changes are reflected in the wage index, which increased from 100.0 in 1970 (1970 = 100.0) to 336.4 in 1975. The index of consumer prices increased from 100.0 in 1970 to only 156.9 in 1975.[13]

To the extent that workers who previously received less than the minimum wage are now receiving the minimum wage or above, and that workers who previously received the minimum wage are now receiving more than the minimum wage, the economic and social welfare of workers as measured by wages has increased. As of the mid-1970s, partial but impressive evidence indicated that both these phenomena had occurred. In many areas it has become difficult or impossible to hire even unskilled workers at the prevailing minimum wage.

INCOME DISTRIBUTION

One of the most controversial issues surrounding the rapid rates of growth achieved by the oil countries has involved changes in the distribution of income. Reliable data for historical comparisons of income distribution are among the most difficult to secure for most countries, and are even more precarious for the developing countries. Nevertheless, several distinct trends in the Iranian income distribution have been clearly identified.[14]

First, the richest urban 20 percent of the population increased their share of total money expenditures from 51.79 percent in 1959 to 55.56 percent in 1973. In other words, as total national income increased, the expenditures of individuals in the top two deciles increased at an even faster rate. In all the other deciles, except the seventh, ninth, and tenth, the relative share of total money expenditures was less in 1973 than in 1959 (see Table 4.3).

While the rich were getting richer, the poor were also benefiting from higher incomes, though perhaps at a slower rate. Income recipients in all deciles had absolute gains in money income adjusted for price increases, with the highest rates of gain in the top categories. The lowest rates of gain occurred in the middle income levels. Urban incomes grew more rapidly than did rural earnings, and those with university education gained at a faster rate than the less educated.

Expenditures are more unequally distributed in the urban areas; that is, the share of the bottom 20 percent of households in urban areas in 1971 was 5.7 percent (see Table 4.4) but it was 6.6 percent in the rural areas. At the same time the share of the top 20 percent of households in urban areas was 48.3 percent, while the corresponding share in rural areas was 45.7 percent.

TABLE 4.3

Decile Distribution of Household Expenditures, Urban Areas
(percentage)

Decile (lowest to highest)	1959	1969	1970	1971	1972	1973
1	1.77	1.59	1.48	1.34	1.37	1.37
2	2.96	2.86	2.62	2.39	2.51	2.40
3	4.09	3.96	4.07	3.60	3.36	3.42
4	5.08	4.58	4.54	4.32	4.64	4.77
5	6.17	5.94	5.60	5.66	5.16	5.08
6	7.37	7.96	7.68	6.94	6.98	6.85
7	8.92	8.48	8.23	8.57	9.51	9.36
8	11.85	11.72	11.48	11.70	11.14	11.19
9	16.42	16.05	16.18	16.00	18.38	11.57
10	35.37	36.86	38.12	39.48	36.95	37.99

Source: Compiled from Bank Markazi Iran, *Annual Survey of Household Expenditures* (Tehran: Bank Markazi Iran, 1959, 1969, 1970, 1971, 1972, 1973).

From 1969 to 1972 the inequality in Iran's expenditure distribution increased (see Table 4.5), as measured by the Gini coefficient, which increased rather sharply during this period. In large part the increasing inequality during this period was caused by widening in the gap between urban and rural incomes. This was particularly pronounced in 1969 and 1970, when the ratio of urban to rural per capita expenditures increased from 1.91 to 2.3.

These and several other patterns (see Appendix B) can be summarized as follows:

1. Between 1959 and 1971 the inequality in income distribution in Iran increased. Over the period 1971 to 1973, however, there was a tendency for inequality of household expenditures (and thus income distribution) to stabilize or even decline slightly.
2. The distribution of income in rural areas is less equal than in urban areas.
3. There is some evidence that in urban areas the share of middle-income classes has been rising.
4. Households in the bottom income deciles, particularly in the urban areas, usually have no literate members and have a high

TABLE 4.4

Decile Distribution of Household
Expenditures, 1971
(percentage)

Decile (lowest to highest)	Urban Areas	Rural Areas	Total
1	2.17	2.79	1.96
2	3.56	3.82	3.51
3	4.56	5.04	4.37
4	5.96	5.90	5.14
5	6.66	6.98	6.24
6	7.67	8.14	8.39
7	9.35	9.56	8.51
8	11.74	12.10	11.88
9	16.21	14.48	15.80
10	32.12	31.19	34.20

Source: Compiled from Statistical Center of Iran, Survey of Household Expenditures (Tehran: Plan and Budget Organization, 1973).

rate of unemployment. Furthermore, their household heads are either self-employed (in rural areas) or wage and salary earners (in urban areas).

5. There are considerable variations in regional expenditure inequality. High income regions, such as Fars and Central Province, show a greater degree of inequality than do poorer regions.

6. The ratio of urban to rural expenditure, government development expenditures, and the overall educational attainment of households have a significant influence upon income distribution in Iran. It follows that a policy that emphasizes reducing the gap between urban and rural areas, and between rich and poor regions, through balanced regional government development expenditures is very likely to succeed in reducing income inequalities in Iran. Furthermore, an educational program with a wide regional coverage (which in the long run reduces regional income disparities) will also be instrumental in achieving an improved income distribution. Finally, the creation of relatively well-paid jobs for unskilled and semi-skilled laborers in small urban centers is also likely to reduce income inequality in urban areas.[15]

The data are seriously limited in several respects: if this could be corrected, a lesser degree of income concentration would undoubtedly be revealed. Nevertheless, the broad pattern would still be one of significant income concentration. Some of the data and conceptual limitations are:

1. End-point comparisons. The data for 1959 and 1973 show increasing income concentration, a trend which was particularly noticeable over the year 1959-71. However, in 1972 and 1973 a stabilization seems to have occurred in the pattern of expenditure.

2. Money expenditures versus economic welfare. The estimates of household expenditures in Iran measure only the change in money expenditures. They do not measure social and economic welfare improvement, which should also include changes in the availability of such services as education, subsidized housing, social security, recreation facilities, and health—all fields in which Iran has sharply increased its government expenditures in recent years.

3. Comparison of Iran with other developing countries. In comparing Iran with other developing countries for which data are available, the Iranian pattern of expenditure is mixed. Based on the percent of income received by the lowest 20 percent of households, Iran appears to have a less equitable distribution than do countries such as Korea and Taiwan. On the other hand, based on the share

TABLE 4.5

Measures of Inequality of Expenditure
in Urban Areas
(percentage)

Years	Gini Coefficient	Share of Top 20 Percent	Share of Middle 20 Percent	Share of Bottom 20 Percent
1959	0.4552	51.79	27.54	13.90
1969	0.4710	52.91	26.96	12.99
1970	0.4849	54.30	26.05	12.71
1971	0.5051	55.48	25.49	11.65
1972	0.4916	55.33	26.29	11.88
1973	0.4946	55.56	26.06	11.96

Source: Compiled from Bank Markazi Iran, Annual Survey of Household Expenditures (Tehran: Bank Markazi Iran, 1959, 1969, 1970, 1971, 1972, 1973.

of income received by households in the top 20 percent income groups, income was more concentrated in such countries as Iraq, Ecuador, and Venezuela.

The criticism of Iran's income distribution pattern has been of two types. One has been on egalitarian and social justice grounds, generally expressed in terms of the rich becoming relatively richer. The criticism further argues that income distribution patterns are generating an explosive potential for popular discontent that will result in widespread disaffection and an erosion of popular support for the government and its development efforts.

The second type of criticism has focused on economic issues: that Iran's development strategy has relied upon income concentration, so that the government may set in motion and maintain the demand for consumer durables as a causal force for industrialization. But, the argument continues, the market for products purchased by high-income families has become saturated, and unless the size of the market is enlarged through a better distribution of income, economic growth in Iran will soon decline.

A possible response to the egalitarian criticisms is that the facts are being erroneously represented. It is true that the rich are getting richer, but the poor are also benefiting, even though the rich are gaining at a faster rate. Furthermore, the income distribution studies do not shed any light on the economic status of specific individuals. The deciles do not necessarily include the same individual in both 1959 and 1969, or 1973. Over the period an individual in the lowest decile may in fact have moved to a higher income decile or vice versa.

The degree of popular discontent that exists in Iran because of differing rates of gain and changes in the distribution of income has been impossible to verify empirically. Income distribution has not been debated in elections and it is probably less of an economic concern to individual voters than is the sharp increase in inflation. Casual empiricism and the weight of logic support the view that Iranian individuals and families are primarily concerned with whether they are making absolute progress compared with their own previous situation. In a relative sense, they compare this past progress to that of their neighbors and co-workers, rather than to that of the super rich.

Even more important as a source of content or discontent is the attitude of the individual Iranian and his family towards continuing to improve his welfare status. To the extent that this reasoning is valid, income distribution patterns have been more an issue in the minds of international agencies, foreign observers, and some Iranian scholars than among the Iranian rank and file.

In this regard one particular pattern stands out—a definite upward trend in the share of the middle 40 percent of urban households, which is a clear indication of the rise of the urban middle class. However, the share of the bottom 40 percent of households in urban areas also increased, if only slightly.

SOCIAL SECURITY AND SOCIAL LEGISLATION

Over the years Iran has created an extensive welfare system, more comprehensive than that of many developed countries. While services are often substandard in comparison with the developed countries, the system operates on a compulsory basis under state management, and is apparently comprehensive enough in coverage benefits to undercut what might otherwise be a source of urban discontent.

The system for workers in the nonagricultural sector provides benefits in cash and kind, such as for employment injury and occupational disease, sickness and maternity disability, and old age and death of the head of household.[16] The declared policy of the government is to extend coverage to the entire nonagricultural employed population. This can only be a long-term objective because the provision of such extensive medical care under social security legislation requires the availability of a much larger network of medical and hospital facilities than are now available. The further extension of the social security system will also raise financial and administrative problems that can only be solved gradually and in the course of time. A realistic timetable would aim for complete coverage by the end of the Seventh Plan period.

The rural population has its own social security system, following the enactment of a law on social insurance for farmers in May 1969. This legislation was subsequently made applicable to agricultural laborers as well, in May 1970. The object of these programs is to provide medical care and cash benefits in the event of sickness, maternity, employment injury, disability, and death of the head of the family. These social security programs are administered by a newly created Social Security Organization. Implementation on a limited basis has begun with the provision of medical care to selected categories of the rural population.

Additional legislation has covered the important area of termination of employment. In addition to 15 days' wages for each year of service, which he receives automatically, a worker may, under the third paragraph of Section 33 of the Labor Act of 1959, claim additional compensation for termination of employment. In practice a worker may thus obtain a termination grant corresponding to three years' wages after three months' service.

The social security and related programs are just beginning in Iran, and a number of problems must be corrected before they will be capable of meeting their intended goals. There are, of course, a number of uncertainties as to whether effective social welfare coverage can be provided to the groups presently excluded from coverage. Probably the greatest deficiency relates to the termination of employment issue. The high benefits received by terminated workers have caused firms to prefer capital intensive, rather than labor intensive, technology when a choice is available. Also, the legislation creates a bias in favor of overtime work as against adding new workers to the labor force.

Other criticisms of the social security system are that resources are too heavily allocated to individual medical assistance programs, in preference to preventive public health programs, and that imbalances exist in the distribution of services among regions and groups of workers. In spite of the numerous shortcomings of social welfare services, the system is realistic given Iran's stage of development, and is steadily being expanded. It is noteworthy that even within Iran's authoritarian political system, welfare services and agencies have continued to be a subject of criticism and evaluation by the press and by numerous studies of official planning agencies.

CONCLUSIONS

Iran, along with a number of other developing countries, has begun to recognize that the most relevant goal of development is the improvement of the quality of life for a nation's people, and that increasing the national output of goods and services should be a means of achieving the development goal, rather than a goal in itself. Nevertheless, until the early 1970s the emphasis of Iran's drive for development was primarily focused on expanding output and increasing the size of national income, rather than on a more equitable distribution of gains in economic and social welfare. The change in orientation toward improved social welfare should in no way detract from the country's continued economic expansion. If anything, this new orientation should assure continued economic advancement.

NOTES

1. Abdolmajid Majidi, "Social Change in the Modern World," in Jane Jacqz, ed., <u>Iran: Past, Present and Future—The Persepolis Symposium</u> (New York: Aspen Institute for Humanistic Studies, 1976), p. 11.

2. Various measurements of welfare are analyzed in Hollis Chenery et al., Redistribution with Growth (London: Oxford University Press, 1974).

3. See International Labor Office, Employment and Income Policies for Iran (Geneva: International Labor Office, 1973) for a comprehensive discussion of employment trends.

4. Iran, Ministry of Interior, The First Census of Iran (Tehran: Ministry of Interior, 1956); Iranian Statistical Center, National Census of Population and Housing (Tehran: Iranian Statistical Center, 1968). An excellent summary of manpower studies and statistics is given in Firouz Tofigh, "Development of Iran: A Statistical Note," in Jacqz, Iran: Past, Present and Future, pp. 57-71. See also Ferydoon Firoozi, "Demographic Review: Iranian Censuses 1956 and 1966–A Comparative Review," Middle East Journal (spring 1970), pp. 220-28.

5. Republic of Iraq, The National Development Plan 1970-74 (Baghdad: Planning Board and Ministry of Planning, 1971), pp. 138-39.

6. Iraq, Ministry of Education, Education in the Republic of Iraq (Baghdad: Ministry of Education, 1973), p. 17.

7. Ibid., p. 49.

8. International Labor Office, Employment and Income Policies, ch. 1.

9. Figures are from F. Aminzadeh, "Human Resources Development: Problems and Prospects," in Jacqz, Iran: Past, Present and Future, pp. 179-87.

10. Ibid., p. 185.

11. See George Baldwin, "The Iranian Brain Drain," in Ehsan Yar-Shater, ed., Iran Faces the Seventies (New York: Praeger, 1971), pp. 260-83.

12. International Labor Office, Employment and Income Policies, p. 81.

13. International Monetary Fund, International Financial Statistics (December 1976), p. 197.

14. The figures for income distribution are based on two primary sources: Bank Markazi Iran, Annual Survey of Household Expenditures, and the surveys conducted by the Statistical Center of Iran for the Plan and Budget Organization.

15. For a detailed analysis of the changes in Iran's income distribution, see M. H. Pesaran, "Income Distribution and Its Major Determinants in Iran," in Jacqz, Iran: Past, Present and Future, pp. 267-86; and Robert E. Looney, Income Distribution Policies and Economic Growth in Semiindustrialized Countries: A Comparative Study of Iran, Mexico, Brazil, and South Korea (New York: Praeger, 1975), especially ch. 7.

16. International Labor Office, Employment and Income Policies for Iran, ch. 7.

CHAPTER

5

THE ECONOMY: FOREIGN TRADE

INTRODUCTION

The amount of available resources and the extent of their utilization are fundamental to the growth of the economy. No economy, including Iran's, can spend more than it produces and imports, nor, in the short run, can it radically change the pattern of its expenditures among different activities without causing inflation. Despite dramatic developments in the last several years, the country's maneuvering capacity with regard to rapidly changing patterns and rates of growth of both imports and exports is still rather limited.

A major problem that the government will have to resolve is of the means by which the country can achieve an optimum balance between the use of imports to alleviate short-run domestic bottlenecks and shortages, and the restriction of certain types of imports so as to provide newly established industries with adequate protection from foreign competition.

COMMODITY COMPOSITION OF IMPORTS

Over the last decade and a half domestic manufacturers have enjoyed a great deal of government protection, especially in the form of high tariffs levied against imported goods competing with their products. This, together with the introduction and expansion of medium-sized and heavy industries, has caused a number of significant changes in the country's import structure.

Consumer goods accounted for slightly over 30 percent of total imports in 1959 (see Table 5.1). By 1969 this figure had declined to 11 percent. Imports of intermediate goods, largely used as inputs

TABLE 5.1

Composition of Imported Goods, 1959-68
(millions of dollars)

	1959	1960	1961	1962	1963	1964	1965	1966	1967	1968
Intermediate goods	267.5	324.6	329.9	313.2	285.1	408.0	518.2	558.2	711.0	856.5
	(49.2)	(42.2)	(53.4)	(57.2)	(55.9)	(55.0)	(57.7)	(57.9)	(59.7)	(61.7)
Industries and mines	217.7	261.9	260.6	234.9	221.9	317.9	410.1	444.5	545.3	641.7
Construction	26.2	40.4	35.5	49.8	34.8	58.8	69.2	74.7	120.8	147.0
Services	22.1	19.9	29.1	23.5	22.1	24.7	30.7	31.3	30.9	52.1
Agriculture and live-stock breeding	1.5	2.4	4.7	5.0	6.3	6.6	8.2	7.7	14.0	15.7
Capital goods	112.1	167.1	129.8	114.9	104.4	162.4	223.0	260.7	329.3	376.3
	(20.6)	(24.3)	(21.1)	(21.0)	(20.3)	(21.9)	(24.8)	(27.1)	(27.7)	(27.1)
Industries and mines	60.1	84.1	74.8	81.0	54.0	72.8	132.1	160.1	230.2	239.1
Services	33.1	69.1	29.4	20.6	26.7	47.7	55.8	63.9	71.5	103.8
Agriculture	19.0	13.9	25.6	13.3	23.7	41.9	35.1	36.7	27.6	33.4
Consumer goods	164.6	196.6	156.9	119.5	124.0	171.9	157.2	144.8	150.0	156.4
	(30.2)	(28.6)	(25.5)	(21.9)	(24.2)	(23.2)	(17.5)	(15.0)	(12.6)	(11.3)
Total	544.2	688.3	616.6	547.6	513.5	742.3	898.4	963.7	1190.3	1389.2

Note: ( ) indicates percent of total.
Source: Compiled from Bank Markazi Iran, Annual Report and Balance Sheet, various issues.

for expanding import-replacing industries, were increasing very rapidly during this period, from 49.2 percent of total imports in 1959 to 64.0 percent in 1969.

The predominant trend—a declining share of imports of consumer goods and a rising share of intermediate goods—has been reversed since 1969. The share of consumer goods in total imports has increased from its low level of 10.9 percent in 1969 to about 15.4 percent in 1974 (see Table 5.2). Since there has not been any significant change in the structure of tariffs or in overall government policy towards imports of consumer goods, the rising share of consumer goods imports during this period was the result of a rapid increase in consumer demand that could not be met by domestic producers (most industries were working at full capacity during this period).[1] Rising real incomes of many Iranians had therefore to be met by foreign products. The failure of domestic producers to increase their capacity in line with rising demand is the main factor responsible for the increasing growth rate of imports of consumer goods.

Inadequate domestic supplies and the government's granting of high levels of protection from foreign competition have strengthened the monopoly position of domestic producers. The reduction in domestic competition has thus put an upward pressure on domestic prices of most consumer goods. Consequently, imports of consumer goods have become more attractive than locally produced goods.

With the prospect of higher oil revenues and appreciably higher real incomes of many middle-income groups, consumer goods imports will probably continue to increase their proportion of the country's total imports unless major steps are taken to expand domestic production and eliminate inefficient plants, and to keep prices and costs down in Iranian industries.

An effective approach in terms of long-run industrial growth would be to encourage imports of consumer goods by reducing tariffs. Such a policy would not only cause downward pressure upon prices but would force the import replacement industries to operate their plants more efficiently and to increase the quality of their products. The reduction in tariffs begun in 1974 is a step in the right direction.

A closer examination of Iran's imports indicates that the country remains dependent on imports of a number of products to satisfy its domestic needs. Imports of the four major groups—machine and transport equipment, chemicals, basic manufactures, and food and live animals—account for over 89 percent of Iran's total imports.[2]

Imports of food and live animals increased sharply from 4.1 percent of total imports in 1970 to 12.9 percent in 1974 largely because of lagging agricultural production. In addition to the rise in food imports associated with the country's growth in real income, increases in world prices, particularly for wheat and sugar, were

TABLE 5.2

Composition of Imported Goods, 1969-74
(millions of dollars)

	1969	1970	1971	1972	1973	1974	Average Annual Rate of Growth	
							1969-72	1972-74
Intermediate goods	987.3	1068.5	1336.3	1596.2	2273.7	4266.4	17.37	38.78
	(64.0)	(63.7)	(64.8)	(62.1)	(60.8)	(64.5)		
Industries and mines	737.4	845.0	1110.9	1265.8	1912.0	3324.5	19.73	37.97
Construction	152.7	145.8	138.5	204.3	237.8	375.8	10.19	22.53
Services	64.8	52.7	57.8	97.4	76.3	444.1	14.55	65.82
Agriculture and livestock breeding	32.4	25.0	29.1	28.7	47.6	122.0	-3.96	61.99
Capital goods	387.2	391.0	482.9	642.6	906.0	1330.9	18.40	27.47
	(25.1)	(23.3)	(23.4)	(25.0)	(24.2)	(20.1)		
Industries and mines	316.2	263.7	316.6	411.9	560.3	770.4	9.21	23.21
Services	30.9	91.2	132.7	168.4	273.0	464.6	75.98	40.25
Agriculture	40.1	36.1	33.6	62.3	72.7	95.9	15.82	15.46
Consumer goods	168.2	217.1	241.7	331.6	557.4	1016.4	25.39	45.26
	(10.9)	(12.9)	(11.7)	(12.9)	(14.9)	(15.4)		
Total	1542.7	1676.6	2060.9	2570.4	3737.1	6613.7	18.55	37.03

Note: ( ) indicates percent of total.
Source: Compiled from Bank Markazi Iran, Annual Report and Balance Sheet, various issues.

also partially responsible for doubling the share of food and live animals in the total imports during this period. The rising growth rate of imports of foodstuffs is clearly going to continue. At present one major obstacle to a higher rate of growth in food imports is the limited unloading capacity of the nation's ports and the deficiency in roads and other infrastructure needed for proper distribution of imported foodstuffs. However, a long term solution to the country's food requirements does not lie in the expansion of port facilities, but in a fast rate of growth of agricultural output.

Chemicals, the second major item in Iran's imports, comprise 10 percent of total imports. This percentage should decrease, however, with the projected expansion of domestic chemical plants.

Basic manufactures account for approximately one-third of total imports. This percentage has declined somewhat since 1970 because of a recent expansion in metal industries and iron and steel foundries. Because most of these products are essential inputs for the country's industries, however, their share in imports cannot be expected to decline much further in the near future.

Machinery and transport equipment constitute the most important group of imported commodities. In 1970, the share of this category was over 40 percent, with imports of nonelectrical machinery accounting for well over half of this amount. As with imports of basic manufactures, this category is vital to a number of rapidly expanding light and heavy industries, thus it is expected that it will retain, or increase, its 40 percent share of total imports in the future.

The rapid rate of industrialization and economic growth experienced by the Iranian economy over the last decade has meant that the country has become increasingly reliant upon imported machinery, capital goods, and services. During this period the ratio of imports to GNP increased from 15.8 percent in 1961 to 24.4 percent in 1972, and to over 25 percent in 1974. Such a steep rise in the import-GNP ratio is nearly without precedent among developed or developing countries; it partially reflects the increasing ratio of oil revenues to total output. Given the levelling off in the rate of increase in oil revenues in the next few years, it is reasonable to believe that the country's ratio of imports to GNP will also begin to stabilize in the next few years.

Iran has encountered several import crises, the last severe one occurring in the late 1960s, before the series of new oil agreements were signed.[3] The country's strategy to meet the current import crisis has both short- and long-range components. The government's response to the short term is a series of measures to curtail imports through reestablishing some customs duties, requiring Iranian importers to pay cash for many import items, and reducing purchases

THE ECONOMY: FOREIGN TRADE 59

abroad by the government and its agencies. A longer range solution is expected from an accelerated drive to substitute local production for imported goods. As Iran expands its fertilizer industry and exploits its newly discovered reserves of nonferrous metals, there will be further import replacement in these categories. In addition to the expansion of steel and petrochemicals, another important contribution is expected from the program to expand the local production of capital goods.

COMMODITY COMPOSITION OF EXPORTS

The economic history of Iran since the late 1950s is dominated by developments in the oil sector. This has been particularly so since the latter part of 1973, when the country's exports of petroleum products began exerting a growing impact not only on the domestic economy but on world economic conditions.

As Iran's economy has developed, the share of exports in GNP has increased from about 20 percent in 1969 to 57 percent in 1974. On the other hand, the rise in nonoil exports and services up to 1973 was only about equal to the growth in GNP. Almost all of the change in the rising share of exports in the GNP has therefore been caused by the rising volume and value of oil exports. Iran's total exchange receipts from exports, including oil (less factor payments from abroad), traditional goods, and industrial goods and services, increased from $528 million in 1960 to $6.2 billion in 1973, and further to $21.1 billion in 1974. Although exports of goods increased at least sixfold, and services almost 28-fold, during this period, the dramatic increase in exchange receipts from the oil sector caused the share of nonoil exports in total exchange revenues to decrease from 32.0 percent in 1960 to 11.7 percent in 1974.

Iran's other exports are mainly of raw materials (minerals) and handicrafts such as carpets, refined cotton, animal hides and skins. Manufactured products such as textiles, soaps, detergents, shoes, clothing, and transportation equipment are, however, becoming more important, as increased labor costs and child labor laws restrict the production of carpets. The value of nonoil exports increased from $112 million in 1960 to $610 million in 1974, a 5.5-fold increase. About one-fifth usually consists of carpets and another one-fifth of cotton. Dried and fresh fruits make up about 15 percent, and animal by-products about 6 percent. The most significant development in Iran's nonoil exports has been the emergence of industrial goods as significant exports, increasing from less than 1 percent of total exports in 1960 to 23 percent in 1974.

OIL AND FOREIGN TRADE

Structure of World Oil Markets

Historically the world oil market has been controlled by a relatively small number of big oil companies.[4] These companies possessed significant monopolistic power since they held a large share of the world market and cooperated with each other in their international activities. With the postwar increase in oil consumption, the companies shifted the center of their operations from their home countries to areas where the new oil reserves were being discovered—especially in the Middle East. Consequently, the Middle East's share in world oil output increased from 15 percent in 1950 to over 40 percent in 1973.

In 1960 OPEC was established;[5] it now includes 11 countries—Saudi Arabia, Kuwait, United Arab Emirates, Iran, Iraq, Libya, Algeria, Nigeria, Indonesia, Venezuela, and Ecuador. By 1970, OPEC had become the strongest entity in the world oil market, due to its large output and the aggressive actions of its members' governments. Of the 16 billion barrel increase in oil output from 1952 to 1974, OPEC accounted for 10 billion barrels; 80 percent of OPEC's output came from its Middle East members.[6]

By 1973 a number of patterns in world oil trade and production were fairly well established, as follows:

1. OPEC members produced 55 percent of the world's output. Their exports constituted 96 percent of international oil trade.
2. Western Europe and Japan imported nearly all of their oil. Their imports accounted for 65 percent of international output.
3. The United States, which is the largest consumer, produced only 63 percent of its own consumption. Its imports constituted 19 percent of world trade.
4. The developing countries imported 12 percent of world trade.
5. Canada, the communist countries, and the rest of the world were self-sufficient, with insignificant surpluses.

In October 1973 the OPEC members increased the posted price of oil to $5.00 per barrel; in December they announced another increase to $11.65 per barrel effective January 1974. After a few months of uncertainty and price fluctuation at even higher levels, the oil prices stabilized in the $10.50 per barrel to $12.50 per barrel range (depending on grade of oil). World inflation, which averaged between 20 and 25 percent from January 1974 to the end of 1975, has, through increasing the price of imports, reduced the real price of oil (as of mid-1976).

THE ECONOMY: FOREIGN TRADE

Oil prices would have to rise to $13.00-14.00 per barrel to maintain the purchasing power of oil revenues at their early 1974 levels. In September 1975 OPEC posted a 10 percent price increase, which compensated for only part of the increase (after January 1974) in prices of imports to the OPEC countries. A number of proposals, such as indexation of oil prices (see Appendix C), have been put forth as means of neutralizing the effect of world inflation on the purchasing power of oil revenues.

OPEC's Impact on Iran

The OPEC price increases in late 1973 and early 1974 resulted in the average price of Iranian oil increasing by $7.00 per barrel. During the rest of 1974 and early 1975, most Iranian policy makers were confident that the newly acquired increases in the country's oil revenues could be maintained for a number of years. Their confidence was enhanced by the solidarity shown by the OPEC member countries and the inability of the consuming countries to mount any effective retaliatory action.

On this basis the Plan Organization made long-term projections for the country's likely levels of oil and gas revenues over the next 20 years that assumed the maintenance of constant production agreements with the Iranian Oil Participants (known as the consortium)* and other oil companies, at OPEC-determined prices.[7] In making these projections economists at the Plan Organization paid only minimal attention to the international financial problems and imbalances that would result from the inability of oil-consuming nations to absorb the transfer of their wealth to the oil-producing countries.

---

*From 1954 to March 1973, Iran's major oilfields were operated by the Iranian Oil Exploration and Producing Company for the Iranian Oil Participants (the Consortium). The Consortium was originally made up of British Petroleum (40 percent), Royal Dutch/Shell (14 percent), Gulf, Mobil, Exxon, Standard of California, Texaco (each 7 percent), Compagnie Française des Pétroles (6 percent) and Iricon Agency. The Consortium was the successor to the Anglo-Iranian Oil Company which operated the area of southern Iran until May 1951 when the oil industry was nationalized. Effective from March 20, 1973, a new agreement came into force governing operations in the Consortium area. The National Iranian Oil Company (NIOC) then took over all operations, including oil production and refining, and the Consortium's role in production was reduced to that of technical advisor and contractor for a period of five years.

As a result, their forecasts were somewhat optimistic. They projected $452.0 billion for the Fifth, Sixth, Seventh, and Eighth plans combined, and revised upward the initial estimates of revenues for the Fifth Plan, from $24.6 billion to $87.9 billion. The country's expanded financial resources meant that a large number of new projects could be included in the revised plan.

Trends in Oil Output and Revenues

Higher prices for oil and the world recession, beginning in 1974 and dragging on into the late 1970s, have, however, reduced the demand for oil. In the first six months of 1975 overall output of petroleum was down 11.8 percent in Iran, compared with the same period in 1974, and by June 1975 production was 15.5 percent below that of 1974.[8] (Production during 1975 averaged 5.35 million barrels per day, compared with 6.02 million in 1974.) This decline in production, though substantial, was nevertheless smaller than Saudi Arabia's 16.9 or Kuwait's 19 percent.

The average production figure, however, is misleading. Demand was reasonably steady in the first part of 1975 when, in anticipation of another increase (in September) in OPEC's price, sales suddenly increased. Once the 10 percent price increase had been agreed upon by the OPEC members, the demand for Iranian oil declined sharply. By December, production averaged 4.8 million barrels per day, 20 percent below the 1974 average.

Much of the decline in oil revenues can be attributed to the difficulty of finding buyers for Iranian heavy crude. Buyers have considered it overpriced, particularly after the September price rise and in view of the slowing increase in fuel oil needs among the industrialized countries. The fall in demand for heavy crude has been most responsible for the lower rate of Iranian exports. Normally, Iranian light crude (34 degrees American Petroleum Institute [API]) comprises about 52 percent of sales, and heavy (31 degrees API) 48 percent. This ratio has altered dramatically in the last few years, with the proportion of heavy crude sales dropping to as low as 31 percent.

As a result of declining demand for its oil, Iran has reluctantly followed Saudi Arabia and Kuwait in lowering the price of heavy crude. In February 1976 Iran reduced the price of its heavy grade by 9.5 cents, bringing it down to $11.40 per barrel. Iran's resistance to the price reductions of other OPEC countries was based in part on the planners' belief that a price cut would not encourage proportionately larger demand (and thus revenues).

THE ECONOMY: FOREIGN TRADE

The Iranian view that price reductions would be detrimental to revenues has been rejected by several of the major OPEC members. Both Kuwait and Saudi Arabia have pressured Iran to follow their lead in making a further cut of 7 cents in the price of heavy crude. In retrospect the Saudi position seems correct: as a result of these price reductions, February production in Iran was 5.6 billion barrels per day, against 4.9 million barrels per day in January.

While Iran has become increasingly opposed to the Saudi position in OPEC, relations between the country and the oil companies operating there remain strained. In January 1976 the Iranian government accused the oil companies known as the consortium of falling short of their production commitment by 14 percent. The companies argued that they were merely responding to market forces—that the 22 percent margin per barrel agreed to in 1973 related to the official market prices, when in fact prices were much lower and the margin was eroded. Now that demand has begun to pick up, this issue seems to be less pressing than before, but it will undoubtedly arise again.

Estimates of Future Petroleum Revenues

Any determination of the country's future level of oil revenues and resulting balance-of-payments position must involve estimates of the country's production levels of oil and consideration of participation agreements with the major oil companies, prices, and the rate of taxation of oil exports. There is no real consensus as to the likely values for these variables over the next two decades. Those estimates that are available vary widely. The problem of forecasting economic developments in the Middle East can be best illustrated by examining the estimates of several leading authorities.

Morris Adelman, forecasting increases in income taxes and royalty payments before the December 1973 price increase, predicted a price of $5.00 per barrel for Middle Eastern oil in 1980. The *Oil Daily* reported, in July 1973, that experts in Iran predicted a price of $10.00 per barrel for Iranian crude in less than a decade if energy substitutes were not developed.[9] James Akins and other authorities on the subject have proposed that $10.00 per barrel is not unlikely, but that prices might peak in the nearer term and then decline by 1980 because of a fall in sales, resulting from conservation measures (in use); a decrease of demand, due to high prices; and the eventual development of alternative sources of energy and supplies of oil.[10]

Estimates of the behavior of petroleum prices and revenues over the next two decades must therefore be considered tentative, as they are subject to many economic variables. Noneconomic factors are also likely to influence Iran's ability to expand oil revenues. Particularly important in this connection will be the relative bargaining strength and attitudes of the various OPEC countries, the energy and import policies of major industrialized countries, and the political situation in the Middle East. Because of the high degree of uncertainty associated with many of the forces shaping world petroleum markets, a realistic approach to Iran's revenues can be made only by accepting a range of likely prices for oil and then establishing the levels of government revenues and foreign exchange savings associated with individual assessments within that range.

Reserves

Any forecast of oil revenues in the long run must take into account Iran's existing reserves and the likelihood that new deposits will be found.

Official Iranian estimates of the country's oil reserves, both proven and recoverable, have not been made public by the government, but most Iranian foreign experts agree that it amounts to approximately 70 billion barrels.[11] If this figure is accurate, Iran could maintain its 1974 production level for 32 more years. In terms of its oil resources and the financial demands that will be made on them, Iran therefore is not as favorably endowed as is Saudi Arabia, or even Iraq. On the other hand, a number of foreign experts feel that there will be a sharp rise in Iran's proven reserves, as more sophisticated recovery methods become available.

Intensive exploration for new deposits is under way but the chances of major discoveries is fairly remote. The bulk of production will therefore continue to be from the Khuzestan fields in the former "agreement area" operated until 1973 on a quasi-concessionary basis by the Western Consortium composed of British Petroleum (40 percent), Shell (14 percent), the other majors—Exxon, Standard Oil of California, Texaco, and Mobil—(7 percent each), Compagnie Française des Pétroles (6 percent), and a handful of U.S. independents grouped under the name Ircon.

The Khuzestan fields, now owned and operated by the National Iranian Oil Company (NIOC), produced 5.57 million barrels per day (including a quantity of gas liquids), which accounted for 92 percent of the nation's 1974 total output. In the first half of 1975, however, output from these fields fell 12.6 percent further than the general national decline. By contrast, output of the four even-split joint ventures between NIOC and its foreign partners rose by 2.2 percent.

Despite the relative production decline of the Khuzestan fields, they continue to bear the main brunt of financing the country's develop-

THE ECONOMY: FOREIGN TRADE   65

ment. When, in 1972, the government started negotiating with the
foreign oil companies for the eventual takeover of the country's main
producing fields, the Iranian authorities assumed that they could be
developed to yield 8 million barrels per day and produce at that rate
until 1993. The 20-year "purchase agreement" with the Consortium
of Western Companies, then known as Iranian Oil Participants, was
eventually reached in 1973. The complicated formula for sharing
of output between NIOC and the members of the old consortium set
no firm projections for future output, but did set the objective of
installing productive capacity capable of producing 8 million barrels
per day. This agreement was hedged with the clause that this capacity
was technically feasible and economically justifiable. Since the signing of the agreement the target capacity for the Khuzestan fields has
been reduced by the operating companies, to 7.2 million barrels per
day. This is compared with an average of 5.57 barrels per day in
1974, and a peak of 5.73 million barrels per day in the spring of
that year. Obviously 1973-74 oil prices and resulting revenue increases made the expansion of capacity less urgent. In the meantime,
a very large investment is being made by the government, not only
to raise production in this area to its optimum but to maintain it at
that point.

The Fifth Plan goal is for a total allocation of 623.7 billion rials
($8.3 billion) for expanding capacity, with the government and NIOC
providing Rls. 535.9 billion for the expansion. The balance will
come from the members of the consortium, who still have a 40 percent investment obligation for the Khuzestan fields. The other foreign
partners of NIOC are involved to a much lesser extent.

More recently, NIOC has announced a $7.5 billion five-year
expansion program, beginning in 1976 and designed to raise production to 7.2 million barrels per day. The investment is also designed
to raise gas utilization from the present capacity of 5 billion cubic
feet per day (all of it currently associated with petroleum production)
to 30 billion cubic feet per day. Obviously the success of these
investments will go a long way towards determining whether or not
Iran will be able to retain its position as a major oil-exporting
country. As the country's position now stands, extraction of oil
from the Khuzestan fields by primary methods can go on for only
another seven or eight years. The prolongation of production from
this area to the end of the century will involve a massive and exter-
nally expensive program of gas injection.

FUTURE DEVELOPMENTS

Despite a number of underlying long-run trends, Iran's foreign
trade patterns should not change drastically in the next several years.

With oil and gas remaining important export products during the next decade, and Iran's plans for building infrastructure and industrial production capacities, it is likely that the average share of imports will remain at about 30 percent of GNP.

An important question is whether the growth in Iran's exports will be adequate to finance such levels of imports. During the next ten years oil should remain Iran's major export and foreign exchange supplier. The rate of growth of oil exports will be dependent on the strength of world demand for petroleum. It is true that the growth of demand for imported oil has been reduced following the price adjustment in 1973-74, a general economic slowdown in the industrial countries, and the efforts of oil-importing countries to conserve energy. With economic recovery under way in Western Europe, however, the demand for oil should continue its recent upswing. In the longer term context, in the absence of a major technological breakthrough replacing oil as a primary source of energy, the demand for oil should continue to grow fast enough for Iran to maintain at least the current level of exports.

On the supply side, Iranian reserves of crude oil are sufficient to last at least 30 years at production levels ranging between 5.5 million and 6.5 million barrels per day. Given this, and the assumption that oil prices will remain relatively constant in real terms, Iran may continue receiving an inflow of over $20 billion annually from crude oil exported during the next decade.

As Iran's economic plans materialize, the country will be drawing on its crude oil reserve for expanding the domestic economy and for providing the raw materials needed in the petrochemical, oil products, and manufacturing industries. It is very likely that in the future Iran will be an exporter of a host of industrial products derived from petroleum. Since the net value added (value added less import requirements) for these products is high, proceeds from oil-related exports should exceed the existing levels of $16 billion to $20 billion per year. Consequently, it is conceivable that, without any major efforts, $25 billion to $30 billion of Iran's import requirements could be financed by the export of crude oil and oil-related products. This means a real rate of growth for the oil-related exports ranging between 3 and 5 percent annually. For financing the remainder, the Iranian policy makers and planners must look hard at Iran's other resources, both actual and potential.

Iran's traditional exports reached the level of $530 million in 1973 but fell to $470 million in 1974, a year in which domestic demand was very strong. The country's future prospects for exporting these products are not high owing to two important factors. First, as the economy develops, a large proportion of mineral production—copper and iron ore in particular—and a number of traditional agricultural exports will be diverted to the domestic market, as input into many of the industries currently being established and, as in the case of food, to satisfy increased consumer demand. In addition, the price of raw materials and wages, particularly of skilled workers, will undoubtedly rise rapidly in the face of strong domestic demand and shortage of supply, making production of many of the country's traditional labor-intensive exports, such as carpets, extremely expensive. Thus, exports of industrial raw materials and agricultural goods cannot grow much beyond 5 to 7 percent annually, in real terms.

The new industrial products, yet to be developed, hold a more promising prospect. Iran's industrial exports have increased from less than $1 million in 1960 to $141 million in 1974, at an average annual rate of slightly over 42 percent.

For Iran to export significant amounts of industrial products in the next decade, at least three events must occur:

1. The cost of production must be reduced to make these exports competitive in international markets. The quality of output must also be improved significantly.

2. Secure markets must be developed by introducing Iranian manufactured goods in foreign markets and by signing bilateral and multilateral agreements for lowering trade barriers and duties.

3. Domestic output must grow fast enough to satisfy a major share of the rapidly growing domestic demand and to have some excess capacity for supplying the export markets. Thus to export, say, $2 billion to $4 billion worth of industrial goods, assuming that 15 percent of domestic production can be exported, value added by industries must rise from $13 billion to $27 billion, at an annual rate of growth ranging between 11 and 19 percent. Whether Iran's physical and human resources permit such a sustaining rate of growth in industrial output depends on factors beyond the scope of this study; nevertheless, in the author's judgment, it is feasible. Given these considerations, it is assumed that the rate of growth of industrial goods exports would be 25-40 percent per year.

CONCLUSIONS

The future prospects for exports of oil, gas and their related products are good, and Iran may count on her rich natural resources for at least one to two more decades. The country's pattern of oil-induced growth has, however, been somewhat of a mixed blessing. On the one hand, the sector's relatively weak linkages with the rest of the economy, its large share of rent and depletion allowance in its value added, and the fact that income generated by production and export of oil and gas do not accrue equitably to all strata of the society have resulted in the formation of a dualistic economy (the coexistence of a high-income sector and the much poorer traditional sector).

Still, large inflows of foreign exchange from the export of crude oil have permitted the public sector to launch massive economic and social development plans and programs for subsidizing basic consumption of agricultural products and services. This has also afforded the citizens a standard of living much above that which the productivity and efficiency of the nonoil economy warrant. On the other hand, an abundant supply of foreign exchange, and the public sector's concern in turning the exchange earned into the domestic currency, have given rise to a market rate of exchange for the rial above that warranted by efficiency and the international competitiveness of the nonoil sectors. These factors have given rise to a rate of exchange too high for the domestic economy to be able to compete effectively with foreign producers under relatively free trade conditions. It is true that the domestic industries have been protected from undue foreign competition by tariffs and commercial profit taxes; however, this situation has left few incentives for the domestic producers to lower their costs of production, to become technological innovators, or to expand their exports.

Iran's balanced growth in the long run cannot be dependent on oil exports alone. Other sectors of the economy, particularly agriculture, industry, and human resources, must develop in harmony with the growth of oil exports. The balanced growth of the above sectors cannot be completely dependent on the national economy. In order to benefit from the advantages of economies of scale and the improvement of quality, the industries in which Iran has actual or potential comparative advantage must be able to compete with others in international markets.

In the longer term, Iran needs to replace her oil exports with exports of energy and raw-material-intensive products. Iran's oil resources, rich as they may be, are bound to be exhausted. The economy must be prepared for this eventuality.

Iran's economy, no matter how fast it grows, cannot become independent of imports. Economic growth, technological change, and the consumer's taste for variety should lead to increasing imports. To finance the costs of these imports, and in order to prevent a deficit from occurring in the balance of payments, thus constraining growth, Iran must develop her nonoil exports.

NOTES

1. See Robert E. Looney, The Economic Development of Iran: A Recent Survey with Projections to 1981 (New York: Praeger, 1973), ch. 6; United Nations Economic Commission for Asia and the Far East, "Iran," Interregional Trade Projections, Effective Protection and Income Distribution, Vol. 2, Effective Protection (Bangkok: 1972), pp. 62-74.

2. Figures on exports and imports in this chapter are taken from Bank Markazi Iran Bulletin, various issues, and Bank Markazi Iran, Annual Report and Balance Sheet, various issues.

3. An excellent account of this earlier period and the events after 1970 are contained in Taki Rifai, The Pricing of Crude Oil: Economic and Strategic Guidelines for an International Energy Policy (New York: Praeger, 1975).

4. The structure of the petroleum industry has been exhaustively surveyed by Edith Penrose. See Edith Penrose, The Growth of Firms, Middle East Oil and Other Essays (London: Frank Cass, 1971), sec. 2.

5. The early origins of OPEC are documented in Mana Saeed Al-Otaiba, OPEC and the Petroleum Industry (New York: Halsted, 1975).

6. Bank Markazi Iran, Annual Report and Balance Sheet 1353, ch. 2.

7. Iran, Plan and Budget Organization, Planometrics Bureau, A Twenty-Year Macro-Economic Prospective for Iran, 1351-1371 (Tehran: Plan and Budget Organization, 1974).

8. Data on recent production trends in world oil markets are taken from Oil and Gas Journal, various issues.

9. Morris A. Adelman, The World Petroleum Market (Baltimore: Johns Hopkins University Press, 1972), ch. 8.

10. For several projections of world oil production, prices, and OPEC revenues, see: H. B. Chenery, "Reconstructing the World Economy," Foreign Affairs (January 1975), pp. 242-63; James Akins, "The Oil Crisis: This Time the Wolf Is Here," Foreign Affairs (April 1973), pp. 462-90; "Why OPEC's Rocket Will Loose Its Thrust," First National City Bank Monthly Review (June 1975); and Paul Eckbo, The Future of World Oil (Cambridge, Mass.: Ballinger, 1976).

11. See particularly Fereidun Fesharaki, Development of the Iranian Oil Industry: International and Domestic Aspects (New York: Praeger, 1976), ch. 8.

CHAPTER 6

ALLOCATION OF OIL REVENUES—AGRICULTURE AND AGRARIAN REFORM

INTRODUCTION

Iran's relatively advanced state of development, its large population, and the high volume of petroleum income that it will obtain over the next two decades will give the government great discretion in disposing of future earnings. By estimating future revenues and analyzing the determinants of the country's past expenditure levels and their patterns, an estimate can be made of Iran's capacity to absorb* oil revenues and to spend them in a manner consistent with national objectives. To the extent that earnings exceed this capacity, Iran will save foreign exchange. Obviously, the greater the level of these savings, the more Iran will emerge as a major lender in international financial markets.

The capital available from the oil revenues is financial capital and represents external purchasing power. Financial capital is not, however, the same as an equivalent amount of capital formation.†

---

*The term "capacity to absorb" has a number of meanings, and can operationally be defined in a number of ways. (The latest attempt at systematically analyzing the conceptual and measurement problems involved in any application of the term to a developing country is given in Willy J. Stevens, Capital Absorptive Capacity in Developing Countries [Leiden: A. W. Sijthoff, 1971].)

†The distinction between financial capital and capital formation is fundamental to an analysis of the Iranian economy. The difference between the two types of capital was first identified and analyzed by Raymond F. Mikesell. (See Raymond F. Mikesell, U.S. Private and Government Investment Abroad [Eugene, Ore.: University of Oregon Books, 1962], pp. 360-76.)

Money available for investment, whether in the form of local currency or the foreign exchange derived from oil revenues, must be employed for the purchase of capital assets and for hiring labor, managers, and technical services, all of which need to be combined into an organization capable of producing goods and services before capital formation can take place. The ability of Iran to transform its vast amounts of financial capital into an equivalent amount of real productive capital (as measured by the discounted value of the net outputs) will ultimately determine whether the country will join the ranks of the world's developed nations.

The task of planning the development of Iran is not as easy as it may seem to analysts who consider capital to be the only, or at least the major, factor determining the country's rate of growth.[1] True, Iran certainly had (particularly in 1974) an abundance of capital in relation to exportable raw materials and available labor. In view of the major aims of Iran's Fifth Five-Year Plan, however, there are two basic economic policy problems facing the planners: how to find the best investment opportunities for the country's substantial savings, and, given the existence of shortages of a number of domestic materials and skilled labor, how best to explore and expand the opportunities for investment within the country. Both problems involve decisions as to the optimal manner in which the country should adopt capital-intensive technologies, raise the level of the technological skills of the work force, and encourage the country's latent entrepreneurial talent. There is no doubt that the costs of experimentation and learning have been extremely high since 1973, and will continue to be so in the near future. To an important extent, the final success of the control of waste will depend on the vitality and adaptability of the entrepreneurial class, and on the willingness of the Iranian citizens to acquire new skills and improved working habits.[2] Until the country's work force is upgraded to levels commensurate with the requirements of a modern industrialized country, the nation's ability to utilize its oil revenues in productive domestic investments will continue to fall considerably short of the volume of financial capital accruing to the government.

As with other oil-exporting countries, the rate at which a predominantly agricultural Iran can become industrialized is certainly not governed only by the amount of capital available for investment. Inadequate education, lack of technical know-how, social customs, religious beliefs—all these may limit the rate of economic growth. Furthermore, the processes of economic and social change cannot be accelerated beyond a certain point without disrupting the fabric of society and inflicting intolerable hardship on the people concerned. In some OPEC countries, lack of capital will soon cease to be the limiting factor in economic development. (This is already the case in the larger OPEC countries, particularly Nigeria and Indonesia.)

The use of oil revenues for accelerating development in Iran is in itself not a new problem. A system for allocating the income from the oil sector towards the attainment of the country's national development objectives and targets was set up over 20 years ago. What is new is the magnitude and volume of these resources and the prospect of their limitation in time. Rightly or wrongly, the country has accepted a time horizon of about 30 years for the exhaustion of its oil resources as a major exporting asset.[3] The combination of having immediately available both a high level of resources and the prospect of their limitations has created a sense of emergency that is not conducive to satisfactory and realistic planning. It is conceivable that under these circumstances oil income may have an unfavorable impact on the country's social and political stability, on the decision-making process, and even the country's long-run growth potential.

The agricultural sector illustrates a number of problems that Iran has encountered in effectively utilizing its oil revenues. There is no doubt that public officials responsible for agricultural development, and other enlightened citizens in the country, have given serious attention and devoted considerable effort and funds to agricultural development. At the same time, performance has fallen substantially short of projected or desired targets. The growth of agricultural income has not kept pace with the average growth of total national product. The result has been increasing tension in the rural sectors, and massive migration to the larger towns. There is no simple explanation for the discrepancy between expenditure, effort, and achievement. The rate of development of any sector, and particularly the rural sector, is obviously not exclusively a function of government expenditure, but instead is bound to the entire social, political, and economic environment. The success of efforts in this area depends quite often on the coordination of the efforts of several government departments. When coordination falters, good plans frequently sustain damaging delays in implementation, and sometimes never come to full fruition.

Clearly, if oil revenues are to be utilized efficiently in improving the country's agricultural performance, the government will have to deal simultaneously with three major problems that have characterized Iranian agriculture: the slow, and at times negative, growth of the sector; the continuing low level of technology used in agriculture, and the resulting low levels of productivity per hectare; and rural poverty, particularly in a number of isolated areas in the western part of the country where agriculture is characterized by small farming units and surplus labor.[4]

CHARACTERISTICS OF THE AGRICULTURAL SECTOR

Two popular opinions concerning the country's agricultural potential are widespread both within and outside Iran. One is that Iran's soil resources are played out and will be worthless forever; that is, that the nation has exhausted its soils, denuded its forests, and generally worn out its (agricultural) resources beyond repair. The other looks to water as the rejuvenator that can, in short order, restore the country to its former productiveness. Experience in the last several years has shown that both judgments are myths. First, the country is not played out: with appropriate modern farm technology, practices, and management, and freed from the restrictions, inhibitions, and rigidities that lie in the political, social, and institutional field, the natural resources of Iran could permit production on a vastly higher level. As for the second point, the results obtained from massive irrigation schemes have been notably poor.

Owing to the quadrupling of oil prices in December 1973, funding for the agriculture sector has increased markedly. The government expenditure of 239.6 billion rials together with investments expected to be made by the private sector, $1 billion for rural development and $2.4 billion for irrigation work, means that the country will be spending an unprecedented $8.0 billion for agricultural development during the Fifth Plan period. Not even the government's recent decision to tighten its budget and modify its priorities is likely to diminish agriculture funding.

As in many other sectors of Iran's economy today, however, bottlenecks have developed that are threatening to slow down progress temporarily. Imported equipment is not getting through the badly congested ports fast enough, projects have been held up because of a nationwide shortage of construction materials, and the Ministry of Agriculture is lacking in field staff capable of educating farmers in the use of new techniques and seeds.

PROGRESS IN LAND REFORM

Agricultural production in Iran has been largely influenced by a series of land reforms, the first of which was attempted by Reza Shah, the present Shah's father, in 1932 and 1937.[5] It was his intention to distribute the public domains that had fallen into the hands of the tribal chiefs among the farmers. Both attempts were unsuccessful.

In 1950 another attempt at land reform was made by the Shah, who ordered the distribution of crown lands by a royal decree. Between 1955 and 1960 a series of decrees followed regarding public domains and private estates, but these were obstructed by the still powerful vested interests of the landlords. The 1956 census indicated that during this period Iranian agriculture was still characterized by a great complexity of tenures.[6] Under the existing system the landlords shared from 10 to 87 percent of the product, depending on the crop and the geographical area—the remainder went to the sharecropper. The problem was accentuated by the pattern of land ownership: 10 percent of the land belonged to public domains and 4 percent were crown lands. The latter, though small in percentage, were the very best agricultural areas.

In 1962, however, the Shah abolished the feudal system and significant progress toward land reform took place. The first phase of the reform concentrated on the principle that only one village could be retained by the landlord. The rest of his holdings were to be expropriated (with compensation) and redistributed. As of 1963, 8,000 villages had been purchased; 271,000 peasants had received conditional titles; and 2,000 cooperatives (with 243,000 members) had been established.

It became increasingly clear in the late 1960s, however, that land reform, as it was originally conceived, could not be counted upon to solve the multitude of problems that had existed for centuries. Land reform was conceived by the Shah primarily as a political—not economic—tool, and to this end the initial reforms worked with exceptional efficiency. The redistribution of the huge private estates removed much of the power possessed by Iran's all-powerful landowning classes. In the late 1950s and early 1960s these groups were able to block many of the Shah's early attempts at reform. More importantly, perhaps, land reform won grass roots support for the Shah among the new class of farmer-cultivators and enabled him to proceed with even more difficult reforms (in education, for example) that would have proven next to impossible without the support of at least one sector of the Iranian people.

To make up for some of the economic deficiencies of earlier reforms, a third phase of land reform was started in 1968. During this phase land was to be redistributed in three parts: one-third to the original landlord and two-thirds to the peasants. A deadline of August 1972 was set for the completion of this phase of reform.

It is too early to evaluate precisely the country's attempts at reforming the rural sector, but three results can be assessed: production increased by 30 percent during the 1960s (this may, however, simply reflect the drought in the early 1960s, and the relatively good rainfall in the latter 1960s); the agricultural labor force, which constituted nearly 50 percent of total employment in the early 1960s, dropped to less than 40 percent by the early 1970s, thus raising the average income of rural workers; and there has been a tendency for farmers to invest larger amounts in the sector, to use fertilizers more extensively, and to improve their levels of educational attainment.[7]

Despite the new importance attached to agriculture, however, the late 1960s saw the Iranian farmer still left without any appreciable material well-being. The economy seemed finally poised to make its long-awaited takeoff but, largely because of an acute lack of agriculture funding in the Third and Fourth Plans, the income of the farmer was rapidly falling behind that of his contemporaries in other sectors. Instead of applying the new technical know-how that was starting to yield results on the farms of the more prosperous Iranians, most of the country's farmers were barely able to support their families and relatives, let alone the seemingly insatiable appetite of the increasingly affluent urban Iranian.

GROWTH IN PRODUCTION

Partially as a result of the land reform programs, Iran's agriculture has undergone a number of significant changes. Field crops increased by about 60 percent during the 1960s, largely owing to the gradual breakdown of the five-shares system (land, water, seed, draught animals, and labor), growing mechanization, and the spread of cooperatives and land under irrigation. In the late 1960s performance significantly exceeded that of the earlier period. However, even as late as the mid-1970s only 6 million hectares, out of a possible 50 million, were being cultivated.

The result has been one of the least-publicized, but most disturbing, trends in the Iranian economy—the country's growing dependence upon agricultural imports. In 1966 Iran was a net exporter of agricultural products, yet by 1976 it had become a substantial importer. Admittedly, demand for most food items has risen to unprecedented levels as a result of the government's food subsidy program for low-income families. The overall increase in purchasing power associated with the new oil wealth has especially increased the demand for meat, fresh fruits, and vegetables—items the country has never produced in abundance.

By the mid-1970s sales of foodstuffs (including imports) were increasing at approximately 12.5 percent a year, a rate much higher than the ability of the domestic agricultural sector to supply. Official Ministry of Agriculture figures tend to be optimistic, indicating a domestic production rate of 8 percent.[8] These estimates are undoubtedly on the high side, but still show a rapidly widening gap between domestic consumption and imports—a gap even more alarming when a number of experts in the field indicate that the real growth rate in agriculture is considerably lower than the official figures; that is, little more than 2.5 percent, or less than the annual increase in population.

Whichever figure one accepts, the reality remains that in 1975 foodstuff imports tripled over their 1974 level, rising to $1.4 billion. This figure could easily rise to $4 billion by 1980.[9]

It is becoming apparent that money alone will not solve the multitude of problems currently facing Iranian agriculture. In fact, halfway through the Fifth Plan (1973-77), progress in the sector is still very uneven. Despite a massive channeling of funds (in the form of loans and subsidies) to the Iranian farmer, the arrival of all the latest equipment from the West, and the launching of some 500 small- and large-scale mechanized projects, agriculture is still lagging behind the country's booming industrial sector.

The government contends that such measures are highly preferable to becoming increasingly dependent on imported foodstuffs. Projections of consumption indicate that the country's food requirements are likely to increase from 245 billion rials in 1971 to 1,300 billion rials in 1987. To counter the trend towards having to import increasingly large amounts of food, the government seems to be making a very determined attempt to achieve some degree of self-sufficiency in agriculture.

CURRENT PROBLEMS

Such major goals as the government's professed aim of achieving relative self-sufficiency in the production of food by the mid-1980s may fall far short of achievement. Several major studies have recently concluded that food imports are likely to increase rapidly over the next decade regardless of any steps taken by the government.[10]

The government's major problem is that of overcoming the problem of rural illiteracy. A secondary one involves the failure of many excellent programs simply because the Ministry of Agriculture still lacks the qualified personnel to demonstrate the operation of new machines or to ensure that the new and improved seed varieties associated with the "green revolution" (brought to Iran in the late 1960s) are delivered in time for planting. As a result, most of the ministry's programs have had virtually no impact on the level of food production.

Although increased consumption of meat, cereals, sugar, and oils is an important factor affecting the increase in imports, it is clear that the government's agricultural strategy has not been as successful as hoped. Indeed, the main source of new and increased production—large-scale commercial farming—has not lived up to expectations and gives no indication of improvement in the near future. Problems in agriculture have reached such a level that the Ministry of Agriculture is being forced into reassessment of both the concepts and methods behind the nation's agricultural development.

In order to stimulate production, a massive new loan and subsidy program was set up in the summer of 1974, through which farmers can obtain low-interest credits and help from the government in the form of improved infrastructure. Furthermore, under a ten-year tax holiday farmers are guaranteed an annual return of at least 20 percent. In addition to these benefits the Ministries of Agriculture and Natural Resources are willing to arrange payment for 50 percent of feasibility study costs and 60 percent of all land-leveling work. Large subsidies are given for seed; in 1975, for example, 11 crops, including wheat, rice, grapes, and potatoes, were eligible for the subsidy program. The ministry has also volunteered to pay all freight costs on the 200,000 dairy cows that are now being imported.

Equally important, but of more long-term significance, is a series of recently enacted laws that could be the key to agricultural development in the Sixth Plan (1978-82). Aiming at consolidating Iran's rural areas, the Ministry of Agriculture can now legally limit grazing on the country's already badly overgrazed pasture lands, prevent farmers from selling prime agriculture lands to either speculators or home builders, control the use of lands bordering the country's waterways, have a greater say in the development of lands adjoining urban areas, and set up agricultural centers to stimulate mechanization.[11] These programs have not brought the success hoped for.

The government's input subsidies and minimum price support programs have not fared much better. In theory relatively sophisticated and, in some cases, very generous, unfortunately they are based, more often than not, on poor data and also suffer from a lack of skilled administrators. These deficiencies in turn lead to poor food import planning and seasonal shortages.

More pressing in the long term, perhaps, is the current lack of security felt on many farms. The land reforms begun in the early 1960s have not been completed. While the third phase is near completion, another phase, that of land consolidation, is already being discussed. Land consolidation is necessary because the relatively high proportion of small farms in the country makes extension work extremely costly and inefficient. As an indication of the magnitude of the problem, over four-fifths of the farmers' work holdings are of less than 11 hectares. These farmers own 40 percent of the country's richest agricultural land yet provide less than 20 percent of the crops actually sold in urban areas. By comparison, farmers with medium-sized holdings, of between 11 and 100 hectares, have been producing almost three-quarters of the nation's marketed supplies, while cultivating less than 50 percent of the country's arable land.

Compounding the problem of small farms is the fragmented pattern of land ownership. Farms of 10 hectares are often divided into a number of separate plots, rendering useless many of the agricultural ministry's plans for high technology. In an attempt to overcome this problem the government, in 1975, decided to establish a number of agricultural centers (or poles) where all farms will be combined into units of not less than 20 hectares—the size considered to be economically viable for large-scale farming. By mid-1976, 20 such centers were already established. Ultimately they will be turned into what may be described as state-sponsored agribusinesses.

The success of this innovative approach will depend largely on how the government proceeds with its implementation. Despite the urgency of land consolidation, experts feel that the government must use persuasion and not coercion in inducing farmers to participate in the program. Rumors that those farmers who turn down the government's offer of membership in the new agribusiness ventures will find their land automatically bought up by the Ministry of Agriculture and either rented to the private sector or farmed by the government itself have caused great consternation in several areas. The result has been a drop in investment and levels of production on small farms. A number of farmers are reported to be leaving their land in fallow, and are seeking nonagricultural employment.

The government's antiinflation program, begun in early 1975, is also causing great discontent in rural areas. Many farmers consider the government's target of a zero rate of inflation—through controlling food prices—unacceptable and unrealistic. Quality has slipped noticeably in the fruit and vegetable market, and a number of large farms have closed, charging the government with mismanagement. Retailers are also unhappy, claiming that shortages of a number of crops are becoming commonplace. Bigger shortages, particularly in processed foods, are predicted for 1977.

THE FAILURE OF COMMERCIAL FARMING

In 1967, the Ministry of Agriculture decided to promote large-scale commercial farming. Methods used to develop this pattern of farming emphasized both the encouragement of foreign participation and the provision of substantial local finance through the Agricultural

Development Bank (ADBI). The area singled out by the ministry for the country's first experiment at large-scale commercial farming was the province of Khuzestan in the southwest, where there were huge tracts of flat and largely uncultivated land. The ministry felt that this area had the greatest potential to be brought under modern agriculture with the use of irrigation, fertilizers, and good management.

Under the ministry's direction, four ventures were formed with foreign partners: Iran Shellcott (Royal Dutch Shell 70.5 percent, Mitchell Cotts 4.5 percent); Iran California (Bank of America, 10.02 percent; Transworld, 18.11 percent; John Deer, 4.14 percent); Iran America (Citicorp International Development, 7.64 percent); and Iran International (Mitsui, Diamond A Cattle Ranch, Chase Manhattan Bank, Hawaiian Agronomics, all 15 percent). All were well-qualified companies. Hawaiian Agronomics had experience in the province, in sugarcane growing in particular; Mitchell Cotts had extensive knowledge of cotton growing in Ethiopia; and Transworld was based in California, where growing conditions were similar to those in Khuzestan. Unfortunately, of the 60,800 hectares allocated by the ministry to the four groups between 1969 and 1973, only 8,200 hectares, or 13.4 percent, have been brought into cultivation.

This failure dramatically illustrates the problems that have resulted from Iran's attempt to grow too fast. Projects have not been well-conceived, nor has coordination between different participants been very effective. In the example of Khuzestan, the ministry had assumed, without any real supportive studies or field experience, that there were large economies of scale in Iranian agriculture in that province. Thus the land allocated was in large blocks (the ventures were given 30-year leases): farms averaged 15,000 hectares, with Iran America taking the largest (19,000 hectares). The advantages of economy of scale, however, proved illusionary against the complex problems of management and cultivation of such large holdings.

In practice, the high temperatures (40-50° C in summer) and poor soil meant that winter crops like sugar beets and wheat have been the most successful. Growing more valuable crops such as cotton has proved disastrous. The foreign firms admit now that they should have made more independent tests to gauge the most suitable crops instead of relying on information provided from the undermanned Iranian experimental station at Safiabad. These problems were compounded by poor utilization of machinery, lack of skilled manpower (drawn away by higher wages in nearby Ahwaz), and such normal occurrences in a fast-developing country as, for example, crop-spraying aircraft arriving too late, spare parts being held up in overcrowded ports, and essential infrastructural items such as water coming behind schedule.

Finally, all the projects have run into a series of problems created when some 6,500 families were moved from the land to be developed. The government's plan was to remove these people, who had traditionally used it for grazing and cropping, into resettlement centers, and then rely on them as the source of labor. Not only have these people been reluctant to move, they have also been reluctant to work for others on the lands which historically they regarded as theirs, especially as most of the work offered to them has been low-paid manual labor.

The agribusiness failures exemplify the type of problems the government has run into in the rural sector. As a result of these setbacks, the Ministry of Agriculture must decide whether investments in large-scale agriculture will ever prove as profitable as similar investments in industry. If the initial problems can be overcome and large-scale farms can be shown to have a high potential, then substantial new development costs will have to be borne by such institutions as the ADBI. More importantly, the payment of higher prices to the producers and the development of a new system of market distribution would be necessary.

FUTURE TRENDS IN POLICY

The setbacks suffered by the farm program are reportedly prompting the government to reexamine its agricultural program. One outcome has been a noticeable renewal of interest in the middle farmer (with 11-100 hectares), who received 83 percent of the loans distributed by the ADBI during 1975. During that year, ADBI also established three regional development banks intended to mobilize local savings and to make access to loans easier for small farmers. In the same vein, the Ministry of Cooperatives and Rural Affairs recently announced the creation of a 200 million rial rural aid fund that is open, not to agribusiness, but to members of farm corporations and to farmers with less than 2 hectares.

Despite the difficulties with agribusiness, the government appears determined to go ahead with the largely unpopular farm corporation program. The 85 such organizations existing in 1976 was expected to expand to 140 by the end of the Fifth Plan. Membership in these organizations requires that the farmer exchange the title deeds of his land for a share in the government-financed agribusiness company. The economic viability of many of these farm corporations is highly questionable, however, and even government officials have conceded privately that few farmers are happy working under such a system. Far more popular are the production cooperatives that were instituted by the government, which are basically organizations of like-minded farmers who agree to pool their resources in the name of more mechanization and higher crop yields.

The Iranian economy has reached a stage where further progress depends increasingly upon achieving a balance in sectoral growth rates and, in fact, upon an integration of sector policies. It will not be possible, for instance, to meet the effective demand for agricultural crops, livestock, and primary products without substantial increases in agricultural production and value added (of the order suggested by the Fifth Plan, that is, 5.5 percent annually). At the same time, further expansion of the industrial sector itself has come to depend, among other things, on an adequate increment of domestic demand among the poorer (largely rural) population.

CONCLUSIONS

Two long-range solutions are possible: higher prices might increase the land under cultivation, and local farm subsidies to increase domestic production, rather than the present massive subsidies of $1 billion a year to finance food imports.

More immediately, however, indications are that the Ministry of Agriculture is looking towards renewed emphasis on medium-scale farms. In its efforts to restructure and salvage the Khuzestan projects, parcels of land are expected to be taken from the areas allocated to the four ventures. At the same time, foreign companies are likely to participate more as managers than as venture partners.

Developments over the last few years, therefore, cast some doubt on the government's agricultural strategy, which presumably has been oriented towards achieving some degree of national self-sufficiency in food production. Whereas only a year ago F. R. C. Bagly concluded that (based on initial successes) the great increases in oil revenues would enable the Khuzestan to be developed in a manner that would assure the country a large degree of self-sufficiency in food,[12] now authorities are proceeding with caution and some doubts as to the best means of developing the area.

The government is working hard at setting up a coordinated and comprehensive agriculture policy, but unless some basic reforms are undertaken at both the institutional and farm levels—to say nothing of reevaluating and cutting back on a number of questionable programs—Iran's agricultural sector could remain troubled for many years to come.

NOTES

1. See, for example, the approach taken by Michael Bruno in his analysis of the Israel economy. Michael Bruno, "Economic

Development Problems of Israel, 1970-1980," in Charles A. Cooper and Sidney S. Alexander, eds., Economic Development and Population Growth in the Middle East (New York: Elsevier, 1972), ch. 3.

2. Increased Iranian concern with waste and corruption associated with the oil boom is reported by Robert Graham, "When the Dreaming Had to Stop," Financial Times (February 26, 1976), p. 18.

3. At least this is the view expressed in Iran, Plan and Budget Organization, Planometrics Bureau, A Twenty-Year Macro-Economic Perspective for Iran, 1351-1371 (Tehran: Plan and Budget Organization, 1974). This is also the view of the Shah. In a recent speech to a labor congress he noted that in 30 years time, "your agricultural exports and your industrial exports must compete with those of other advanced countries of the world. . . . Otherwise, it will be impossible to maintain the present standard of living." See "A Survey of Iran," The Economist (August 28, 1976), p. 5.

4. An excellent and recent survey of the Iranian agricultural sector is given in Oddvar Aresvik, The Agricultural Development of Iran (New York: Praeger, 1976). See particularly Chapter 3 for an overview of the sector.

5. An extensive outline of the country's land reform efforts is given in Kenneth B. Platt, "Land Reform in Iran," in Agency for International Development, Land Reform in Iran, Iraq, Pakistan, Turkey, and Indonesia (Washington, D.C.: Department of State, 1970), pp. 1-102.

6. See A. K. S. Lambton, Landlord and Peasant in Persia (London: Oxford University Press, 1969).

7. S. Thomas Stickley and Bahaoldin Najafi, "The Effectiveness of Farm Corporations in Iran," Tahqiqat-e Eqtesadi (winter 1971), p. 24.

8. As reported in Bank Markazi Iran, Annual Report and Balance Sheet, 1353.

9. A number of projections of this magnitude are given in Allen LeBaron et al., Long Term Projections of Supply and Demand for Selected Agricultural Products in Iran (Logan: Utah State University Press, 1970).

10. Ibid.; Abdolhossain Zahedani, Iran: Evaluation of Agricultural Development Strategy, 1962-1972 (Ph.D. dissertation, University of California, Davis, 1974); H. Kaneda, "Agriculture," (Tehran: International Labor Organization, 1973), mimeo.

11. Harry W. Richardson, "Regional Planning in Iran," Growth and Change (July 1975), pp. 16-19.

12. F. R. C. Bagley, "A Bright Future After Oil: Dams and Agro-Industry in Khuzestan," Middle East Journal (winter 1976), pp. 25-35.

CHAPTER

7

THE USE OF OIL REVENUES FOR NATIONAL DEVELOPMENT

INTRODUCTION

The Iranian government, pursuant to the policies it has set for the country, is spending its oil revenues toward the following goals: developing the economy so that it will eventually be self-reliant and independent of events and developments in the oil sector; increasing the standard of living of the majority of the population; increasing Iran's national security; maintaining and strengthening the country's political and institutional organizations; and increasing the country's influence in international affairs.[1]

If it is to achieve these goals, the government must control utilization of the oil revenues in four main types of activities:

1. increased private and public consumption so that the standard of living will be raised, not only in the short run, but over time
2. increased domestic investment in either public or private projects that have a positive rate of return and thus are capable of contributing to the country's growth and development both now and in the future
3. discretionary spending by the government (including military expenditures), which does not directly increase the economy's productive capacity, yet is considered desirable on noneconomic grounds
4. increased investment in foreign countries, either in the form of aid, loans, or direct purchase of equity shares

A further consideration for the government is that it must decide when the expenditures are to be made.

Since oil is an exhaustible resource, Iran cannot continue to expand oil discoveries at rates equivalent to (or higher than) rates of production; that is, beyond some rate of production, the country's rate of production will in effect be equal to its rate of depletion. The higher the rates of production, the shorter will be the production horizon financed from the country's given stock of oil. Given these realities, the problem of intergenerational comparisons of utility or welfare becomes increasingly relevant to policy making as the rates of production and current consumption increase. Higher rates of current consumption financed from oil revenues mean that the production horizon shortens, thus increasing the conflict between the welfare of the present and future generations.*

DOMESTIC CONSUMPTION AND INVESTMENT

Domestic Consumption

In determining the level of domestic consumption financed by oil revenues, the government has two broad options: to increase public expenditures on imports of consumer goods and subsidization of housing, perhaps producing a sharp acceleration in the growth of domestic expenditures; or to continue the policy of rapid expansion of government investment that characterized the 1960s. The latter would mean that the government would concentrate its expenditures on social welfare; agriculture; the petrochemical and other selected heavy industries, such as steel and aluminum production; the operating expenses of the ministries; and national defense.

---

*The optimal allocation of resources over time is one of the most difficult problems, both operationally and conceptually, a government must solve. Unfortunately, temporal welfare economics remains one of the least understood areas in economic theory. (For a clear discussion of the relevant issues, see Otto Eckstein, "Investment Criteria for Economic Development and the Theory of Intemporal Welfare Economics," Quarterly Journal of Economics [February 1957], p. 57. An excellent discussion of the problem in the context of oil-producing countries is given by Naiem A. Sherbiny, "Arab Oil Production Policies in the Context of International Conflicts," in Naiem A. Sherbiny and Mark Tessler, eds., Arab Oil: Impact on the Arab Countries and Global Implications [New York: Praeger, 1976], pp. 47-54. A survey of the literature is given in Paul Samuelson, "Interest Rate Determinations and Oversimplifying Parables: A Summing Up," in M. Brown et al., Essays in Modern Capital Theory [Amsterdam: North-Holland, 1976], pp. 3-24.)

Whichever option is chosen, the result will be an immediate increase in the people's standard of living. However, increased consumption may detract from the achievement of the government's other goals; that is, long-run growth may be lower if large-scale investments (which imply reduced consumption) are not undertaken at the present time.[2]

The conflict over the allocation of expenditures for consumption or investment occurs in Iran (in contrast to Saudi Arabia, which has much larger oil reserves) because the country's accelerated levels of petroleum output cannot be maintained for more than several decades, due to limited deposits. Obviously, this being the case, consumption will fall drastically as soon as the flow of revenues drops if part of current revenues are not saved and invested.

In any event, it is quite unlikely that the increased oil revenues could be channeled into efficient short-run consumption. The government, in fact, might find it difficult to induce the public to increase their rates of consumption voluntarily. Individuals in Iran usually base their decision to consume on changes in their long-run incomes, rather than on temporary windfalls (see Appendix D). The government might be able to increase consumption at a greater rate, by increasing transfer payments and gifts to the population, but such a policy might run the danger of undermining the country's social and economic viability. It seems, therefore, that only a fraction of Iran's increase in oil revenues can (or should) be directed towards increased private consumption.

Investment

The government has also found that expenditures for investment are, as in the case of consumption, difficult to expand in the short run (again note investment equations in Appendix D). Since 1973 government income has outrun the ability of the authorities to identify and invest in productive projects. Obvious potential still exists for investment in petrochemicals and other industries, particularly where natural gas and petroleum can be utilized. The implementation of such projects, however, given shortages of skilled labor and domestic resources, will be slow. The authorities simply have not demonstrated that they have identified and can implement a large number of directly productive and economically feasible investment projects during the balance of the decade. Government investments are therefore likely to remain concentrated in social overhead capital (roads, schools, and power). In any case, since proven and potential petroleum reserves are likely to expand somewhat as exploration continues, the government should proceed in developing complementary inputs, primarily in administrative and labor skills. When these inputs are more readily available, the government's investments aimed at diversifying the economy will be more feasible.[3]

Constraints on Government Policy

While economic arguments can be used to establish a framework in which the government allocates its revenues between consumption and investment over time, this framework must remain flexible. Clearly the government does not have complete control over expenditures, however. A number of pressures are continually being applied, urging the government to allocate its revenues to the benefit of various constituencies or interest groups in the country.

The importance of internal pressures placed on the authorities for specific undertakings has been largely neglected by outside observers, who often have a number of misconceptions about the degree of freedom Iranian authorities have in the formation of policy. Iran's political system is a constitutional monarchy. This, together with the creation of a one-party system in 1975, has led to such observations as "political activity is virtually nil" and "the Shah of Iran shows no interest in political institutions."[4] If these comments are interpreted to mean that Iran has few of the political institutions common to Western political democracy, they are accurate. But if they mean that the Shah and other public figures can ignore the interests and aspirations of such groups as the nomadic tribes, religious groups, a growing educated class, and large numbers of civil servants, and still stay in power, these observers are mistaken. Government policies and actions in Iran emerge from a mix of diverse interests and conflicting goals similar to those in any of the Western democracies. As in the Western countries, it is difficult for government leaders to ignore pressures from the various elements of the population, each of which wants to share in the country's growing wealth.

DISCRETIONARY SPENDING

Discretionary spending includes a wide range of expenditures which do not directly (or sometimes even indirectly) contribute to economic growth or to an increase in the material standard of living of the population. However, these expenditures are not necessarily wasteful, in that they may contribute to national security or long-run regional harmony. Thus, Iran's foreign aid to Afghanistan has undoubtedly reduced tensions between the two countries and thus created a stable atmosphere in which Iran's development can proceed. In another example, the lavish celebration of the 2,500th anniversary of the monarchy at Persepolis, in 1973, undoubtedly contributed to national pride.

FOREIGN AID

A major factor affecting the government's expenditures in the future is the Shah's concern for the reactions of other less-developed countries, particularly other Middle East states, to Iran's rising income and regional power. Given the scarcity of resources in some of these countries, an accumulation of revenues and wealth by Iran has led to pressures on the country to make loans and grants to its poorer (nonoil) Arab neighbors. Iran's foreign aid expenditures have increased in the last few years* and may increase substantially in the next decade, since its income and wealth create a larger per capita income gap between it and other countries in the region, such as Pakistan and Afghanistan.

Following the 1973-74 price increases the government also decided to come to the aid of industrialized countries. To this end it lent $1.2 billion to Britain and $1 billion to France. It also raised its commitment to the World Bank and the International Monetary Fund (IMF). By the end of 1974 it had made bilateral and multilateral commitments totaling $10 billion. Admittedly, many of the commitments were not binding and were cut back following the 1975 reduction in oil revenues. The figures are still indicative, however, of the international implications and forces that Iran will face in the future, particularly if oil revenues should increase fairly rapidly in a short period of time.

DEFENSE EXPENDITURES

While levels of discretionary spending and foreign aid are hard to forecast, there is no question that major increases in defense spending will continue.

---

*Iran's lending program in 1974 included a line of credit to the IMF for 580 million SDRs to finance purchases under the fund's oil facility, the purchase of 290 million SDRs of IBRD bonds, a contribution of about 16 million SDRs to the United Nations Emergency Fund, and financial commitments to aid other developing countries. (For a breakdown, see International Monetary Fund, IMF Survey [February 17, 1975], pp. 58-59.)

Military expenditure, as published in the 1976 budget, amounted to $8.1 billion (exchange rate of 69.14 rials to the dollar). At that time military expenditures accounted for 27 percent of the general budget and represented over 12 percent of GNP. Few countries not at war have such a high defense expenditure.[5]

The official figures also conceal a number of expenditures that probably should be included as military expenditures, by placing them in other categories. For example, the budget does not give figures for military-related construction or the establishment of military industries.[6] A scrutiny of the budget reveals that, under the heading of public affairs, $1.7 billion has been allocated for government buildings and construction—a 66 percent increase over that spent in 1975. Most of this is for fixed capital investment, but some experts feel that up to 70 percent of this figure, or $1.2 billion, covers military construction—new air and naval bases, expansion of army buildings, plus housing and related infrastructure. Elsewhere in the budget, $106 million was allocated to the Military Industries Organization for expansion of the electronics, ordnance, and vehicle assembly areas. If these allocations are included with the military budget, it increases to $9.5 billion in 1976, or about 17 percent of GNP.

Iran has not reduced its defense expenditures in line with its decline in oil revenues. The only effective constraint on its expenditures appears to be the willingness of the United States and other Western countries to sell new and highly advanced weapons systems to the country.[7] Iran's extremely sophisticated weapons include Gruman F-14 Tomcats and Chieftan tanks from England, and the government, because of its current shortfall in oil revenues, is looking into the possibility of bartering oil in payment for aircraft from General Dynamics (F-16), McDonnell Douglas/Northrup (F-18), and Boeing (AWACs—Airborne Warning and Control System). Over 300 aircraft are said to be involved. Those familiar with both the arms and the oil industries are skeptical as to whether such an arrangement will be consummated. On the other hand, most believe that, one way or another, Iran will be able to acquire a substantial amount of the military hardware she feels she needs.

Official government justification for such a big military buildup is straightforward. Because the nation has nearly 35 million people and is in the process of becoming an industrial power, it needs powerful modern armed forces, both as a reflection of its own importance and as a means of safeguarding its security.[8] Government policy is implicitly based upon the <u>tous-azimuts</u> theory, which states that a country must be ready to defend itself against all comers, rather than against one specific threat.[9] Even on this basis, however, particularly discounting any credible Iranian defense against Soviet attack, Iran appears to many of its neighbors as possessing more weapons than it needs.

The Iranian answer to this is that its armed forces with their sophisticated equipment are intended to act as a deterrent, and they must look as impressive as possible so long as the country lacks nuclear weapons. Iranian strategists also claim that a high level of military preparedness is necessary to cope with five major potential threats to the country's security: instability in the Persian Gulf, particularly if a radical change in government occurs in Saudi Arabia; a breakup of Pakistan; a move by Afghanistan towards closer ties with the Soviet Union; the destabilizing factors of the Arab-Israeli conflict; and the rapid increase in India's power and influence in the East.

As part of the country's concern with national security, much effort has been put into improving relations with the country's Arab neighbors in the gulf. A final agreement has been reached with Iraq on all details of frontier demarcation and navigational rights (although as of late 1976 there was some doubt concerning the good faith in which the treaty is likely to be observed).[10] The Shah has also initiated discussions on an agreement for a gulf security pact that would bind the states of the region to mutual aid and would establish a framework for regional cooperation on such matters as pollution control, protection of shipping, and offshore exploration.

While Iran's relations with Iraq and the gulf states have improved since 1971 (when Iran occupied the Thum Islands and Abu Musa), the barrier of distrust between Iranians and Arabs has not been broken—undoubtedly the major reason for the military buildup. This conclusion is supported by the fact that Iran has demonstrated that it will use its arsenal of weapons where it considers its vital interests to be at stake. The first instance of military action was in the country's occupation of the Thum Islands after the withdrawal of British forces in 1971. The Iranian authorities considered these islands essential for maintaining the free flow of oil to world markets. Equally, in Oman, Iran perceived a threat to its own security if the Marxist-oriented liberation movement in Dhofar was not checked. Accordingly, the Shah dispatched special forces to fight there (at the request of Oman's leader, Sultan Zaboos).[11]

DOMESTIC VERSUS FOREIGN INVESTMENT

Once the government has decided the approximate division of oil revenues between investment and consumption, it must decide the optimal proportion between investment in the domestic economy and investments that could contribute more to the nation's goals if made in foreign countries. Since both domestic and foreign investments potentially further the nation's goals, the major question facing the government concerns the proportion of total investments that should be allocated to each type in order to maximize the achievement of those goals. Clearly this can be done by obtaining a diversified portfolio.

If the government is able to achieve a minimum risk level for a given level of expected return, then it will have achieved an efficient portfolio: in strict economic terms, the country's portfolio should maximize the rate of return on invested funds. The condition (assuming no uncertainty) necessary for achievement of this target is that the rates of return on domestic and foreign investments are equal to each other. Given uncertainty and noneconomic considerations, the country must adopt a mixed investment strategy that includes a number of considerations in addition to monetary rates of return.

Foreign investment may take any of three forms. The first type is equity investment, and is typified by Iran's original proposed joint venture with Ashland Oil Company. In this agreement Iran would have acquired a 50 percent share of Ashland's refining and marketing operations in New York State in return for a guaranteed long-term oil supply. Equity investment in petroleum-related activities would seem to be mutually advantageous for Iran and the foreign firm it buys shares from.

Given the massive capital requirements in the petroleum industry, together with forecasts of an impending shortage of financing in the Western countries, Iran could not only increase the yield of its portfolio by investing in these industries, but would also be assuring itself of secure and growing markets for its oil exports. World capital requirements for the petroleum industry over the 1970-85 period were estimated at $565 billion by the Chase Manhattan Bank.[12] Iran should, therefore, be able to invest profitably in a wide range of energy-related ventures in the United States and Western Europe.

A second type of foreign investment is portfolio investment of blue chip securities issued and sold in the major world capital markets. Iran could acquire income-earning assets of this type and thus quickly reduce dependence on petroleum activities, whether at home or abroad.

A third type of foreign investment involves the government's obtaining controlling interest in nonpetroleum enterprises. These companies would then become, essentially, Iranian national companies under Iranian managerial control. During the next two decades, however, it is not likely that Iran will attempt much investment of this type. The country is already short of top-caliber managerial talent and can hardly spare executives for overseas assignments. The long-run interests of the country would therefore seem to be best satisfied by diversifying its sources of foreign exchange earnings through the first two types of investments.

Four major considerations dictate the size and composition of the Iranian government's investment portfolio and the manner in which it is to be managed. The portfolio must maintain a degree of liquidity consistent with regulations and operating requirements, maintaining liquidity in the highest-yielding or most strategic short-term instruments; maintain a desired level of income, consistent with the ability to assume risk and absorb loss; maintain a strategic outlook on markets so that opportunities to increase profits will be recognized; and maintain a flexible approach to changes in market conditions.

Thus, within the framework, a desirable portfolio would include two separate types of funds: short-term assets capable of being redeemed at or near par, which could be drawn upon to meet any emergencies that may arise; and long-term funds designed to meet the income needs of the portfolio, such as investments in more liquid assets—those yielding a higher rate of return, but also having greater risk. The proper combination, in term of weights to be assigned to each asset, will be a function of the portfolio's objectives.[13]

For Iran, a possible set of objectives would include developing the domestic economy, both socially and economically. Consequently, the placement of funds abroad should not be used to increase political influence, but should simply reflect the inability of the domestic economy to absorb these funds productively. Iran needs a portfolio capable of generating income on which the national economy will be free to draw (that is, to repatriate) as the need manifests itself, given, on the one hand, the nature of the Iranian economy and its dependence on increasing oil revenues to maintain a steady growth path, and, on the other, the fact that oil revenues will ultimately begin to decline. The liquidity needs of the portfolio, therefore, must be guided by the annual rate of domestic growth and the welfare requirements of the economy vis-a-vis government revenues. A portion of Iran's surplus must be set aside for low-interest "recycling" purposes, either on a bilateral government-to-government basis or through the proper international agencies. Obviously, it is in Iran's own interest to give support of this nature to the countries it traditionally trades with—the industrialized countries of Western Europe and Japan. To accommodate humanitarian and political needs, another portion of the portfolio should be in the form of loans to those nonoil developing countries that have encountered severe economic difficulties stemming from the deterioration of their balance of payments since the 1973-74 oil price increases. Finally, to assure adequate food supplies (given the country's limited agricultural potential with respect to the size of its population) the government's portfolio should include joint ventures and investments in countries where such commodities can be produced to advantage (for example, beef in Australia and wheat in the United States). These investments would not only yield a high rate of return but would secure supplies of these essential items when a need for them develops.

Holdings of foreign assets will require a highly efficient and specialized organization such as that established in Venezuela. (A full description of the Venezuelan approach to the problem is given in Chapter 10.) This agency must be capable of sophisticated financial analysis. It is particularly important, in the case of equity investments and loans, that the organization be able to evaluate the economies of the countries in which the investments are considered. Risk evaluations, both from an economic and political point of view, are essential to the proper geographical management of the surplus. Moreover, the agency must be capable of forecasting changes in exchange rates if losses are to be minimized. Naturally, the bulk of relatively lower-risk investments will take place in the industrialized countries, that is, Canada, Japan, Australia, New Zealand, and members of the European Economic Community (EEC). The size of investments in particular countries should probably be related to GNP so that political risks can also be minimized.[14] In any case, a well-diversified portfolio, both geographically and according to assets, is the best protection against the risks involved in investing beyond Iran's borders.

OIL REVENUES AND INFLATION

One of the major determinants of the allocation of oil revenues between domestic consumption and investment, on the one hand, and foreign assets, on the other, is the ability of the local economy to expand without producing an unacceptable level of inflation.

Inflationary pressures arise in any economy whenever expenditures are greater than the amount of savings voluntarily undertaken by the nation's citizens.[15] Whether or not the inflationary pressure will result in price increases depends primarily upon the ability of the economy to expand output commensurate with demand. For instance, if the economy possesses unemployed labor and excess capacity in those sectors where demand is increasing, inflationary pressure will lead to both greater output and income, and there will be no price inflation. However, if the economy has full employment prices will begin to rise and will keep rising as long as aggregate demand in monetary terms is greater than aggregate supply.

Inflation in Iran is a relatively recent phenomenon. The period from 1959 to 1970 was characterized by rapid growth with little or no inflation. By contrast, the period from 1971 to 1976 (see Table 7.1) has been characterized by an inflation rate that accelerated from 2.17 percent in 1970 to nearly 20 percent in 1974.

TABLE 7.1

Variation in GNP Deflator and Oil Revenues

Year	GNP Deflator (1972 = 100.0)	Rate of Increase in GNP Deflator (percentage)	Oil Revenues (billions of rials)	Annual Rate of Increase in Oil Revenues (percentage)
1959	73.2	—	19.4	—
1960	75.7	3.41	21.4	10.3
1961	75.8	0.13	21.8	1.9
1962	76.9	1.45	25.7	17.9
1963	77.0	0.13	29.1	13.2
1964	79.0	2.59	35.0	20.3
1965	80.0	1.26	38.6	10.3
1966	79.8	0.25	45.6	18.1
1967	79.3	0.63	56.4	23.7
1968	80.9	2.10	64.0	13.5
1969	82.9	2.47	72.9	13.4
1970	84.7	2.17	87.2	19.6
1971	92.9	9.68	152.1	74.4
1972	100.0	7.64	182.9	20.2
1973	111.1	11.11	477.5	161.1
1974	133.1	19.18	1297.4	171.7

Source: Bank Markazi Iran, <u>Annual Report and Balance Sheet,</u> various issues.

Historically, inflation in Iran has been closely correlated with increases in oil revenues. In the 1960s the economy had enough capacity to expand output sufficiently rapidly to meet the increased demand stemming from rising oil revenues. In the early 1970s this was clearly no longer the case. At that time scarcities began developing in a number of areas—skilled labor, natural resources, and infrastructure. By the mid-1970s, domestic expenditures were incapable of going beyond a certain level without inflationary pressures. Because the economy had little slack, these inflationary pressures were incapable of eliciting a corresponding increase in real output of goods and services.

Under these circumstances, expenditures in the domestic market financed by oil revenues represented a permanent loss of real resources to the nation. In addition, the amount of real resources lost—in the sense that they are represented by exported barrels of oil—are resources that could have been used to expand productive capacity during periods of stable prices in the future. When spent at such high levels as in 1974-76, these resources are simply dissipated in the form of higher domestic prices and imports.

The current inflation has lingered much longer than the authorities anticipated, and is now threatening to erode many of the gains made in the early 1970s. Although the government has initiated a number of controls that have prevented the price level from rising as fast as it might otherwise have done, they have not destroyed inflation; it continues to increase, expressing itself in shortages, long delays in delivery, and black markets.

By mid-1975, inflation in Iran was still running at a rate in excess of 25 percent (see Table 7.2), and was certainly above levels considered acceptable by the authorities. There is a very real possibility that, unless inflation is curbed, it will slow the country's ambitious development plans.

The government's ability to control inflation caused by its expenditure of oil revenues will no doubt determine the proportion of these revenues that can be efficiently spent within the country. The remaining oil revenues must be channeled into expenditures outside the country.

CONCLUSIONS

It is clear that the amount of oil revenues that Iran can productively spend in the domestic economy is limited, and that increased expenditure during a given time period will eventually result in inflation above tolerable levels. Accordingly, Iran's aggregate ability to spend oil revenues domestically equals the total amount of finan-

TABLE 7.2

Rate of Inflation, First Half of 1975 Compared
to First Half of 1974

	Percent Increase
GNP	150
Investment by public sector	30
Imported goods	110
Retail store sales volume	150
Savings and bank deposits	70
Bank system lending to private sector	42
Locally manufactured autos	20
Tires	25
Lubricating oil	20
Antifreeze	75
Bricks	94
Tea	30
Textiles	25
Colored thread	240
Linseed oil	400

Source: Bank Markazi Iran, Bulletin, various issues.

cially sound private and public investment opportunities that can be undertaken and successfully implemented within a given inflation range. The amount of funds allocated for foreign investments should be that part of the aggregate investment program that cannot be financed without exceeding this inflation limit.

Because of the persistent threat of inflation, the utilization of the nation's oil revenues for domestic expenditures must not exceed a certain limit. Conceptually, given the maximum rate of inflation considered acceptable by the authorities, it is possible to establish a basis for the optimal division of those funds destined for internal use and those destined for foreign investments. This allocation is clearly dependent on the ability of the authorities effectively and efficiently to control domestic inflation induced by these expenditures.

NOTES

1. The general tone is set in Iran, Plan and Budget Organization, Iran's Fifth Development Plan, 1973-1978, Revised—A Summary (Tehran: Plan and Budget Organization, 1975).

2. See G. W. Irvin, Roads and Redistribution: Social Costs and Benefits of Labor Intensive Road Construction in Iran (Geneva: International Labor Office, 1975) for a series of illustrative calculations.

3. Willy J. Stevens, Capital Absorptive Capacity in Developing Countries (Leiden: A. W. Sijthoff, 1971), pp. 64-70.

4. Bahman Nirumand's, Iran: The New Imperialism in Action (New York: Monthly Review Press, 1969) is representative of Marxist antigovernment writings.

5. Emile Benoit, Defense and Economic Growth in Developing Countries (Lexington, Mass.: D. C. Heath, 1973), p. 26.

6. One of the few estimates of Iran's defense expenditures is given in Economic Survey of Asia and the Far East, 1970 (Bangkok: Economic Commission for Asia and the Far East, 1971), p. 225.

7. Robert Looney, "Iran: Rise of a World Power," Countermeasures, no. 2 (May 1975), pp. 10-16.

8. Justifications are given on a fairly regular basis by the Shah in interviews with the domestic and foreign press. See, for example, his interview in Kayhan International (December 18, 1976), p. 1.

9. An interesting application of this theory is given in S. Swamy, Indian Economic Planning: An Alternative Approach (Delhi: Vikas, 1971).

10. See the Economist Intelligence Unit, Quarterly Economic Review—Iran, no. 2 (1976), p. 3.

11. The Economist Intelligence Unit, Quarterly Economic Review—Iran, no. 4 (1974), p. 7.

12. A survey of various forecasts is given in Henry Wallich, "Is There a Capital Shortage?" Challenge (September-October 1975), pp. 30-43.

13. A similar view is held by Firouz Vakil, Director of the Planometrics and General Economy Bureau of the Plan and Budget Organization. See his Determining Iran's Financial Surplus, 1352-1371 (Tehran: Institute for International, Political, and Economic Studies, 1975).

14. Vakil, Iran's Financial Surplus, p. 44.

15. A number of mechanisms of inflation are outlined in V. Corbo Lioi, Inflation in Developing Countries: An Econometric Study of Chilean Inflation (Amsterdam: North-Holland, 1974), ch. 1.

CHAPTER

8

INFLATION

INTRODUCTION

Recent price increases in Iran cannot be pigeonholed into any of the standard types of inflation.[1] Since 1972 inflation in Iran has been a hybrid of the major inflationary mechanisms found in most developing countries. Four inflationary forces are, to one extent or another, currently at work in Iran: cost push—resulting from wages increasing more rapidly than labor productivity; demand pull—resulting from rapidly expanding levels of both private and public expenditures, made possible by the inflow of oil revenues; structural—resulting from rigidities in certain key sectors such as agriculture, causing production in these sectors to lag behind demand and, thus, prices to rise; and import—resulting from the general worldwide increase in the prices of commodities and manufactured goods. Higher prices of imports are, in turn, reflected in the country's wholesale and consumer price indexes.

Data limitations make precise quantitative estimates of the contribution of these four inflationary sources to the country's price indexes impossible. Still, it is possible to arrive at a tentative assessment of the relative impact that two major factors, world inflation and increased oil revenues, have had on the country's major price indexes.

INCREASES IN IMPORT PRICES

The impact of increased import prices on the domestic price level began to be felt in the early 1970s. At that time most of Iran's major trading partners had already been experiencing inflationary pressures in their own economies for several years.

Using a weighted average of the exports of these countries (see Table 8.1), with the weights based on the proportion of imports from each, a clear pattern between their inflation rate and Iran's emerges; during the early 1970s a one percent increase in the export prices of Iran's major trading partners resulted in an immediate 0.5 percent increase in import prices paid by Iran. After an average lag of about one and a half years Iran's import prices had risen by 1.33 percent.[2]

The impact of increased import prices during the next two decades, and the overall increases in the Iranian price structure, depends on the weight of these prices in the country's wholesale price index. This was 17.5 in 1969, but has been rising as a result of the larger share of consumer goods imported and the rising share of imports in GNP. As a result, the weight of imports in the wholesale price index had increased to nearly 20 percent by 1974. If the weight of imports in the wholesale price index remains around 20 percent, then a one percent rise in the export prices of Iran's major trading partners would cause the Iranian wholesale price index to increase by 0.1 percent in the short run, and by 0.27 percent in the long run.

Using these relationships it is possible to obtain a rough estimate of the contribution that increased import prices have made to the increase in the Iranian wholesale price index.

In 1973 and early 1974 the increase in U.S. export prices was approximately 28 percent per annum, and 13 percent for West Germany. Iran's other major trading partners also had double-digit rates of inflation. As a result, their weighted average increased by 25 percent per annum. This increase resulted (if past patterns held) in a 2.5 percent increase in the Iranian wholesale price index in the short run and a 6.5 percent increase within two years.

The average rate of increase of the wholesale price index over the first six months of 1974 was around 20 percent. Based on past relationships, about one-third, or 6.67 percent, of the observed rate of domestic inflation was related to price increases of imported goods.

Since 1974 there has been a deceleration in the rate of increase in the export prices of Iran's major trading partners. The low level of activity in all industrialized countries, and a drop in the growth rate of the volume of world trade, have accounted for this trend. The 1976 rates of inflation in Iran, therefore, were not, to any appreciable degree, caused by external factors. Other elements, mainly expanded domestic credit, must be largely responsible for the unprecedented increase in prices over the last several years.

TABLE 8.1

Imports from Iran's Leading Trading Partners
(millions of dollars)

Country	1959	1963	1965	1970	1972	1974
West Germany	124.3	106.6	180.5	347.9	474.1	1185.0
	(22.8)	(20.8)	(20.1)	(20.8)	(18.4)	(17.9)
Japan	54.7	37.0	71.5	201.2	359.5	999.4
	(10.1)	(7.2)	(7.9)	(12.0)	(14.0)	(15.1)
United States	94.6	81.3	170.4	217.4	428.2	1321.5
	(17.4)	(15.8)	(19.0)	(13.0)	(16.7)	(20.0)
United Kingdom	78.2	75.0	114.7	162.7	297.5	529.5
	(14.4)	(14.6)	(12.8)	(9.7)	(11.6)	(8.0)
France	21.2	28.8	45.1	77.5	120.5	242.1
	(3.9)	(5.6)	(5.0)	(4.6)	(4.7)	(3.7)
Italy	19.5	22.2	41.4	67.9	112.9	199.4
	(3.6)	(4.3)	(4.6)	(4.0)	(4.4)	(3.0)
Others	151.7	162.6	274.8	572.0	777.8	2136.8
	(27.8)	(31.7)	(30.6)	(34.1)	(30.3)	(32.3)
Total	544.2	513.5	898.4	1676.6	2570.5	6613.7

Note: ( ) indicates percent.
Source: Compiled from Bank Markazi Iran, Annual Report and Balance Sheet, various issues.

DEMAND PULL INFLATION

Iran's financial sector has expanded rapidly following the steep rise in oil receipts and the expanded development efforts and security expenditures of the government. While the government has begun to play an important role in influencing the pattern of credit from the country's commercial banks, through the promotion of specialized banks and new banking regulations, the country's financial sector remains relatively undiversified. The stock market has expanded its volume in recent years, but it too cannot transfer funds from savings to investors as efficiently as in many other countries at Iran's stage of development.[3] Traditionally, the central bank (Bank Markazi Iran) has had great difficulty channeling credit into productive investments (mainly agriculture, construction, and industry). The last few years have seen the bank improve its control over the distribution of credit among various uses, albeit at the expense of control over the volume of credit extended.

Determinants of the Money Supply

Credit in Iran is closely related to the money supply, which in turn is largely determined by oil revenues (see Appendexes E and F). The supply of money is also determined by central bank monetary expansion, bank reserve policies (deposit/reserve ratio), and the public's preference between holding currency and deposits (deposit/currency ratio).[4] The expansion in domestic credit has therefore been influenced by the country's foreign exchange reserves, the Bank Markazi's loans to the government and various public enterprises, and the ability of the country's commercial banks to attract deposits. (See Table 8.2.)

The rapid expansion of the government's expenditures after 1973, together with a considerable increase in the loans and credits to the private sector has been largely responsible for the increased liquidity of the economy and has contributed significantly to acceleration in the rate of increase of money (see Table 8.3) and credits (see Table 8.4). The sum result has been to sharply increase the inflationary pressures in the economy.

The government's 1974 market was the first year that local expenditures were wholly financed by the increased foreign exchange revenues from oil exports. Government expenditures were the major factor responsible for the unprecedented rise of money and quasi money during 1974-75; this action alone was to expand the money supply by 419 billion rials in 1974. The potential for oil revenues to expand the money supply is even more sharply illustrated by the fact that a considerable proportion of the government's foreign exchange revenues were not spent—they simply went into the country's foreign exchange reserves. If they had been fully utilized by the government, the money supply might have nearly doubled in 1974.

Several other salient indicators illustrate the magnitude of the financial sector's expansion after 1973. These include the following: the growth of the assets and liabilities of the banking system reached 77 percent in 1974, as compared with a 41 percent increase in the previous year; the banking system's foreign assets increased by 376 billion rials, a 224 percent rise over 1973; the private sector's increased demand for loans and expanded production and trade caused loans and credits to this sector to rise by 43 percent (the figure for the previous year was about 35 percent); the government sector's net indebtedness to the banking system, in spite of the increase in oil revenues, increased by over 49 percent (as compared with 35 percent in 1975). This was wholly due to the considerable utilization of the banking system's loans and credits by government institutions and government-affiliated companies; and the government sector's deposits with the banking system increased by 74 percent, the largest proportion of which was in the form of deposits with the Bank Markazi.

TABLE 8.2

Consolidated Balance Sheet of the Banking System—Liabilities, 1968-74

	1968	1969	1970	1971	1972	1973	1974
Money	87.9	90.4	97.4	117.0	158.7	202.7	327.2
Quasi money	87.4	115.3	138.3	179.3	240.7	313.1	502.9
Total money	175.3	205.7	235.7	296.3	399.4	515.8	830.1
Public sector deposits	40.1	52.2	57.2	99.9	132.1	209.9	364.3
Treasury General	9.5	11.6	48.0	90.1	110.3	180.0	294.6
Other government agencies	30.6	40.6	9.2	9.8	21.8	29.9	69.7
Capital account	35.9	38.5	44.5	48.0	59.5	81.5	154.4
Private sector import restriction deposits	7.3	7.8	7.5	10.3	15.7	26.1	22.1
Advance payment on letters of credit of the public sector	3.4	4.9	5.3	9.5	14.1	30.7	158.3
Foreign loans and credits received and foreign exchange deposits	12.8	21.7	43.4	43.8	38.3	59.3	85.5
Miscellaneous	5.5	11.9	12.4	12.2	19.1	32.1	73.7
Total liabilities	280.3	342.7	406.0	520.0	678.2	955.4	1688.4

Source: Compiled from Bank Markazi Iran, Annual Report and Balance Sheet, various issues.

TABLE 8.3

Factors Responsible for Changes in Money Supply, 1962-73
(billions of rials)

Changes in	1962	1963	1964	1965	1966	1967	1968	1969	1970	1971	1972	1973
1. Money (4+7+10+11)	3.7	5.2	4.9	6.4	6.5	10.3	10.8	2.5	7.0	19.6	41.7	44.0
2. Credits of banks to the private sector	10.8	11.4	15.2	14.1	19.0	21.1	24.9	31.4	31.6	47.4	84.8	126.7
3. Quasi money	8.6	7.7	5.9	6.8	8.7	13.3	20.2	27.9	23.0	41.0	61.4	72.4
4. Net debt of the private sector (2-3)	2.2	3.7	9.3	7.3	10.3	7.8	4.7	3.5	8.6	6.4	23.4	54.3
5. Credit of the banking system to the public sector	-2.0	6.3	6.3	6.0	6.0	19.7	16.8	27.2	23.0	41.0	61.4	72.0
6. Deposits of the public sector with the banking system	-0.6	5.4	14.1	-7.3	3.8	7.1	1.0	12.1	5.0	42.7	32.2	77.8
7. Net debt of the public sector (5-6)	-1.4	0.9	-7.8	13.3	2.2	12.6	15.8	15.1	26.7	-13.3	12.8	12.8
8. Foreign assets	1.8	2.5	7.7	-3.8	-1.7	6.4	-4.6	3.8	0.0	37.2	28.4	73.5
9. Foreign debts	-1.2	-0.2	0.1	0.6	0.8	8.7	1.4	8.9	20.9	0.4	-5.4	21.1
10. Foreign assets (net)	3.0	2.7	7.6	-4.4	-2.5	-2.3	-6.0	-5.1	-20.9	36.8	33.8	52.4
11. Other (net)	0.1	-2.1	-4.2	-9.8	-3.5	-7.8	-3.7	-11.0	-7.4	-10.3	-28.3	-61.9

Source: Bank Markazi Iran, Annual Report and Balance Sheet, various issues.

TABLE 8.4

Credits of the Banking System
(billions of rials)

	1961	1962	1963	1964	1965	1966	1967	1968	1969	1970	1971	1972	1973	1974
Credits to the private sector	50.7	61.5	72.9	88.1	102.1	121.2	142.3	167.2	198.6	230.2	277.6	362.4	489.1	698.3
Credits to the public sector	29.0	27.0	33.3	39.6	45.6	51.6	71.3	88.1	115.3	147.0	176.4	221.4	298.4	445.9
Total	79.7	88.5	106.2	127.7	147.8	172.8	213.6	255.3	313.9	377.2	454.0	583.8	787.5	1144.2
Nonsight deposits of the private sector	16.2	24.8	32.5	38.4	45.2	53.9	67.2	87.4	115.3	138.3	179.3	240.7	313.1	502.9
Deposits of the public sector	16.6	16.0	21.4	35.5	28.2	32.0	39.1	40.1	52.2	57.2	99.9	132.1	209.9	364.3
Total	32.8	40.8	53.9	73.9	73.4	85.9	106.3	127.5	167.5	195.5	279.2	372.8	523.0	867.2
Net credits to the private sector	34.5	36.7	40.4	49.7	57.0	67.3	75.1	79.8	83.3	91.9	98.3	121.7	176.0	195.4
Net credits to the public sector	12.4	11.0	11.9	4.1	17.4	19.6	32.2	48.0	63.1	89.8	76.5	89.3	88.5	81.6
Total	46.9	57.7	52.3	53.8	74.4	86.9	107.3	127.8	146.4	181.7	174.8	211.0	264.5	277.0

Source: Bank Markazi Iran, Annual Report and Balance Sheet, various issues.

In short, the liquidity of the private sector increased at an accelerating rate, and the growth rate of volume of money and quasi money reached a level of 61 percent (see Table 8.2), which has been without precedent since the establishment of Bank Markazi Iran.

Monetary Policy and the Money Supply

Since the oil boom, the Bank Markazi has pursued a policy of "restricting the increase of loans and credits which were inflationary in nature and encouraging the expansion of loans and credits for productive purposes and imports." The single most important aim of the Bank Markazi's monetary and credit policy during the post-1973 period has been "to ensure that the growth in bank loans and credits to the private sector is such that, on the one hand, it does not harm the private sector's productive activities, and, on the other hand, it does not cause the rate of price increases to accelerate."[5]

This statement of policy is indeed unfortunate, particularly since it is based on several assumptions usually associated (at least in the United States) with a variation of the real bills doctrine.[6] Monetary authorities in the United States and other countries have often used that doctrine to defend their expansion of credit, even during times of inflation, on the grounds that certain types of investments do not have a significant inflationary impact. The argument is simple: any loan which helps generate output is noninflationary, since the loan facilitates the production of goods and services (as opposed to consumption). Since the loan is repaid when the goods are sold their increased supply would, according to this line or argument, diffuse any temporary inflationary pressures. The real bills doctrine sounds plausible—all the more so because it has a tinge of moral beauty about it. Unfortunately, countries have found that its conceptual limitations make it a poor foundation upon which to design monetary policy. At least in the United States, the theory is considered fallacious.*

---

*For example, assume that all banks are making loans for real goods and service and that one bank needing cash starts to reduce its loans. As old loans fall due, the bank insists on payment; as new loans are applied for, the bank refuses to grant them. If the other commercial banks are also striving, for one reason or another, to reduce their loans, the first bank's debtor may not be able to liquidate its "self-liquidating" loans. The merchants to whom these debtors must sell their goods would themselves have trouble obtaining loans, and so would have difficulty financing their purchases. One

The Bank Markazi may not base its monetary policies on the real bills doctrine, yet the bank's actions indicate it is extremely reluctant to limit the availability of credit to certain commercial banks—the rapidly expanding specialized banks that lend primarily to sectors producing real goods and services in industry, agriculture, and construction.

Banks remain the most important financial institutions in Iran. They are expanding at a fast rate and their operations are becoming more specialized and sophisticated. As long as a large proportion of government expenditure is financed by oil revenues, however, monetary policy will be very much influenced by the fiscal and external trade policies of the government. Over the last few years Iran's monetary policy has been devised mainly to balance the expansion of private and public sector investments. It is clear, however, that in pursuing the goals of channeling credit into what it considered productive investments, the Bank Markazi has lost whatever minimal control it has over the country's money supply.

More specifically, monetary policy in Iran must operate in an environment where the quantity of money is completely outside of its control. The country's money supply (see Appendix E) is determined largely by the oil revenues received by the federal government and the manner and speed with which the government spends these revenues. As a result, the main variable usually controlled by central banks—the monetary base—is not amenable to central bank manipulation in Iran. Instead, the scope of monetary policy in Iran has been confined to changes in the level and structure of interest rates and to changes in the reserve requirements of the (nonspecialized) commercial banks. While these measures may to some extent influence the amount and type of credit generated by oil revenues, they are, for all practical purposes, incapable of influencing the overall stock of money.

The central bank's inability to control the monetary base has forced it to resort, with increasing frequency, to the use of credit ceilings on the commercial banks as a means of controlling credit and channeling it into certain key sectors. For example, during 1975-76 the target level for the expansion of private sector credits

---

part of the banking community could succeed in reducing its outstanding loans by these processes only if other bankers stepped up their lending.

Shiftability of assets is, however, a more fundamental argument against the real bills doctrine, at least the Bank Markazi's version. (See A. Hart and P. Kennon, Money, Debt and Economic Activity [Englewood Cliffs, N.J.: Prentice-Hall, 1961], pp. 37-38.)

was set by the Bank Markazi at 260 billion rials. This represents a credit ceiling of 35 percent for each commercial bank over the level of credit outstanding on March 20, 1975.[7] While in most countries credit ceilings might enable a central bank to maintain some control over the money supply, the Bank Markazi has abandoned any attempts along these lines, refusing to place restrictions on the level of credits granted by the specialized banks. Furthermore, the government continues to provide these banks with loans, credits, and other funds in order to strengthen their lending capabilities. Bank Markazi therefore has no control over the lending of specialized banks or of government revenues. Thus it has no effective control over the money supply or, ultimately, over the rate of domestic inflation.

To summarize, inflationary pressures in Iran since 1971 are a symptom of the monetary policy pursued by the Bank Markazi and the government's ambitious development plans—the nation is trying to do too much in too short a time. Admittedly, world inflation has been responsible for some of the price increases experienced during this period. Most experts feel, however, that international inflation has not been a major contributing factor to the increase in domestic price levels, thus leaving the main thrust of the inflationary pressures to be accounted for by domestic factors. In this regard it should be noted that Iran's inflation has followed a pattern similar to that found in other oil-exporting countries (see Table 8.5).

Any inflation is either open or repressed, depending on a government's reaction to inflationary pressures. If the government maintains a hands-off policy and relies primarily on the price mechanism to ration and distribute goods and services, then the inflation is open and market prices usually reflect the excess of demand pressures over available supplies. If, on the other hand, the government interferes with the working of the distributive functions of the price system through controls, then a repressed inflation exists. Iran has experienced both these phases since early 1974.

The country's current inflation began to accelerate in 1972. In contrast to the country's earlier inflations, which were characterized by rising prices and money scarcity, this inflation has been associated with a scarcity of goods and an overabundance of money and credit.

THE GOVERNMENT'S STABILIZATION PROGRAM

With the acceleration of inflation, the major problem facing the government is one of devising a set of policies that can effectively utilize oil revenues to optimize real increases in GNP, while containing inflation at levels that are economically, socially, and politically

TABLE 8.5

Measures of Inflation

Country	1969	1970	1971	1972	1973	1974	1975
Iran (1970 = 100.0)							
Wholesale prices	96.5	100.0	106.0	112.8	125.2	145.8	154.4
Home goods	96.7	100.0	106.9	113.0	123.2	144.1	154.1
Consumer prices	98.3	100.0	104.2	110.9	126.8	138.9	156.9
Wages	—	100.0	121.0	146.2	185.2	243.3	336.4
Import prices	96.5	100.0	102.0	110.8	125.2	143.0	148.8
Iraq (1970 = 100.0)							
Wholesale prices	91.2	100.0	106.4	102.3	107.1	120.4	133.0
Consumer prices	95.8	100.0	103.6	109.0	114.3	123.8	135.5
Import prices	93.6	100.0	106.0	110.9	125.2	182.8	217.2
Venezuela (1970 = 100.0)							
Prices: home and imported goods	98.5	100.0	103.5	107.1	113.9	132.7	150.6
Prices: home goods	99.5	100.0	102.4	105.1	112.7	131.5	150.2
Consumer prices	97.5	100.0	103.2	106.2	110.6	119.7	132.0
Ecuador (1970 = 100.0)							
Consumer prices	95.2	100.0	108.4	117.0	132.2	163.0	188.0

Source: IMF, International Financial Statistics, November 1976.

tenable. In reacting to the danger of increased rates of domestic inflation, the government has already undertaken a number of policies, each designed to control price increases in the various segments of the economy. Many of these have been well conceived from a theoretical standpoint, but the government's success in this area has been mixed and, in general, unsatisfactory.

In attacking inflation the country has used monetary, fiscal, and income (or price control) policies. Monetary and fiscal policy have been generally geared towards increasing savings and directing investments into productive channels. Monetary policy, as noted, has been used to increase interest rates on deposits and advances and to tighten credit availability to the private sector, without diverting credit for productive investment. Fiscal policy has been geared towards reducing private sector liquidity through the issuance of attractively priced securities.

Finally, in attacking inflation the government's income policy has entailed the enactment of a number of laws and regulations designed to control wage and price increases. The government has established several organizations to administer its income policies. They are charged with the task of not only depressing rates of price increases, but, in many cases, of reducing prices to those of the early 1970s.[8]

Operation of the Antiinflation Program

The major announced objective of the government's antiinflation program was to roll back prices as rapidly as possible to levels 10-20 percent below the existing level (summer 1975), to levels that the economy could afford and still yield a fair profit to firms. In implementing this program an ad hoc policy committee was first established, made up of ministers from a number of state organizations, that had the ultimate responsibility for the program. Under the direct jurisdiction and control of the policy group, a committee was organized to investigate the cost of producing a number of products commonly consumed in Iran, and to use this information to establish official prices for commodities, products, and services.

Another organization created by the authorities to deal with inflation was made up of thousands of young members of Iran's single political party, the Rastakhiz (Resurgence) party. It was formed to seek out and report deviations from the officially set prices. As a beginning, it specified 640 commodities and products considered essential to consumers. This was followed by a number of additional lists of goods whose prices were established by the authorities. Those who were accused of delinquency in following posted prices were tried before the fourth group in the system, the special courts, which were part of the Iranian Department of Justice. Those found guilty of setting prices over the official limit received sentences ranging from suspension of their businesses, to fines, to imprisonment or a combination of these penalties, depending upon the seriousness of the offense.

At the height of the price control action, pressures for price reductions and for moves against profiteers and hoarders occurred in all areas and at all levels of the manufacturing-distribution chain, and in every sector of the commercial-industrial establishment. Managing directors of nationally known companies, small merchants, street vendors, and government officials were brought to court for price violations and penalized if found guilty. In a period of approximately three months, over 10,000 cases were tried, millions in fines were assessed, and many were sent to prison, including people in high circles.[9]

The program reached its zenith of intensity and general community interest in the fall of 1975, and then seemed to move quickly from the public scene. At the close of 1975, little space was allotted to the price control situation in the daily English-language newspapers, compared to space allotted in the summer and autumn.[10] The programs under the antiprofiteering campaign are still enforced, however, and are becoming part of the Iranian way of life.

Obviously, any price control scheme such as the one initiated in Iran encounters a number of technical problems in its enforcement. For example, considerable confusion has occurred concerning how new products (products not produced at the time the stabilization plan was initiated) should be priced. In practice each new product has been considered on its own merit. The result has been delays in production and a general air of uncertainty in the business community. A uniform base for establishing new prices has still not been clearly articulated to the public by the minister of commerce and his policy committee. Arguments in official circles continue to take place over the validity or lack of it in using such pricing methods as cost plus. In addition, it is difficult for most firms to ascertain what pricing method is actually being used in setting the official prices.

As for the antihoarding and antiprofiteering campaigns, they will have some effect on the prices of essential commodities if profiteering has, in fact, contributed to price increases in the recent past. There is evidence that this has been the case. It is not uncommon in Iran for shopkeepers to take advantage of higher prices by exploiting the situation and by creating artificial shortages. In campaigns such as those implemented in Iran, the ultimate results will largely depend on the efficiency and integrity of the implementing staff; without this, there is great scope for corruption and black marketing to flourish.

Results of the Stabilization Program

In the year since July 1975, when the rigorous system of price control was enforced, rate of increase of the consumer price index has declined to around 10 percent a year. Rents, however, do not come under the price control system, and have been increasing in some cases by 50 percent, reflecting pressure on housing and continued land speculation. At the present time rents comprise between 30 and 60 percent of wages.

Until food supplies increase and rents can be controlled, it will be very difficult to control wages: these rose 35 to 45 percent in 1975, and in 1976 a number of increases of 30 percent or more were granted. This is in defiance of a government-imposed limit of one percent and 20 rials per day (28 cents). A number of industrialists feel that wages in manufacturing have become so high that Iran will have a very difficult time competing against potential export rivals. If that is the case, Iran will be left with cheap energy as its sole advantage in international trade.

The problem of productivity and wage costs strikes at the heart of Iran's ambitions. The country's long-run aim is to transform the economy in a comparatively short time—20 years or so—into an industrialized society capable of breaking its dependence upon oil revenues, substituting a strong manufacturing base capable of sustained growth and sizable export earnings. Iran is acquiring an impressive industrial base, but it is highly questionable where competitive nonoil exports will come from beyond the capital-intensive sectors of steel and petrochemicals.

Implications of Repressed Inflation

The price controls have repressed inflation in Iran, but they have not eliminated it. Two signs of inflationary pressures remain: excessive money demand, and the legal actions prohibiting that demand from exerting its influence on the prices of a number of goods. When, as in 1975, monetary demand threatened to outstrip the productive resources of the economy, the government initiated price controls and rationing to restrain the excess demand from producing inflation. Its success in repressing inflation, and the side effects upon the economy, will, to a large extent, determine the country's growth pattern over the next two decades.

Unfortunately, repressed inflation is extremely conducive to a wage-cost inflation, one of the most serious of the effects of repressed inflation in Iran. The government's controls and the excess demand are likely to combine in several ways to bring about a loss in productivity. This, in turn, will lower consumers' potential real

INFLATION

incomes. The loss of productivity may arise from a number of sources, all primarily the result of the government's policy of repression. These include the increasing reluctance of labor to exert effort when real purchasing power declines (due to shortages of goods at the controlled private levels) and the declining productivity of capital as greater amounts of investment, relative to labor hirings, occur (due to the uncontrolled increase in wages).

The above are likely to appear under repressed inflation, and will tend to reduce the productivity of the economy, thereby increasing pressure against controls. Thus the country's attempt to repress inflation is not likely to be successful in maintaining stable price levels. Costs, particularly wage costs, are always tending to push prices up. Repressed inflation is unlikely to stabilize the general level of prices; it can only control the rate at which prices are rising.

A SUGGESTED INCOME POLICY

What is needed is a policy on incomes to accompany an existing or modified version of the country's price policy. The antiinflationary programs to date have attacked only the most apparent symptoms of inflation—high prices—and not the underlying causes, excessive expenditures financed by the banking system. If the authorities continue simply to control prices and not incomes, then domestic purchasing power will continue to increase as the economy expands.

As a first step in designing a stabilization program, the Bank Markazi should assume its responsibility as a central bank, to control the annual amount of new commercial bank credit. In this regard the bank need not fear that credit ceilings on the specialized banks will result in a relative decline in the private sector vis-a-vis the public sector (see Tables 8.6 and 8.7). In fact, through controlling the credit ceilings on commercial banks the Bank Markazi should have no trouble in maintaining price stability (that is, a rate of inflation of 2-5 percent per year) while the economy continues to grow at real rates in the 10 percent (of GNP) range.

When the price controls are removed, this pent-up demand will cause a price explosion that may result in a higher increase in prices than if the authorities had not imposed price controls in the first place.

Even within a framework of credit control, price controls must be administered skillfully if the confidence of the business community is to be maintained. While price controls are helpful in controlling inflation induced by cost and wage increases, care must be exercised by the government to assure that sufficient stability exists to enable businessmen to make long-term projections of prices, costs, and hence, profits. The price control system must be rational in the

TABLE 8.6

Credit Requirements for Ten Percent Real GNP Growth, 1975–82
(billions of rials)

Year	Inflation 2 Percent			Inflation 5 Percent			Inflation 10 Percent		
	Private Credit	Public Credit	Total Credit	Private Credit	Public Credit	Total Credit	Private Credit	Public Credit	Total Credit
1975	985.9 (62.6)	587.5 (37.3)	1573.5	1010.4 (62.5)	605.8 (37.5)	1616.2	1051.1 (62.3)	636.3 (37.7)	1687.5
1976	1091.4 (61.1)	694.0 (38.9)	1785.5	1186.4 (61.5)	744.1 (38.5)	1930.5	1347.9 (61.9)	829.9 (38.1)	2177.9
1977	1117.3 (59.0)	777.5 (41.0)	1894.8	1285.9 (59.7)	869.5 (40.3)	2155.4	1583.2 (60.5)	1032.3 (39.5)	2615.5
1978	1147.7 (57.6)	845.8 (42.4)	1993.4	1392.9 (58.5)	988.1 (41.5)	2381.0	1842.0 (59.6)	1247.8 (40.4)	3089.8
1979	1183.0 (56.7)	904.3 (43.3)	2087.3	1508.7 (57.7)	1103.8 (42.3)	2612.5	2128.4 (59.0)	1480.2 (41.0)	3608.6
1980	1222.1 (56.1)	956.6 (43.9)	2178.7	1632.5 (57.2)	1219.6 (42.8)	2852.1	2444.8 (58.5)	1732.7 (41.5)	4177.5
1981	1263.8 (55.7)	1005.1 (44.3)	2268.9	1764.1 (56.9)	1337.3 (43.1)	3101.4	2793.6 (58.2)	2008.4 (41.8)	4802.0
1982	1307.7 (55.4)	1051.2 (44.6)	2359.0	1903.3 (56.6)	1458.3 (43.3)	3361.6	3177.8 (57.9)	2301.2 (41.9)	5488.1

Note: ( ) indicates percent of total credit.
Source: Compiled by the author, based on Appendix E.

TABLE 8.7

Credit Requirements for Ten Percent Real GNP Growth, 1983–90

(billions of rials)

Year	Inflation 2 Percent			Inflation 5 Percent			Inflation 10 Percent		
	Private Credit	Public Credit	Total Credit	Private Credit	Public Credit	Total Credit	Private Credit	Public Credit	Total Credit
1983	1353.4 (55.3)	1096.2 (44.8)	2449.5	2050.1 (56.4)	1583.7 (43.6)	3633.8	3600.9 (57.7)	2641.4 (42.3)	6242.2
1984	1400.5 (55.1)	1140.6 (44.9)	2541.1	2204.7 (56.3)	1714.3 (43.7)	3919.0	4066.5 (57.5)	3005.0 (42.5)	7071.5
1985	1449.0 (55.0)	1184.9 (45.0)	2633.9	2367.3 (56.1)	1850.6 (43.9)	4218.0	4578.8 (57.3)	3404.6 (42.6)	7983.4
1986	1498.6 (54.9)	1229.5 (45.1)	2728.2	2538.2 (56.0)	1993.3 (44.0)	4531.6	5142.4 (57.2)	3843.9 (42.8)	8986.3
1987	1549.5 (54.9)	1274.6 (45.1)	2824.1	2717.9 (55.9)	2142.8 (44.1)	4860.7	5762.5 (57.1)	4327.0 (42.9)	10089.4
1988	1601.4 (54.8)	1320.3 (45.2)	2921.8	2906.6 (55.8)	2299.5 (44.2)	5206.1	6444.6 (57.0)	4858.2 (43.0)	11302.8
1989	1654.5 (54.8)	1366.7 (45.2)	3021.3	3104.8 (55.8)	2463.9 (44.2)	5568.8	7195.0 (56.9)	5442.5 (43.1)	12637.5
1990	1708.7 (54.7)	1414.0 (45.3)	3122.7	3313.0 (55.7)	2636.5 (44.3)	5949.5	8020.4 (56.9)	6085.2 (43.1)	14105.6

Note: ( ) indicates percent of total credit.
Source: Compiled by the author, based on Appendix E.

sense that businessmen are still capable of forecasting (based on market forces) relative price changes over time. Unless businessmen can make these forecasts with a certain degree of confidence, it will be impossible for them to maintain high levels of investment. Similarly, price controls must allow for an adequate profit margin to make business investment sufficiently attractive. If price controls can meet these conditions, the required capital formation will be realized at home, and the optimum rate of capital flow in and out of the country will be obtained.

The authorities responsible for price controls must therefore exercise great care in arriving at a reasonable rate of return on investments and business ventures. Above all, price control policy must provide for long-term financial security while checking inflation, profiteering, and speculation.

Realistically, a policy of price control cannot provide long-term solutions for controlling demand, inflation, and excessive imports unless administrative controls on a very large scale become a permanent feature of the economy. What is needed, therefore, is a policy on credit and income controls to supplement the government's price policy. With an integrated income policy and controlled credit the authorities regulating the price policy should be able to control incomes and regulate demand for foreign and imported goods. They should also periodically review and post prices to stop profiteering and, when needed, could increase efficiency by making allowances for special cases. For example, low-paid workers might be excluded from income controls to enable them to increase their real incomes and thus reduce the existing disparities in income distribution. To maintain productivity, the authorities could also eliminate restrictions preventing skilled labor from earning additional income.

Most importantly, a board should be established to coordinate the stabilization activities of the various agencies and ministries. For example, to reduce inflationary pressures the central bank could restrict credit, increase the reserve requirements of commercial banks, issue high-yield bonds, or restrain the expansion of the money supply. Simultaneously, the Ministry of Economic Affairs and Finances could increase direct taxes to reduce the personal disposable income of individuals. In short, if a deflationary policy is to be followed, all agencies should work together in order to achieve the maximum possible results.

CONCLUSIONS

Increases in the domestic money supply have been closely associated with the country's recent inflation. Significant increases in the quantity of money are to be expected as oil revenues continue to grow. The effect on prices will depend on how such excess liquidity is oriented. The foreign sector, through increased imports of goods and services, has traditionally been important in absorbing increased demand associated with excessive liquidity. Because of the bottlenecks associated with the nation's ports and transport system, however, this sector may not be very effective in providing an outlet for domestic demand, at least in the short run. On the other hand, increased purchases of foreign securities and foreign investments are not hindered by bottlenecks in the transport system. If the foreign sector is used as an outlet for liquidity, through import of securities, with proper monetary management domestic prices need not rise much more than international prices.

NOTES

1. One of the better discussions of the inflation experienced throughout the world in the 1970s is given in Irving S. Friedman, Inflation: A Worldwide Disaster (Boston: Houghton Mifflin, 1973). A number of mechanisms and semantic problems surrounding the discussion of inflation are excellently detailed in Fritz Machlup, "Another View of Cost-Push and Demand-Pull Inflation," in Fritz Machlup, Essays on Economic Semantics (Englewood Cliffs, N.J.: Prentice-Hall, 1963), pp. 241-68. Also see Machlup's "The International Transmission of Inflation," Euromoney (July 1975), pp. 241-45.

2. A detailed discussion of a number of patterns between Iran and her major trading partners is given in M. H. Pesaran, World Economic Prospects and the Iranian Economy (Tehran: Institute for International, Political and Economic Studies, 1976).

3. Gunter Rischer, "The Tehran Stock Exchange," Euromoney (May 1975), pp. 32-36. The classic work in this area is still Richard Benedick, Industrial Finance in Iran (Boston: Harvard University, Graduate School of Business Administration, 1964).

4. For an exhaustive application of these concepts, see Maxwell J. Fry, Finance and Development Planning in Turkey (Leiden: Brill, 1972), ch. 5, and Maxwell J. Fry, The Afghan Economy: Money, Finance and the Critical Constraints to Economic Development (Leiden: Brill, 1974). Of particular interest in both studies is the difficulty Fry encounters in determining the most appropriate definition for money. It should be noted that in this study we have defined money as currency and coins, demand deposits, and quasi money. This follows Friedman's approach of including time deposits in the definition of money. See Milton Friedman and Anna Schwartz, A Monetary

History of the United States, 1867-1960 (Princeton: Princeton University Press, 1963). In the context of Iran, Friedman's theories are articulated in M. Friedman, "Monetary Policy for a Developing Society," Bank Markazi Iran, Bulletin (March-April 1971), pp. 267-86.

5. Bank Markazi Iran, Annual Report and Balance Sheet, 1353, p. 53.

6. The real bills doctrine has a number of interpretations. See A. Hart and P. Kennen, Money, Debt and Economic Activity (Englewood Cliffs, N.J.: Prentice-Hall, 1961), pp. 36-37, for a summary of several variants.

7. M. H. Pesaran, "Banking and Credit Control in Iran," Euromoney (May 1975), pp. 51-52.

8. The following description of the government's antiinflationary drive has been gleaned from various issues of Kayhan (weekly international edition).

9. V. Ray Vicker, "Caveat Vendor—Merchants in Iran Face Citizen Army of Price Policeman," Wall Street Journal (October 5, 1976).

10. Kayhan (international edition).

CHAPTER

9

THE EXPERIENCES OF IRAQ, ALGERIA, ECUADOR, AND VENEZUELA

INTRODUCTION

Despite the obvious temptation to treat the oil-exporting countries as one economic group, the fact remains that even in a relatively small geographic region such as the Middle East the differences between national economies are in many respects greater than are the similarities, if not so much in terms of resource endowment as in terms of the political and institutional framework. On the other hand, the four countries examined here do share, as a result of the increase in oil revenues, a number of features with Iran (see Chapter 2).

All four are countries with populations and resources large enough to absorb most of their oil revenues in productive investments in the short run. Growth in these countries, despite their post-1973 windfalls, will not be automatic. What is required is enlightened effort. Each of these countries provides useful insights into just how difficult the development process is even for countries that, for all practical purposes, are not constrained, as are most developing countries, by severe shortages of foreign exchange.*

---

*Whether foreign trade can be an independent limit on economic growth is a controversial issue. Most development economists tend to accept the thesis that, at least in the short run, foreign exchange shortages can place a limit on a country's growth. A number of economists, however, take issue with this theory. (A balanced view is given in Thomas Weisskopf, "An Econometric Test of Alternative Constraints on the Growth of Underdeveloped Countries," The Review of Economics and Statistics [February 1972], pp. 67-78.) Of the

Thus far our examination of the Iranian economy has indicated the country has, in large part, been fairly efficient in adjusting to its new level of oil revenues. However, a number of deficiencies, particularly the ability of the government to control inflation, remain. Before projecting the outlook for Iran and making recommendations as to ways the country's economic performance can be improved through the period up to 1990, an examination of the experiences of the four countries selected for comparison should be instructive. Their ability (or, in several cases, inability) to deal with the problems associated with the massive inflow of oil revenues will give a number of insights into the variety of means oil-exporting countries have at their disposal to significantly modify their development processes.

Iraq illustrates the problems of planning in a socialist environment where the private sector plays a much smaller role than in Iran. Algeria, while socialistic, illustrates the potential for coordination between the public and private sectors for direct utilization of oil as a basis for broad-based regional and industrial development.

Venezuela illustrates several ways in which oil revenues, incapable in the short run of being invested in productive domestic expenditures, may be put to best use until the economy is prepared to utilize them.

Ecuador is a relatively new oil producer. The country illustrates how a coordinated effort among various government agencies can avoid waste and loss of potential income from the mismanagement of its revenues.

IRAQ

Iraq is firmly committed to what is often referred to as Arab socialism. Broadly defined, Arab socialism is a political ideology that combines elements of Islamic egalitarianism, Eastern political tradition, modern social democracy, latter-day anticolonialism, and a dash of socialist orthodoxy.[1] The Islamic version of Arab socialism as practiced in Iraq is embedded in a commitment to equality of opportunity, and a fair share of national wealth for all. Its Eastern centralist character is rooted in the notion of a powerful, paternalistic, and avowedly benevolent government that serves as both the apex of nationhood and the arbiter of individual fights. A penchant for modern social democracy is found in public guarantees

---

44 countries studied by Weisskopf, only Iran, Iraq, Venezuela, Malaysia, South Africa, and Trinidad and Tobago had trade surpluses (Ecuador and Algeria were not included in the study).

for economic equality, and related welfare measures for all citizens. Its attitude towards colonialism underlies hostility towards foreign aid and loans and suspicion of multinational private investments; it is inclined instead towards intense nationalism. Socialist orthodoxy is partly reflected in the advocacy of nationalization of basic industries.[2]

For almost two decades, the ruling socialist governments have assumed responsibility for developing the resources of the country toward a rapid attainment of its economic potential, and in fact of all the four countries under examination, Iraq is considered by most observers to have the greatest untapped potential for economic development.[3] Still, the government has had little success in utilizing its oil revenues for such development.

The present government (the Ba'ath party) has described the period 1960-70 as the decade of wasted opportunities, a designation that fits the facts extremely well. Intensive water resource developments begun in the early 1950s resulted in rapidly increasing incomes, only to be brought to a halt by a breakdown in political stability.[4] The political turmoil that still characterizes Iraq began in 1958 with the overthrow of the monarchy. A succession of uneasy and politically isolated groups have come and gone since that time. The result has been the alienation of the mass of people from government, discontinuity in economic planning and administration, and a series of violent and unsolved conflicts between the national government and groups both within and outside the country.

Still, the period from 1950 to 1970 was one of relatively rapid growth, with national income (in constant 1963 prices) rising by an annual average rate of 8.4 percent, or 5.3 percent per capita[5] (see Table 9.1). However, an examination of subperiods suggests that the July 1958 revolution resulted in a very marked slowdown in Iraq's pace of economic development. National income during the prerevolutionary period (1950-58) increased by an annual average rate of 13.9 percent (10.9 percent per capita). During 1958-64 the growth rate fell sharply, to 4.7 percent (1.5 percent per capita), and in the subsequent six-year period (1964-70) was but slightly better, 5.1 percent (1.9 percent per capita).

Three critical problems have inhibited economic development since 1958: the Kurdish war for autonomy, the oil dispute with the Iraq Petroleum Company (IPC), and the lack of a permanent and nationally accepted constitution. The civil war in Iraq between the central government and the Kurdish tribe has diverted much of the nation's oil resources from the national development effort to military expenditures. Meanwhile, confrontation with IPC led to a total cessation of exploration and development activity in the oil sector. The result was that Iraq had the lowest rate of growth in oil exports of

TABLE 9.1

Iraq: Major Economic Trends, 1955-75
(millions of dinars)

	1955	1958	1960	1965	1970	1971	1972	1973	1974	1975
National income accounts										
Exports	204.4	226.2	251.0	344.4	437.5	596.5	505.7	720.5	—	—
Imports	121.0	129.4	164.3	205.9	236.6	314.2	294.2	382.7	—	—
Gross domestic product	412.0	514.0	565.4	857.0	1287.6	1483.9	1475.0	1664.1	—	—
Gross national product	340.8	435.6	470.1	728.0	1121.6	1269.0	1338.5	1582.1	—	—
National income (1963 prices)	288.4	373.4	447.4	659.3	897.1	—	—	—	—	—
International transactions										
Exports	185.4	202.2	233.6	315.0	365.5	535.2	453.4	696.2	1254.8	2582.1
Crude petroleum	168.1	185.5	222.6	293.6	329.8	492.7	408.5	638.2	2044.9	2465.4
Imports c.i.f. (cost, insurance, freight)	97.2	109.8	139.0	162.2	181.7	247.9	234.7	270.3	700.1	—
Monetary sector										
Money	64.5	95.7	103.3	143.6	217.6	227.1	259.8	322.6	462.4	625.6
Quasi money	11.7	20.3	28.8	45.2	73.9	85.8	95.2	122.4	172.8	257.0

Source: Central Bank of Iraq Bulletin, various issues; Central Bank of Iraq Annual Report, various issues.

all Middle East producers in the 1960s.6 Lack of a permanent constitution has encouraged political instability, since governments have been representative of small interest groups, often of a violent nature, that could be replaced only by force and often with bloodshed.

Economic Planning

Iraq's planning experience, in contrast to Iran's, has been erratic. The government formulated four development plans between 1951 and 1958, of which the first and the third (both five-year plans) were in effect for less than a year. The situation improved somewhat in the postrevolution (1958) period: the first four-year provisional plan ran for less than two years, but the detailed five-year plan lasted about four years. The subsequent (1965-70) plan largely completed its course.7

Iraqi planning has never lived up to expectations. Actual expenditures have usually fallen far short of the planned levels. For example, in the 1950-65 period, actual expenditures fell short of planned allocations in industry, agriculture, and transport and communications, by 54 percent, 57 percent, and 48 percent, respectively.8 In part, shortfalls were a result of poor administration and project identification. Planning failures, however, were largely the result of the government's continual change in priorities from industry to agriculture, back to industry and, from both industry and agriculture, to housing and construction.

The chronic state of flux in the government was reflected in the planning ministry's lack of direction, continuous shuffling of key personnel, and bitter bureaucratic infighting.

Iraqi planning is of interest because in spite of all its difficulties the economy still achieved a fairly respectable economic performance. The early plans are also of interest simply because there is little evidence that many of the shortcomings associated with them have been corrected. In fact, the same deficiencies that characterized those plans persist today, and are likely to affect the future performance of the economy. To summarize, frequent changes took place in the planning and implementation bureaucracy; whole sections of plans were changed, often before the plan was even put into operation; and projects were included, then dropped, with sectoral allocations frequently being revised for no apparent reason. In addition, the government's fiscal, monetary, and trade policies were not undertaken in coordination with the plan. Worse yet, the annual budget was not drawn up in relation to the financial requirements of the plan. Finally, there was inadequate coordination between the Ministry of Planning and other government agencies involved in the country's development effort.

On balance, it is clear that although the Iraqi economy achieved an overall rate of GNP growth close to, or exceeding, 7 percent per annum on the average between 1950 and 1970, this was at best underachievement in the sense that it fell short of what might have been achieved, given the large volume of investable funds available from oil revenues—agriculture's contribution to growth was particularly disappointing. These trends continued into the last (1970-74) plan. Again there was little connection with projects completed previously; the plan itself was little more than a limited number of engineering projects, irrigation schemes, and scattered industrial ventures.

Outlook for the Future

The rise in oil revenues in 1973 and a number of lessons learned from past failures have radically altered Iraq's economic course. Disbursement for projects in all sectors rose from 70 to 80 percent in 1973. Expenditures reached twice the level achieved in the preceding decade. A new five-year plan was announced in March 1974 under which total expenditure is expected to be about $7,500 million.[9]

Despite the government's desire to diversify the economy, thus reducing its dependence on petroleum, the major part of the government's current development program concentrates on oil-related activities. Iraqi policy is designed to achieve political and economic independence of the petroleum sector through the nationalization of nearly all of the remaining interests of the international oil companies. As part of Iraq's development strategy, a number of large-scale petroleum-related projects are now underway or planned for the immediate future. Because of their great cost, these ventures will dominate the development budget of the state for some time to come. The new development plan lists petrochemical plants for production of olefins, aromatics, basic petrochemicals, fertilizer, and so on.[10]

The implications of Iraqi concentration in the oil sector are clear. First, the government apparently hopes to make up much of the ground lost in the 1960s through developing the petroleum sector in a more balanced manner. Second, its emphasis on the oil sector, where success, given the high world demand for petroleum and its products, is assured, will, it is hoped (from the government's point of view), divert attention from past failures in industry and agriculture.

There are signs that Iraq may have overextended its resources. The drop in world demand for oil and the increase in the bureaucracy needed for the stepped-up development planning have combined to create a temporary but awkward cash shortage. The government has refrained from signing any further large contracts through early 1977. By mid-1976 Iraq had become a net borrower in the world financial markets.[11]

Certainly, if Iraq's reported aim of compressing its original 1976-80 development plan (which has already been revised several times) into two and a half years is to be fulfilled, then the problems of major manpower shortages and infrastructure weakness will have to be overcome. But if the country can solve these problems and maintain some semblance of political stability, then the nation's economy may finally achieve its vast potential.

Contrasts with Iran

Since Iran and Iraq are conterminous and have different political ideologies, comparisons are inevitable. Both neighbors possess large oil reserves, as well as other natural resources (in relation to population, those of Iraq are far greater). Proven crude oil reserves as of the end of 1971 were (in billions of barrels): Iran, 48, and Iraq, 35. Furthermore, a number of surveys have indicated that Iraq's crude oil reserves may be as high as 75 billion barrels– estimates of Iran's reserves are classified by the government, but many observers feel they are lower than Iraq's.[12]

Iran, by exerting pressure on the international oil companies operating in that country, sought to maximize the exploration and exploitation of its oil reserves. Iraq, in contrast, pursued a number of policies throughout the 1960s that discouraged the foreign oil companies from expanding their investments in the country. Moreover, the government has done very little through its national oil company to exploit the reserves under its control (such as the North Rumaila field) or in discovering new reserves. The consequences are clear– though Iraq's proven reserves in 1971 were 73 percent of Iran's, its crude oil production was only 37 percent of its neighbor's.

The contrasting policies of the two countries are even more evident in the widening gap between the oil revenues received by each. In 1960 oil revenues of the two countries were almost equal– Iraq, $266 million, and Iran, $285 million. By 1966, oil revenues received by the governments were $394 and $607 million, respectively. In 1971 (as a result of the new international price agreements) Iraq's oil revenues rose to $840 million, and Iran's to $1,870 million. In 1972, Iranian oil revenues were over three times those of Iraq, and its oil production was about 3.5 times as great.[13]

In 1958, Iraq introduced a program for land reform: in the early 1960s Iran initiated its White Revolution that, in addition to land reform, initiated a variety of additional programs to stimulate farm production. As with oil, a gap in agricultural output has widened between the two countries. Per capita production in Iran in 1967-69 was 5 percent higher than in 1957-59; in Iraq, it was 13 percent lower.

With a population growth rate of 3 percent in each country, the 1970-72 per capita agricultural production in Iran was 3 percent higher than in 1961-65, while in Iraq there was a decline of 11 percent. Similarly, there was a growing disparity between the two countries in manufacturing. Between 1963 and 1970 the growth rate of this sector in Iran was about twice that of Iraq—11.8 percent versus 6.0 percent.

Other differences between the two countries show the same trend. Since the early 1960s Iran has moved rapidly to exploit its vast natural resources. Petrochemicals have become a major new industry, and a wide range of minerals are now being exported. Foreign capital is welcomed and, through local Iranian partners, is rapidly expanding the country's industrial potential. There is little foreign capital in Iraq, and as a result the country's technology is falling far behind Iran's. Education is another area where the two countries have diverged. In Iran education has been stimulated by large budgetary allocations for schools on all levels, as well as the utilization of the armed services as a "literacy corps," whereby educated recruits are assigned to the more outlying rural areas where educational levels are particularly low. The percentage of 7-18-year-olds in school in Iraq was far higher than in Iran in 1960, rose slightly (in Iraq) from 44 to 50 percent in 1965, and then declined slightly to 49 percent in 1969. In Iran the percentage of 7-18-year-olds in school was but 27 percent in 1960, rose to 36 percent in 1965, and was 45 percent in 1969. Vocational education was at a low level in both countries in 1960, with fewer than 10,000 pupils in each country. This number was still unchanged in Iraq in 1969; in Iran, on the other hand, it rose to 23,000.[14]

Iran's industrial development has, on the other hand, a number of similarities with Iraq's. Both countries began their industrial development in the early 1950s with the establishment of fertilizer, cement, textile and sugar milling and refining plants. In Iraq most of the plants built at that time were producing light consumer goods and were located in the capital and its environs.

Also as was the case in Iraq, Iran's industrial sector did not significantly increase its share of GNP until the early 1970s. The main causes of the sector's relatively slow development were similar to those experienced in Iraq, that is, lack of technology, know-how, management, and credit facilities. Recently, however, Iran's industry has been much more dynamic than Iraq's, with an average annual growth rate of 15.6 percent between 1965 and 1970, and later steeper rises of 16 percent in 1971, 18.5 percent in 1972, and over 20 percent average annual rate of growth between 1973 and 1976. The sector's development is much broader than Iraq's, with its structural changes reflected in the development of durable consumer and capital goods such as motors, metals, tires, and chemicals. The petrochemical industry is also making big strides, particularly in sulfur, ammonia, plastics, detergents, and caustic soda.

ALGERIA

Algeria's approach to industrialization has in large part concentrated on areas overlooked by Iranian and Iraqi planners—extensive utilization of the oil industry for industrialization, and decentralization of industry. Both of these factors have allowed Algeria to exploit its major resources, cheap rural labor and inexpensive energy.

Algeria is a socialist state, but with an ideology somewhat different from Iraq's in its view towards the role the state should play in the country's development. Algeria, like Iran, has a large private sector. The country is of interest to Iran primarily because of the apparent success achieved by the government in regional development. Regional development has been one of the main failures of Iranian planning; the country cannot help, therefore, but gain from an examination of Algeria's approach to this increasingly important area of concern.

Industrial Development

Before independence, Algeria had several light industries, including food processing and assembly plants. But the dislocations resulting from the war for independence from France, beginning in the mid-1950s and finally ending in 1962, are still present. Only recently has the economy been able to begin absorbing significant numbers of workers into the industrial labor force.[15]

Algerian energy policy is geared to the utilization of the vast natural gas fields that have made the country the leader in gas liquefaction facilities in the Middle East and have enabled her to push ahead in the development of industries utilizing hydrocarbons. Investment in industry, particularly in such fields as iron, steel, and petrochemicals, has had priority in planning and spending in recent years.[16] In 1972 over 50 percent of investment allocations went to industrial development, and in 1973 industry absorbed over 46 percent of total allocations.

Yet, while growth rates of exports accelerate (see Table 9.2), the unemployment rate remains high. By the end of 1971, with an additional 150,000 jobs created in the preceding 24 months, about one quarter of Algeria's adult male workers were still jobless. As a result, the 1974-77 development plan is changing the emphasis

TABLE 9.2

Algeria: Major Economic Trends, 1965-75

	1965	1969	1970	1971	1972	1973	1974	1975
National Income Accounts (billions of dinars)								
Exports	n.a.	4.5	5.4	-2.2*	-2.3*	-2.2*	n.a.	n.a.
Government consumption	2.8	3.7	4.0	4.3	4.5	4.7	n.a.	n.a.
Gross fixed capital formation	1.6	5.7	7.6	8.5	11.0	12.7	n.a.	n.a.
Imports	n.a.	5.1	7.0	n.a.	—	—	—	—
Gross domestic product	14.1	20.5	22.9	23.5	27.4	29.7	n.a.	n.a.
International Transactions (millions of dinars)								
Exports	3146	4609	4980	4208	5854	7479	19241	17535
Crude petroleum	2294	3117	3360	3016	4614	6214	17538	16026
Imports c.i.f. (cost, insurance, freight)	3314	4981	6205	6028	6604	8876	16922	23148
Monetary Situation (millions of dinars)								
Money	5128	11010	11625	12951	16746	21483	23431	30547
Quasi money	127	1110	1451	974	1393	1437	1524	1773

*Net.

Source: Department of Statistics, Bulletin of General Statistics, various issues.

from heavy to lighter and more labor intensive industries. The plan's objective is to eliminate unemployment by 1980. Indicative of the new direction of industrial development policy is the emphasis being placed on industries that will promote agricultural production on a regional basis. Food processing industries are expected to expand and, as they are relatively labor intensive, 23,000 jobs are expected to be created by the end of 1976.[17]

Structure of the Petroleum Industry

The petroleum industry is playing a major role in the country's regional and industrial development. Algeria's petroleum sector comprises three easily identifiable (mainly by their geographic location) branches: prospecting and production, transport and storage, and processing (refineries, petrochemicals).

Because of technical requirements of construction, the prospecting and producing sector is very capital intensive. Thus this branch of the industry cannot be counted upon for the creation of much local employment.

Since the oil deposits in Algeria are located inland in the Sahara Desert, crude petroleum must be transported by pipeline to the coast, both for domestic use and export. The terminals along the coast offer ideal locations for industries utilizing hydrocarbons as raw materials or that are dependent on cheap energy, but, to be efficient in contributing to regional development, they must be integrated into a comprehensive national development plan. The importance of regional planning as a prerequisite for effective utilization of terminals as industrial centers is clearly illustrated by the difference in regional impact that has resulted from contrasting government policies.

Regional Industrialization

The difference in regional impact as influenced by government policies is shown in the examples of the terminals in two areas. For example, the terminal at Bejaia has never played a significant role in the country's regional development, apart from creating a small demand for local labor to transfer oil from the pipeline to awaiting ships. In part the terminal's minimal linkages with the local economy stem from the fact that until 1971 the facility was foreign-owned and operated. The controlling companies had little reason, in making their production and investment decisions, to take into account the nation's development effort. Consequently, crude oil simply passed through the terminal and on to export markets, leaving little opportunity for local industry to develop.

In contrast, the two other Algerian coastal terminals, at Arzew and Skikda, are government-owned. They are the terminals of pipelines controlled by SONATRACH, the state-owned and operated oil and gas monopoly. SONATRACH designed these terminals to perform a dual role—carrying on the usual functions associated with terminals, and also economically integrating the coast and the interior.[18] The government's regional integration plan has been a marked success. Natural gas liquefaction plants, refineries, and fertilizer factories (at Arzew) and plants for basic materials for the plastics industry (Skikda) and synthetic resins (Arzew) have either been erected in these regions or are under construction. These plants already provide direct employment for 2,500 (Arzew) and 3,400 (Skikda) relatively well-paid and highly qualified workers. Even larger numbers of workers have been employed in related industries.

While the coastal terminals have begun to thrive, the government has remained concerned with the lack of employment opportunities and the low incomes of families located in the hinterlands, the highlands and dry grasslands between the coast and interior desert. Before 1970 there was little industrialization in these areas. The government's plan has been to establish labor-intensive factories in this area capable of producing and competing in domestic markets. Such industries have a competitive advantage over imports because of their low energy and labor costs.

The program has been a great success. Projects in Setif alone (mainly plastics) will give employment to about 3,100 workers by 1978. The output of these plants, a number of which have already been completed, will consist largely of consumer goods (household equipment, toys, packaging material, plastic furniture, and floor coverings) and articles for agriculture (plastic sheeting, nets, boxes, and buckets).

The Algerian planners select industries on the basis of their ability to stimulate local investment; that is, each industry is expected to have linkages to other sectors (for example, to agriculture). The activities they induce are also expected, in turn, to utilize local materials and labor.

Lessons for Iran

Economic activity in Iran is very unbalanced. The Central Ostan (the province containing Tehran) has less than one-fifth of the total population, yet produces over one-third (more than 40 percent, when oil is excluded) of the net national income, produces more than two-fifths of the consumer goods output, and accounts for more than one-half of the country's investment and manufacturing production.[19] Although no precise regional income data exist, crude estimates indicate that the poorer provinces in the south (actually closer to the oil fields than Tehran), such as Bushehr, Sheli, and Sistin-Baluchestan, have per capita incomes of between one-sixth and one-tenth those found in Tehran.[20]

The uneven distribution of economic activities and associated regional disparities of income have been of concern to the government for some time, but it was not until the late 1960s that a systematic policy for regional development was initiated by the government. Regional policy, as outlined in the Fourth Plan, was based on: controls that made establishment of new factories within 120 kilometers of Tehran extremely difficult, tax exemptions for plants locating in the provinces, minor incentives to relocating firms, and the establishment of industrial estates near the larger cities.

While the plan contained a number of regional projects, the country still did not have a consistent regional policy. Instead, individual ministries (such as the Ministry of Economy and the Ministry of Roads) continued to pursue policies without explicit consideration of their regional impact. There was also little cooperation in determining whether their projects were complementary on a regional basis.[21] Increased government concern resulted in the specific regional objectives outlined in the Fifth Plan, among them: to prevent a widening of interprovincial income disparities; to coordinate regional investment and development so as to use resources more efficiently; to improve local authority and public participation in regional development; and to reduce migration and control internal population movements. More generally, the Fifth Plan placed particular stress on the twin policies of agricultural development and expanded social welfare in Iran's vast rural areas. Still, regional policy remained vague, and the government has made little attempt to integrate the oil industry directly into the nation's regional development effort.

In contrast to the Algerian policies, Iranian planners have always conceived of the oil industry as playing an indirect role in the national development effort through its revenues to the central government, and as a source of input to heavy industries serving the entire domestic market—in the case of petrochemicals, to export markets as well. Planners have simply underestimated the potential the oil industry has for regional development. Instead, their approach to regional planning has been provincial, in that they see regional planning as occurring in each individual province through the utilization of resources located in that province.

Iranian planners have also ignored the need and potential for integrated urban and rural development strategies based on utilization of the petroleum sector. Their approach has thus been characterized by an emphasis on social services, to the neglect of regional economic problems (particularly regional manufacturing expansion); the lack of any provision for coordinating interprovincial investment decisions (for example, major pipelines to Tehran could take routes dictated by regional considerations); and their ignorance of the interdependence of public and private sector investment decisions in regional planning. Since Iran, unlike Algeria, has no mechanism for linking provisional planning with national development plans, regional policies, as in the Fourth Plan, are often inconsistent with the nation's overall development objectives. Similarly, the regional policy instruments designed to influence the location decisions of private enterprise are not effective in integrating the oil industry into the nation's development effort.[22]

VENEZUELA

The year 1973 marked a very special juncture for Venezuela. The quick and substantial increase in its petroleum revenues meant that the country had a unique opportunity to develop itself through investments in new areas and in human capital, thus enabling the nation to lay the foundation for greater future independence from petroleum. On the other hand, it also entailed inflationary problems for an economy characterized since World War II by price stability.

The first impact of the new oil situation was a sharp increase in fiscal revenues. While the government's revenues had risen steadily over the years to a level of $4,000 million in 1973, they increased to $10,000 million in 1974—an increase of 150 percent over the 1973 level, and 285 percent over the average revenues in the 1970-72 period.[23] Although recorded revenues for 1975 were somewhat lower than in 1974, at $9,500 million, the funds available to the government were still considerable.

By early 1974 many government officials were becoming increasingly concerned about the appropriate use of the enormous oil revenues. They underscored the nation's urgent need to raise its absorptive capacity and adopt measures to control its surplus of funds with a view to achieving an appropriate measure of control over the money supply. These considerations have led the government to revise its development strategy, undertake long-range institutional reforms, and to channel part of its funds abroad in the form of investments and financial aid.

As a result of these events, the government faced a conceptual as well as managerial problem of how to make proper use of the newly acquired funds and, in particular, of how to achieve a reasonable measure of price stability while fostering an acceleration in the economy's rate of growth.

In these circumstances immediate government attention was given to:

1. establishing mechanisms and adopting measures that permit the optimal utilization (in terms of both the magnitude of resources utilized and their allocation) of the additional funds available
2. finding ways in which the resources, whose absorption may not be possible in the short run, may be utilized so as to ensure their orderly availability in the future (while preserving the value of these assets)
3. intensifying efforts at improving the systems for the definition of priorities; for the identification, formulation, and appraisal of projects; and for their execution and control. The fiscal surplus stemming from the increased oil revenues, far from reducing the need for programming, has made its usefulness more evident.[24]

With these factors in mind, the Venezuelan government began to revise its development strategy and reorganize its institutional structure in 1974. To this end it was successful in enacting the following measures:

1. Amendment of the Organic Act of the National Treasury, which allocated to the new Venezuelan Investment Fund 50 percent of the government's revenue from taxes on hydrocarbon operations, as well as the tax on income derived from that sector; in addition, the setting up of the mechanisms required to maintain an adequate ratio between the amount earmarked in the annual budget and the resources set aside for the Fund.
2. Establishment of the Venezuelan Investment Fund as an autonomous legal entity for the administration and investment of its own assets. The Fund's objectives include the financing of the expansion and diversification of the economy, making profitable placements abroad, and promoting programs of international cooperation to help achieve the nation's financial and economic stability.
3. Creation of the Agricultural and Industrial Development Funds to stimulate private investment in those sectors. The Agricultural Fund offers credit at interest rates ranging from 3 to 7 percent for 20 years with a maximum grace period of five years. Its operations are handled by commercial banks, the Agricultural and Livestock

Bank, and the Agricultural Development Bank. The Industrial Development Fund is authorized to make loans at interest rates of between 6 and 9 percent, on terms of up to 15 years and a three year grace period. These loans are channeled through the private banks, the Industrial Bank, and the Venezuelan Development Corporation. Each of the Funds has an authorized capital of 2,000 million bolivars.

4. Revision of the Income Tax Law to increase collections from the petroleum companies by levying an additional progressive tax on remaining income, or by using other mechanisms deemed appropriate within the framework of recommendations made by the OPEC members—and modification of the system of tax exemptions and rebates in order to utilize it as an instrument of national economic policy.25

The Operation of Venezuelan Investment Fund

Undoubtedly, the most important of these changes was the establishment of the Venezuelan Investment Fund (VIF). The purpose of the fund was to set aside a significant proportion of the surplus funds to be invested abroad in safe and profitable assets while suitable domestic projects were being identified.26 The fund was assigned $3,000 million in 1974, accounting for 36 percent of that year's oil revenues; in 1975, the fund was assigned $1,750 million (24 percent of the oil revenues).

The VIF also centralizes the country's international financial transactions in coordination with the major lending agencies. For example, the fund has aided many of the nonoil developing countries in financing their balance-of-payments deficits resulting from the increase in oil prices. By early 1976 Venezuela had committed $680 million to this purpose through international mechanisms such as the IMF oil facility, World Bank, Inter-American Development Bank, Caribbean Development Bank, Finance Corporation of the Andean Pact Countries, and Central American Integration Bank. It has also directly lent money to some Latin American countries.

Three other special funds were created that committed a proportion of the surplus funds to direct financing of agricultural and industrial development, and for export diversification—$620 million have been devoted to this purpose since 1974. In January 1976 a fourth special fund has started, operating with an initial capital of $115 million and aimed at stimulating urban and rural construction.27

The overriding policy for internal investments is conservative. So far the fund's portfolio policy has been closely linked to the liquidity demand for financing of projects to which it has committed itself. Most internal investment has been on a short-term basis: only 16 percent of the portfolio is medium and long term, and approximately 10 percent has been put into national agencies. About half the money is on deposit with banks in the United States and their affiliates operating in the Eurodollar market, and the other half is with short-term government securities, principally in the United States. The average transaction is in the $25 million to $50 million range and is rigidly controlled.

The return on the medium-term portfolio was just 9 percent in 1975, and of the medium-term investments almost half were in deutschemark denominated vehicles, with a further 30 percent in U.S. dollars, 8 percent in Canadian dollars, 4 percent in Dutch florins, and 3 percent each in Kuwaiti dinars and French francs. Eurocurrency bonds, usually held to maturity, are the primary instrument. Over half of these are sovereign or state-guaranteed bonds, with a minority of first-class corporate notes.[28]

Antiinflation Program

The VIF has played an important part in the government's antiinflation program. Despite the government's concern with inflation, the rate of increase in the money supply accelerated in 1974. In that year, money in circulation rose 41 percent, compared to an average annual 15 percent increase during the 1970-73 period. The most significant growth was in demand deposits (75 percent of the money supply), which increased by 38 percent (see Table 9.3). Rapid expansion of money in circulation reflected a sharp increase in credit to the private sector and a tripling in net international reserves (oil revenues). In part the extraordinary inflow of foreign exchange that resulted from higher petroleum prices was neutralized by the VIF; by the end of 1974 the VIF had absorbed nearly 12 billion bolivars for investment outside the country.

In spite of the VIF's actions, however, government fiscal expenditures still rose significantly (51 percent in 1974 and 16 percent in 1975), reaching a level that was 122 percent above that of their average in the 1970-72 period. This increase is, as in the case of Iran, directly responsible for the sharp increase in aggregate demand. Private consumption and investment expenditures grew correspondingly and the result was excess demand. As in Iran, demand became excessive because increases in domestic supply of goods and services were inadequate; that is, existing domestic production capacities were small relative to the growth in demand, and full capacity levels of output were quickly approached in many areas of production. In addition, the expansion of domestic capacity in the short run was constrained by normal bottlenecks in transport. The country was

TABLE 9.3

Venezuela: Major Economic Trends, 1955-75
(billions of bolivars)

	1955	1960	1965	1969	1970	1971	1972	1973	1974	1975
National income accounts										
Exports	5.910	8.270	11.650	12.750	13.110	15.880	17.400	25.150	66.210	49.460
Government consumption	2.240	3.680	4.680	6.140	6.890	7.950	8.730	9.770	12.790	15.940
Gross fixed capital formation	4.410	4.800	6.970	11.450	11.320	13.160	15.640	18.950	20.700	30.970
Private consumption	9.130	14.350	21.690	25.110	27.950	29.420	32.100	34.340	44.860	54.960
Imports	4.010	5.140	8.000	9.760	10.360	11.550	12.590	14.390	21.330	29.270
Gross domestic product	17.890	25.670	37.930	47.220	52.010	56.970	63.300	76.340	126.700	124.070
Gross national product	15.990	23.570	34.430	43.540	48.970	53.030	58.660	69.620	108.450	112.070
Gross domestic product (1970 prices)	—	—	—	48.030	52.010	52.520	54.380	57.550	60.160	—
International transactions										
Exports	5.870	7.720	10.926	11.104	11.691	13.893	13.754	21.020	46.418	37.706
Petroleum	5.491	6.642	10.144	10.141	10.550	12.814	12.571	18.632	44.185	35.668
Imports	3.156	3.537	5.664	6.749	7.382	8.252	9.471	10.856	16.249	22.829
Monetary sector										
Money	2.414	3.574	4.705	6.465	6.955	8.116	9.731	11.597	15.975	24.034
Quasi money	0.669	1.691	2.806	4.286	4.702	5.550	6.774	8.189	9.735	14.866

Source: Banco Central de Venezuela, Informe Economico, various issues.

also confronted with acute shortages of skilled manpower. In contrast to Iran, however, Venezuela has not resorted to the wholesale importation of foreign technicians and professionals. Still, imports rose sharply by 46 percent in 1974 and 33 percent in 1975, to a level of about $5,000 million.

The government has been particularly concerned not only by the rate of increase in imports but because of their composition. A greater need for capital goods for private and public investment explains part of the increase, but growing consumption has stimulated imports of a great variety of finished consumer goods and intermediate products that the country is capable of producing locally.

Although import prices have risen (a result of world inflation in general), their massive increase to supplement local supply has helped keep the rate of inflation within reasonable bounds. Nevertheless, the traditional Venezuelan price stability (prices rose at approximately 2 percent per year for decades) was seriously affected by the sharp growth in aggregate demand coupled with government increases in the minimum wage. Venezuela's cost of living index rose by 8 percent in 1974 and by 10 percent in 1975. Wholesale prices rose 16.5 percent in 1974 and 8 percent in 1975.

The government has responded to the resulting increases in prices by initiating a series of price controls.[29] Decrees related to price controls were issued in March, June, and September 1974. Prices were fixed on approximately 70 articles--articles which constituted most of the basic diet of lower-income families. In another attempt to protect the real incomes of the poorer segments of the population, the government established a minimum wage of 15 bolivars per day, and also increased most wages and salaries by 5 to 25 percent.

While some of the inflation in Venezuela has undoubtedly been caused by wage and other increases in costs, most of the increase in prices reflects the sharp increase in money supply in recent years.[30] The money supply has always been determined almost exclusively by government expenditures financed by oil revenues. These expenditures exert upward pressure on prices, which historically have been diffused through outflows of money via imports and capital movements. This self-adjusting mechanism, without significant government interference, enabled the economy to absorb a growth in money supply that traditionally exceeded that of real increases in GDP. The increases in money after 1973, however, were simply too great for the economy to accommodate.

No doubt the inflationary problem is one of the most menacing at this juncture of the Venezuelan economy. If government is intent on maintaining a fixed exchange rate, as it has affirmed on several occasions, then domestic inflation must be kept equal to or below the rates of inflation of its major trading partners. The inflationary impact of the rapid expansion of money indicates that the VIF must play a greater role in the government's antiinflationary program.

Lessons for Iran

With central government revenue from the petroleum sector more than trebling—from 11 billion bolivars in 1973 to 37 billion in 1974, or about one-third of the GDP—the principal policy issue confronting the Venezuelan authorities was how to allocate the increased public revenue so as to satisfy the social and economic needs of the country without producing undue inflationary pressure. The Venezuelan government responded with an imaginative fiscal policy based on the extensive use of special funds, seeking to limit cash expenditure in the short run while diverting a large proportion of public revenue to productive investment projects.

One of the main goals of the government has been to expand the absorptive capacity of the economy so as to invest future resources in new development projects in an orderly and efficient manner. The VIF has been an integral part of this policy. The principal objective of the fund is to finance the importation of materials needed for development projects. It also serves as a complementary source of financing for large agricultural, industrial, and export promotion projects. In addition, a major role of the fund is to maintain the value of government assets. To do this the VIF invests large amounts of funds abroad; the corresponding budgetary allocations constitute an adequate instrument for sterilizing an important portion of the expanded oil revenues. On the other hand, with the creation of the agricultural, industrial, and mortgage credit funds one of the basic mechanisms for stimulating the productive sectors has been established, thus correcting the excessive emphasis formerly put on economic infrastructure works.

Iran has no such fund. Given the country's inflationary pressure and inability to absorb all of its oil revenues efficiently, the country should carefully examine the possibility of creating a fund similar to the VIF.

ECUADOR

The economic growth of Ecuador prior to 1973 can best be characterized as slow, fluctuating, and dependent on foreign trade.[31] As a result of the discovery of great amounts of oil, and its subsequent exploitation in the early 1970s, greater dynamism and favorable prospects for the future are appearing in the economy.

Impact of Oil Revenues

The oil bonanza has revolutionized Ecuador's prospects and has increased the annual value of goods and services from 40.06 billion sucres in 1971 to 108.11 billion in 1974. While in 1971 total exports were $222 million, by 1974 they amounted to $1,061.6 million (see Table 9.4), an increase of nearly 500 percent. For the first time in its history, Ecuador was able to import most of the items its citizens wanted from abroad. The balance of payments, which had in the past generally been in deficit, changed to a positive balance of $54 million in 1973 and $100 million in 1974. By the end of 1974 the reserves had risen to a record level of $345.7 million and in January the nation's currency, the sucre, was declared a hard currency by the IMF.[32]

The government, which had always been limited in its action by revenue shortages, found its income increasing from 9.2 billion sucres in 1972 to 14.4 billion sucres in 1974, an increase of 56 percent. Government spending over the same period went up by only 32 percent, but there was still a budget surplus of 4.5 billion sucres in 1974.

The state had money for projects it could never have considered before, and public investment over the period rose 147 percent, despite the fact that some major plans could not be put into operation. Domestic savings doubled between 1971 and 1974, to a record 14 billion sucres. Opportunities for immediate investment at home being inadequate, Ecuador, despite its great necessity for putting capital to work, found itself, as was the case with Venezuela, actually exporting capital.

Inflation

The great inflow of wealth has not arrived without creating many and diverse problems for the Ecuadorean economy. The most pressing issue facing the authorities is the worst inflation in the country's history.

The National Statistical Institute's food index, which stood at just over 130 in mid-1970, increased to 270 during 1974. The impact of oil revenues, and specifically the resulting increases in inflation, has been a disaster for the mass of families that spend the bulk of their income to nourish themselves. The average working-class family in Quito, the capital, spends up to 81.8 percent of its income on food.

The major factors in the price increases were the strong money expansion, the slow growth of farm output, and the increase in the price of imports caused by world inflation. The consumer price

TABLE 9.4

Ecuador: Major Economic Trends, 1955-75

	1955	1960	1965	1969	1970	1971	1972	1973	1974	1975
National income accounts (billions of sucres)										
Exports	2.07	2.53	3.62	4.14	5.59	6.93	6.20	15.63	30.85	26.91
Government consumption	1.37	1.81	2.84	4.85	5.35	4.63	5.34	6.66	9.58	11.37
Gross fixed capital formation	1.54	1.90	2.41	4.74	7.46	10.21	9.76	11.88	19.93	29.32
Private consumption	7.85	10.12	15.12	23.37	25.85	28.95	34.27	38.41	52.71	66.00
Imports	2.05	2.48	3.57	5.20	7.63	11.45	11.95	12.34	24.64	28.99
Gross national product	10.74	13.74	20.22	31.76	36.20	38.78	45.91	59.35	85.50	105.23
Gross domestic product	11.05	14.14	20.79	32.49	37.34	40.06	47.45	63.14	91.50	108.11
Gross domestic product (1970 prices)	—	—	—	34.60	37.34	35.71	38.70	45.00	52.14	100.30
International transactions (millions of dollars)										
Exports	113.8	144.5	169.5	193.0	221.1	222.1	342.6	547.9	1061.6	910.3
Crude petroleum	—	—	—	0.6	0.8	1.2	59.5	282.1	614.6	515.9
Imports c.i.f. (cost, insurance, freight)	114.0	114.3	167.8	241.8	273.9	340.1	318.6	379.3	958.5	943.2
Monetary sector (millions of sucres)										
Money	1193.0	1732.0	2577.0	4341.0	5404.0	6020.0	7321.0	9568.0	13064.0	14817.0
Quasi money	352.0	469.0	898.0	1705.0	1984.0	2557.0	3018.0	3598.0	4605.0	4873.0

Source: Banco Central, Boletin Stadistico, various issues.

index increased by 12.3 percent in 1973, and by 23.3 percent in 1974, in sharp contrast to the annual average of 7.6 percent in the 1970-72 period. Price increases were highest for food products, which rose by 17 percent in 1973 and by 32 percent in 1974.[33]

Money and quasi money expanded by 42.8 and 23.5 percent, respectively, in 1974, compared to the 23.8 and 19.4 percent annual averages of the 1972-73 period. Their ratio to GDP declined from 20.5 percent in 1974, while the ratio of money alone to GDP decreased from 15.6 to 14.1 percent.

Accumulation of international reserves during 1973-74 was a major factor in the expansion of the money supply, while credit to the public sector, in comparison to previous years, served as a constraining element. Another important expansive factor was domestic credit to the private sector, which rose 42 percent in 1974 and 23 percent in 1973, compared to an annual average of 11 percent in 1971-72.

In 1974 a number of measures were adopted to restrict short-term loans in order to reduce monetary expansion, among them: the minimum legal cash reserve on slight deposits was raised during the second half of the year, and portfolio ceilings were established for private banks and for commercial loans granted by the National Development Bank. The government also adopted several other anti-inflation measures in 1974: it fixed and controlled prices for the major basic consumer goods and essential raw materials; it prohibited the inclusion in prices of wage increases granted; and it subsidized the importation of basic goods. As a result of these measures, together with slower monetary expansion in 1975, inflation declined to an annual rate of 11 percent that year.[34]

The government's chosen instrument to finance the subsidization of food imports has been the Fondo de Inversiones de Venezuela (FONADE). This organization was set up at the end of 1973 to manage government income accrued from oil sales above a reference price of $7.80 per barrel. In addition, FONADE, like the Venezuelan VIF, was directed to facilitate the supply of equipment and seeds for the farm sector.[35] Directives were also given to the commercial banks (which have always complained that lending to the farm sector was unremunerative) that one-quarter of their total loans advanced should be made to farmers. The government's own National Development Bank increased its farm loans from 800 million sucres in 1972 to nearly 3 billion sucres in 1974. With this crash program the government hopes that productivity on the land will improve more rapidly than it has up to now, and that one of the principal economic bottlenecks causing inflation in the country will slowly open up.

FONADE is but one of a number of agencies and devices used by the government to put its new money to work. Given the lack of immediately usable plans waiting to be financed, National Pre-

Investment Funds has been established as an offshoot of the national planning board charged with overseeing the execution of the National Plan for Transformation and Development, the overall set of guidelines for Ecuador's economic future.36

Ecuador, while not as systematic as Venezuela, has undertaken several measures to assure that its oil revenues will be spent in a productive noninflationary manner. Beginning in 1972, the National Planning and Economic Coordination Board was given the power to develop and review public sector investment plans in order to assure their conformity to long-term national development objectives. In addition, an economic council was formed at the ministerial level to oversee budget execution and to establish short-term economic policies. A special section was also established in the central bank to increase banking system's flow of resources for agricultural and industrial projects considered of high national priority.

Lessons for Iran

The experiences of other oil-exporting countries indicate that growth and equilibrium, both internal and external, are now the key issues for these economies and the greatest challenges facing their governments. To achieve accelerated, self-sustained, long-term economic growth without creating internal or external disequilibrium, various interrelated measures and policies must be created.

The main purpose of the economic policy in these countries, with respect to surplus savings derived from oil revenues, is to adjust the composition of the national portfolio over time between financial investments and investments in physical and human capital, according to that country's absorption capacity and development needs. Within this intention, and in the institutional field, the Venezuelan Investment Fund (VIF) seems to be the most effective institution created to date.

As oil revenues are capable of being invested domestically, diversification of the economy, particularly in agriculture, is essential if oil is to be displaced as the primary source of income.

SIMILARITIES IN DEVELOPMENT

Considerable variety exists among these four nations in the ways they have utilized their oil revenues, though they have encountered a number of common features and development problems as a result of the oil boom. The first and most important of these is the fact that, although finance is no longer an immediate constraint, each is currently faced with acute shortages of a number of inputs vital to its development effort. This is most evident in construction, where it is impossible to import all of the necessary materials, such as cement and semiskilled workers.

In addition, the increased oil revenues have had little impact in rural areas; they remain highly concentrated in the capital city and, at most, in one or two other towns. The consequence has been a high rate of migration from the poorer to richer areas, resulting in urban slums, overcrowding, and discontent.

Each country has, through its rapid growth, imposed severe strains on its domestic transport system. Delays in the movement and arrival of goods, particularly into and out of the ports, are often substantial. The result has been increased costs, long delays in implementing development projects, and increased inflation resulting from the inability to import large quantities of food at world prices.

In recent years each country has also tended to select capital-intensive, large-scale, development projects, and many of the projects begun in 1974 and 1975 represent sizable claims on their limited supplies of skilled labor and administrative capacity.

What's more, the problem of inflation was never really encountered before 1973. Not all the countries have had precisely the same level and pattern of inflation, but in each case inflation was the direct result, not only of higher import prices (a result of the acceleration of inflation in the industrialized countries), but of increasing demands on domestic resources by both government and private enterprise. In general, the authorities have reacted to inflation by initiating price and wage controls, instead of reducing expenditures (Venezuela and Ecuador are notable exceptions). In addition, the concern over inflation has caused planners to place increased emphasis on developing the agricultural sector as a means of reducing pressure on food prices. Increased agricultural production is a long-run solution, however, and may take several years to have a significant impact on domestic prices.

A pattern of internal budgetary surpluses and external payments deficits for goods and services has developed in each country since 1973, reflecting the scarcity of domestically produced goods. A related pattern has been the tendency for private sector imports to rise at a significantly faster rate than public sector imports. Internally, this is reflected in the balance sheets of the commercial banks, which show the private sector's demand for credit sharply outstripping that group's increase in deposits (see Appendix E).

CONCLUSIONS

A flood of unearned or easily earned income has traditionally been a severe test for the character of an individual. How it affects the fiber of a nation is a less known process upon which the curtain is now rising in the oil-exporting countries. Sudden immense wealth is the major factor in the unprecedented inflation that now faces Iran and several others of these countries. The drama lies in the fact that, depending on how each nation handles itself, the chain of events set in motion in late 1973 could either lead to a lasting period of prosperity or to chaos.

Two countries, Venezuela and, to a lesser extent, Ecuador, recognized early the dangers of massive oil revenues, and began siphoning off immense sums of money that could not be absorbed by the country's existing financial mechanisms or dropped into the money supply without significantly accelerating domestic rates of inflation. Through careful investment abroad, however, these funds are expected to keep pace with world inflation and can be utilized when the countries are in a position to implement effectively their ambitious development plans.

Iran, on the other hand, while making some investments overseas, has not followed a systematic policy of diverting its oil revenues into noninflationary investments. It is still not too late for the country to examine and possibly implement an investment program of the sort that appears to have been so successful in Venezuela and Ecuador.

The experiences of Algeria and Iraq are of particular relevance for Iran. In considering their experiences, it becomes clear that successful development on a regional or local level depends on five primary factors: the use of oil and gas to promote industrialization directly; the achievement of a satisfactory balance between the agricultural and industrial sectors; the utilization of inexpensive energy to enable industries to be competitive in international markets; the integration of regional and national development plans; and the encouragement of private investment to complement and aid in the implementation of the government's economic and industrial planning.

Historically, the oil-exporting countries have tended to view industrial development apart from the oil industry. In part this stems from the traditional foreign-owned and enclave nature of the oil sector. But as governments have begun to gain greater control over their oil resources, it is evident that petroleum may be one of the best fields for industrial expansion, especially in the case of products that require high imports of energy or petroleum derivatives.

Industrial expansion alone, however, is insufficient to sustain their economic growth and development. Increased production in agriculture will be needed to meet rising demands for food and employment opportunities. Insufficient development of the agricultural sector has already led to rising food prices, thus contributing to inflation. With water resource development, given the temperate climates of these countries, they should have a good chance of achieving a proper balance between industry and agriculture.

A final lesson for Iran is the importance of industrial efficiency. Despite the growth of industrial output in Algeria and Iraq, manufacturing contributes only modestly to each country's exports. A major problem still to be faced by those countries is how to improve the international competitiveness of their industrial products. Rising per capita productivity is the only solution.

Efficiency and productivity can be improved by specialization in industries that require low-cost energy inputs and that are located in areas with adequate labor supply. The debates of the 1960s and 1970s in most oil-exporting countries, about whether or not to industrialize, are no longer relevant. Rather, the major problem facing these countries is to identify those industries capable of making the greatest contribution to their overall development.

While a number of factors have played both positive and negative roles in affecting the growth of Iran and Iraq—independent of political ideology—the divergent patterns of the two countries seem to indicate an especially close correlation between the faster growth in Iran and her sustained political stability and pragmatism in internal socio-economic policies. The more rapid pace of development has been achieved by Iran, where internal social frictions and external political conflicts have been minimal, and domestic socio-economic policies have been tailored to fit national requirements.

In marked contrast to Iraq, Iranian policy has been relatively free of ideological constraints. Under a political leadership that has frequently marched ahead of inescapable events, Iran has been able to maintain a high degree of political stability and domestic social accord within its borders, thus ensuring its sustained economic growth. The wide latitude given to economic freedoms in Iran is in sharp contrast to the top-heavy bureaucracy of Iraq. Undoubtedly, Iran's more flexible economic system has allowed the country to take fuller advantage of its increased oil revenues. The title of a recent article about Iraq in the Financial Times—"The Reality Beneath the Dogma"—signifies the ideological straightjacket within which Iraq has placed herself.[37]

NOTES

1. An excellent summary is given in Charles A. Cooper and Sidney S. Alexander, eds., Economic Development and Population Growth in the Middle East (New York: Elsevier, 1972), pp. 18-19.

2. A detailed description of the nationalization process is given in F. Jalal, The Role of the Government in the Industrialization of Iraq, 1950-65 (London: Frank Cass, 1972), especially pp. 69-79.

3. Albert Y. Badre, "Economic Development of Iraq," in Cooper and Alexander, Economic Development and Population Growth in the Middle East, p. 283.

4. P. J. Vatikiotis, "The Politics of the Fertile Crescent," in Paul Y. Hammond and Sidney S. Alexander, Political Dynamics in the Middle East (New York: Elsevier, 1972), pp. 245-46.

5. Data on Iraq are sparse. Much of the national income data has been estimated and reconstructed by foreign observers. The national income account data used here is from E. Kanovsky, Economic Development of Iraq (Tel Aviv: Tel Aviv University, David Horowitz Institute for the Research of Developing Countries, 1974), p. 2.

6. A number of Iraq's internal problems are excellently summarized in Abbas Alnasrawi, Financing Economic Development in Iraq (New York: Praeger, 1967). See also Ahmad Abdul Kader, "The Role of the Oil Export Sector in the Economic Development of Iraq" (Ph.D. dissertation, University of West Virginia, Morgantown, 1974).

7. Badre, "Economic Development of Iraq," pp. 283-88.

8. A. Y. Hershlag, The Economic Structure of the Middle East (Leiden, Neth.: Brill, 1975), pp. 245-47.

9. The Economist Intelligence Unit, Quarterly Economic Review of Iraq, no. 2 (1976), p. 9.

10. Ibid.

11. "Symptomatic of the country's financial problems and its frustration in putting in hand its development program is the announcement that final agreement has been concluded between Iraq and Japan on a loan to finance the costs of five major hydrocarbon and industrial projects." The Economist Intelligence Unit, Quarterly Economic Review of Iraq (4th quarter 1976), pp. 9-10.

12. See Yusuf J. Ahmad, Oil Revenues in the Gulf (Paris: OECD, Development Center, 1974), pp. 27-49.

13. The Economist Intelligence Unit, Quarterly Economic Review Special, no. 18, Oil Production, Revenues and Economic Development (London, 1974).

14. Hershlag, Economic Structure of the Middle East, ch. 1.

15. Ragaei El Mallakh, "Industrialization in the Arab World: Obstacles and Prospects," in Naiem A. Sherbiny and Mark A. Tessler, Arab Oil (New York: Praeger, 1976), p. 65.

16. Middle East Annual Review (London: Middle East Review Co., 1975), p. 97.

17. The Economist Intelligence Unit, Quarterly Economic Review of Algeria (4th Quarter 1976), pp. 8-9.

18. An excellent account of this program is given in Konrad Schliephake, "Regional Development and Oil Strategy: The Case of Algeria," Intereconomics, no. 7 (1975), pp. 202-06.

19. See Robert Looney, Income Distribution Policies and Economic Growth in Semiindustrialized Countries: A Comparative Study

of Iran, Mexico, Brazil, and South Korea (New York: Praeger, 1975), ch. 1.

20. M. H. Pesaran, "Income Distribution and Its Major Determinants in Iran," in Jane Jacqz, ed., Iran: Past, Present and Future—The Persepolis Symposium (New York: Aspen Institute for Humanistic Studies, 1976), p. 274. See also E. Haraghi, "Regional Studies in Iran," in Multidisciplinary Aspects of Regional Development (Paris: OECD, 1969).

21. Harry W. Richardson, "Regional Planning in Iran," Growth and Change (July 1975), p. 17.

22. Robert Looney, The Economic Development of Iran: A Recent Survey with Projections to 1981 (New York: Praeger, 1973), p. 141.

23. Several recent and quite comprehensive studies are available on the development of the Venezuelan oil industry. See Mostafa F. Hassan, Economic Growth and Employment Problems in Venezuela: An Analysis of An Oil Based Economy (New York: Praeger, 1975); Jorge Salazar-Carrillo, Oil in the Economic Development of Venezuela (New York: Praeger, 1976); and Franklin Tugwell, The Politics of Oil in Venezuela (Palo Alto, Calif.: Stanford University Press, 1975). Data used in this study on the oil sector are taken from the Salazar-Carrillo study.

24. Carlos Andres Perez, "Special Message," mimeographed, (Caracas, April 29, 1974).

25. Inter-American Development Bank, Economic and Social Progress in Latin America (Annual Report, 1974), p. 434.

26. David Nott, "Venezuela: The Apportionment of Oil Wealth," Bank of England and South America (May 1975), pp. 196-99.

27. Richard Ensor, "Brother, Can You Spare a Dollar? Well, the Fondo Has Billions, but. . . ." Euromoney (December 1976), pp. 13-21.

28. Padraic Fallon, "The Man Most Courted by the Leaders Keeps Venezuela on the Path of Sobriety," Euromoney (December 1976), pp. 22-23.

29. The Economist Intelligence Unit, Quarterly Economic Review, Venezuela, no. 1 (1976), p. 3.

30. Several studies have verified this fact. See Mohsin Khan, "Experiments with a Monetary Model for the Venezuelan Economy," International Monetary Fund Staff Papers (November 1974), pp. 389-413; Deena Khatkhate et al., "A Money Multiplier Model for a Developing Country: The Venezuelan Case," International Monetary Fund Staff Papers (November 1975), pp. 740-57.

31. This period has been admirably surveyed by Charles Gibson in his Foreign Trade in the Economic Development of Small Nations: The Case of Ecuador (New York: Praeger, 1971).

32. International Monetary Fund, IMF Survey (January 7, 1974), pp. 15-16.
33. Data taken from Central Bank, Monthly Bulletin, various issues.
34. IMF Survey.
35. Sarita Kendall, "Ecuador: Oil and Development," Bank of England and South America Review (May 1975), pp. 316-22.
36. Early attempts at organization and planning are outlined in R. Echeverria et al., Current Economic Position and Prospects of Ecuador (Washington, D.C.: IBRD, 1973), particularly pp. 40-52.
37. Financial Times (July 30, 1975), p. 7.

CHAPTER

10

A DEVELOPMENT STRATEGY FOR IRAN

INTRODUCTION

On a seemingly limitless tide of oil revenues, Iran began in 1974 to lurch forward towards the twenty-first century. Between now and the end of the century, however, the economy must go through a period of normalization.* Given the current buoyancy provided by petroleum revenues, the country must achieve sufficient momentum before the slow-down in oil revenues in order to consolidate its position and enable the nation to sustain its growth. The dramatic increases in oil prices in 1973-74 have given Iran—the most significant of the Middle East oil producers in terms of population, history, and nationhood—the potential to join the league of fully industrialized states on a permanent basis and establish that "great civilization" that it is the Shah's ambition to create.

---

*The normalization period is the time when Iran's oil revenues will level off and begin to decline. Clearly, if the economy is to maintain a target rate of growth, a number of other sources of demand, particularly nonoil exports, must pick up the slack during this transitionary phase in the country's development. (A detailed discussion of these problems is given in Firouz Vakil, "Iran's Basic Macroeconomic Problems: A 20-Year Horizon," in Jane W. Jacqz, ed., <u>Iran: Past, Present and Future—The Persepolis Symposium</u> [New York: Aspen Institute for Humanistic Studies, 1976]; and Firouz Vakil, <u>Determining Iran's Financial Surplus, 1352-1371</u> [Tehran: Institute for International, Political and Economic Studies, 1975].)

As a patriotic visionary, the Shah set 1990 as the date for Iran to become the fifth most powerful nation in the world.* While that aim may be more of a wish than a realistic goal, the nation does have sufficient wealth and a potential for growth—two factors that have already singled the country out as the dominant force in the region and one of the most advanced countries in the developing world.

The country's vast potential explains and justifies the international attention paid to the Shah's pronouncements, quite apart from his vital position in the Organization of Petroleum Exporting Countries.

PROBLEMS AND POLICY

So far we have gauged the economic potential of Iran and described past development policies within the framework on which development plans were formulated and implemented. It remains now to determine briefly the most salient problems likely to be associated with future development efforts and to examine future policies that might deal with these problems in moving the country further towards the attainment of its great economic potential.

The past decade has been characterized by the very exciting and successful performance of most sectors of the Iranian economy. Clearly Iran was, because of her long history of economic planning and project preparation, in a particularly good position to take advantage of the higher oil revenues resulting from the OPEC successes in the 1973 Tehran agreements; nevertheless, the country must be cautioned against overoptimism.

In realizing its ambitious goals, Iran will have to adjust to a wide range of new uncertainties in the international environment, many of which were not anticipated by Iranian planners in early 1974. In addition, the country must resolve a plethora of domestic, economic, political, and social challenges, many of which are the results of past successes. Iran will also have to defy the conventional wisdom that high growth rates cannot be sustained for long periods without at least a temporary pause. Clearly, any significant slackening of the nation's development momentum will aggravate many persistent social and political problems.

OIL REVENUES

The main determinants of economic growth in the coming decade will continue to be the oil revenues accruing to the government and

---

*With falling oil revenues and the inability to get a higher price for oil at the December 1976 OPEC meetings, the Shah moved this date back to around the year 2000.

A DEVELOPMENT STRATEGY FOR IRAN

the manner in which the authorities spend them. Assuming no substantial change in the allocation pattern of oil revenues or in the average revenue per barrel, the growth rate of oil income will follow closely the growth rates of oil production and exports.

No one can tell with certainty when Iran's oil revenues will begin to decline in relative or absolute terms, nor when oil will be exhausted, in the sense that it cannot compete on an economic basis with other sources of energy. Even the estimates of known oil reserves are to be subject to a large margin of error, and are continually being revised. In addition, there are numerous uncertainties concerning future production rates, which to a large extent must be determined within the framework of OPEC; changes in the structure and organization of the international oil markets; the production policies of non-OPEC exporting countries; the speed with which other sources of energy and fuels become sufficiently competitive; and the unpredictability of future oil discoveries within and outside of Iran. Clearly, considerable variation in Iran's revenues can occur when so many imponderables are involved. These considerations illustrate the futility of attempting any single forecast of Iran's future oil revenues.[1] Realistically, projections can be made only in terms of high, medium, and low forecasts based on a variety of assumptions concerning prices, production rates, and available reserves.

In projecting Iran's oil revenues, several alternative projections of oil revenues were made based on the Plan Organization's estimates of likely price levels, production rates, refinery capacity, and petrochemical expansion over the next 15 years (1975-90).[2] Among the more crucial assumptions behind these projections are that crude oil prices will remain over $10 per barrel and that oil reserves are assumed to total 65 billion barrels. Their rate of extraction is set at a rate permitting investment in refineries to be profitable. It is also assumed that these reserves will be depleted in or around the year 2000 if there are no major discoveries prior to that date.

Three alternative forecasts are considered (see Table 10.1). The total figures vary from a high of 38,912 billion rials to a low of 29,200 billion rials, a difference of 33 percent. It seems reasonable to suggest that the differences are wide enough to cover most eventualities. Yet, in terms of the impact on the economy, not only is the absolute total important, but also the distribution over time, as that distribution that will determine when the adjustment to nonoil sources of growth will have to begin.

FORECASTS

Using the macroeconomic model developed in Appendix F, several forecasts of the economy's major components were made on an annual

TABLE 10.1

Forecast of Oil and Gas Revenues
(billions of rials)

Year	High Forecast	Rate of Growth	Medium Forecast	Rate of Growth	Low Forecast	Rate of Growth
1975	1441.4	—	1414.2	—	1414.2	—
1976	1602.9	11.2	1588.1	12.3	1588.1	12.3
1977	1781.6	11.2	1868.3	17.6	1800.8	13.4
1978	1980.2	11.2	2021.1	8.2	1946.5	8.1
1979	2153.3	8.7	2212.9	9.5	2130.8	9.5
1980	2341.5	8.7	2454.7	10.9	2365.8	11.0
1981	2409.7	3.0	2437.6	-0.7	2349.0	-0.7
1982	2497.8	3.6	2472.2	1.4	2383.8	1.5
1983	2708.1	8.4	2432.6	-1.6	2344.4	-1.7
1984	2787.0	2.9	2425.3	0.3	2338.1	-0.3
1985	2868.1	2.9	2080.9	-16.6	1943.9	-20.3
1986	2868.1	0.0	1791.7	-16.1	1661.9	-16.9
1987	2868.1	0.0	1528.3	-17.2	1406.5	-18.2
1988	2868.1	0.0	1386.2	-10.3	1268.7	-10.9
1989	2868.1	0.0	1285.0	-7.9	1170.8	-8.4
1990	2868.1	0.0	1198.9	-7.2	1086.8	-7.7

Source: Compiled by the author.

A DEVELOPMENT STRATEGY FOR IRAN

basis to 1990. The purpose of these forecasts was to determine the implications of high, medium, and low projections for oil revenues for government policies designed to assure that the country sustains a high rate of real GNP growth without significant inflation.

The results (with the medium forecast), for a 10 percent rate of growth and a 2 percent annual increase in inflation, indicate (see Tables 10.2 and 10.3) that the country is in a relatively favorable position to achieve many of its major economic objectives. But the actual attainment of its goals is contingent on the authorities' ability to reduce consumption levels from their desired (ex ante) levels to the specified or actual (ex post) magnitudes and to prevent imports from rising above 30 percent of GNP. Neither action is extreme and both targets should be well within the range of normal government controls.

Although imports remained below 30 percent of GNP during the 1960s, their growth has been accelerating since 1973. The ex post (actual) consumption targets are also reasonable. Note that consumption still rises from 54 percent of GNP in 1975 to 67 percent in 1982. From 1984 to 1990 the control of consumption is no longer required since the ex ante (desired) figure is lower than the ex post (actual) calculation.

What is striking in the models (see Table 10.4) is the sensitivity of the external gap (exports minus imports and net factor payments) to the rate of inflation. If inflation rises above 5 percent it might be extremely difficult, even under the high oil revenue assumption, for the country to borrow enough in international financial capital markets to finance the external gap, even at an 8 percent growth rate.

The forecasts indicate that Iran must lessen its dependence on oil revenues in order to achieve its longer-term development objectives. Since the country has reserves of approximately 85 billion barrels, oil revenues will most likely taper off and decline sometime in the early to mid-1980s, depending on new discoveries that materialize. It seems evident from the OPEC price agreement of December 1976 that this period may begin much sooner than even the medium-revenue forecasts indicate.

Inflation in the short term, such as the one that has been gradually developing in Iran since 1974 under the push of higher oil revenues and of international inflationary pressures, is bound to affect the longer-term development potential of the country, especially if controls fail to prevent the present inflation from accelerating. Clearly, control of inflation is vital to the country's growth because inflation causes a loss in real resources (barrels of oil)—resources that could be used for future productive capacity expansion.

TABLE 10.2

Domestic and Internal Gaps, 1975-82
(billions of rials)

	1975	1976	1977	1978	1979	1980	1981	1982
Gross national product	3274.3	3669.5	4112.5	4608.9	5165.3	5788.8	6487.6	7270.8
Consumption, ex ante	2788.7	3328.3	3699.0	4032.6	4361.2	4735.0	5141.1	5502.1
Consumption, ex post	1774.6	1989.9	2088.5	2451.0	2826.4	3227.8	4014.4	4836.1
Investment in machinery	337.5	414.3	496.7	557.5	621.5	687.7	761.5	843.0
Investment in construction	522.3	539.9	606.2	648.9	707.9	766.9	835.2	909.5
Total investment	859.8	954.2	1102.9	1206.5	1329.3	1454.7	1596.7	1752.6
Savings, ex ante	485.6	341.2	413.5	576.3	804.1	1053.8	1346.5	1768.7
Savings, ex post	1499.7	1679.6	2024.0	2159.9	2338.5	2561.0	2473.2	2434.7
Exports	1981.6	2225.4	2617.9	2832.1	3100.8	3439.7	3415.7	3464.2
Imports, ex post	982.3	1100.9	1233.8	1382.7	1549.6	1736.6	1946.3	2181.2
Imports, ex ante	1664.9	1893.9	2140.2	2441.6	2683.0	2970.9	3261.0	3416.9
Net factor payments	359.5	399.1	463.0	497.9	541.7	596.8	592.9	600.8
External gap, ex post	639.9	725.4	921.1	951.4	1009.6	1106.3	876.5	682.1
Domestic gap, ex ante	-374.2	-613.0	-689.4	-630.2	-552.2	-400.9	-250.2	16.1
External gap, ex ante	-42.8	-67.6	14.7	-107.4	-123.9	-128.0	-438.2	-553.5
Domestic gap, ex post	639.9	725.4	921.1	951.4	1009.6	1106.3	876.5	682.1

Note: Assumes 2 percent rate of inflation, medium increase in oil revenues, and 10 percent increase in real GNP.

Source: Compiled by the author.

TABLE 10.3

Domestic and Internal Gaps, 1983-90
(billions of rials)

	1983	1984	1985	1986	1987	1988	1989	1990
Gross national product	8148.5	9132.1	10234.5	11469.9	12854.5	14406.2	16145.3	18094.3
Consumption, ex ante	5914.2	6347.6	6818.4	7237.4	7735.8	8317.3	9015.6	9811.9
Consumption, ex post	5849.4	6943.4	8565.5	10271.5	12114.1	13815.8	15445.1	17130.6
Investment in machinery	934.1	1035.7	1149.0	1275.4	1416.5	1574.0	1749.8	1946.3
Investment in construction	992.5	1084.2	1186.0	1298.9	1424.2	1563.3	1718.0	1889.9
Total investment	1926.7	2119.9	2335.0	2574.3	2840.7	3137.3	3467.8	3836.3
Savings, ex ante	2234.3	2784.5	3416.1	4232.6	5118.7	6088.9	7129.7	8282.4
Savings, ex pose	2299.1	2188.7	1669.0	1198.4	740.4	590.4	700.2	963.7
Savings, ex post	2299.1	2188.7	1669.0	1198.4	740.4	590.4	700.2	963.7
Exports	3408.7	3398.5	2915.9	2510.6	2141.6	1942.4	1800.6	1679.9
Imports, ex post	2444.5	2739.6	3070.3	3411.0	3856.4	4132.2	4238.3	4242.2
Imports, ex ante	3611.6	3787.7	3950.5	3951.3	4001.3	4132.2	4238.3	4242.2
Net factor payments	591.8	590.1	511.6	445.6	385.5	353.1	329.9	310.3
External gap, ex post	372.4	68.8	-666.0	-1375.9	-2100.3	2546.9	2767.6	2872.6
Domestic gap, ex ante	307.6	664.6	1081.1	1658.3	2278.0	2951.6	3611.9	4446.1
External gap, ex ante	-794.7	-929.3	-1546.2	-1440.7	-2245.2	-2546.9	-2767.7	-2872.6
Domestic gap, ex post	372.4	68.8	-666.0	-1375.9	-2100.3	-2546.9	-2767.6	-2872.6

<u>Note</u>: Assumptions same as in Table 10.2.
<u>Source</u>: Compiled by the author.

TABLE 10.4

External Gaps, 1975-90—Medium Oil Revenues
(billions of rials)

Year	GNP 12 Percent, Inflation 2 Percent	GNP 10 Percent, Inflation		GNP 8 Percent, Inflation	
		2 Percent	5 Percent	2 Percent	5 Percent
1975	620.7	639.9	607.6	659.1	626.7
1976	681.9	725.4	651.4	767.9	695.6
1977	847.4	921.1	794.7	991.9	870.7
1978	840.3	951.4	759.5	1056.4	875.6
1979	852.2	1009.6	736.1	1155.1	902.6
1980	892.6	1106.3	732.5	1300.1	961.5
1981	594.3	876.5	379.6	1127.4	685.8
1982	317.1	682.1	-34.9	1000.5	436.3
1983	-92.4	372.4	-457.6	769.9	-60.4
1984	-515.8	68.8	-982.5	559.1	-322.4
1985	-1393.9	-666.0	-1984.4	-67.2	-1151.6
1986	-2274.8	-1375.9	-3015.7	-650.8	-1973.7
1987	-3207.2	-2100.3	-4125.8	-1228.2	-2831.0
1988	-4076.5	-2732.6	-5220.1	-1689.9	-3620.6
1989	-5003.2	-3373.0	-6412.5	-2132.7	-4446.6
1990	-6027.3	-4058.7	-7756.5	-2589.8	-5351.0

Source: Compiled by the author, based on forecasts using Table F.1.

The promotion of nonoil exports, derived from the industrial and service sectors, is the key to the success of the longer-term Iranian development effort. On the one hand, the Iranian industrialization process is likely to require increased imports, while on the other, the need for foreign capital and intermediate goods will be growing during the period of slackening oil revenues. It is time, therefore, for the country to plan now for the creation of an internationally competitive industrial sector. The model presented in Tables 10.2 and 10.3 implies that rates of increase of nonoil exports of 20-26 percent are probably necessary to achieve the noninflationary target of 10 percent GNP growth.

The experience of the Venezuelan Investment Fund indicates that it is essential for Iran to look at planning as a decision concerning the division of annual oil revenues between that portion that can be absorbed domestically and that portion that should be invested

A DEVELOPMENT STRATEGY FOR IRAN

abroad in interest-bearing securities, until such time as the local economy is large enough to absorb both the annual oil revenue and the additional funds required to maintain its forward momentum. With national savings managed by an institution such as the VIF, the model (see Table 10.5) indicates that the process of oil-induced growth could be extended in time if excess funds are put aside for purposes of earning interest abroad (8 percent is assumed) until local absorptive capacity becomes adequate.

Indeed, when a comparison was made between the two alternative approaches, that is, spending the oil revenues as they accrue or spending the oil revenues according to absorptive capacity, it was found that the latter approach had many advantages. It avoided the Plan Organization's forecasted downturn in the Iranian economy associated with the peaking and tapering off of oil revenues in and around 1980; greatly extended the period of time when the country would have to resort to international borrowing; smoothed out Iran's growth path avoiding, on the one hand, large jumps in the initial years of oil revenue upsurge and, on the other, significant drops associated with steep declines in revenues; avoided excessive inflationary pressures in the initial years (1975-78); and allowed for the accumulation of substantial funds abroad, on which the economy could draw in difficult times.

Several things seem clear, as follows: oil plays a crucial role in the future growth momentum of the Iranian economy; the economy is highly dependent on the absolute value of total oil receipts in any given period, as well as its annual distribution pattern over that period; given the limitation of total reserves, at some time in the future oil revenues will decline and necessitate major structural adjustments in the economy; and, in order to take best advantage of its oil revenues, the country should phase the domestic spending of oil revenues according to some inflation limit.

FUTURE DOMESTIC ECONOMIC CHALLENGES

The domestic and the external challenges are closely intertwined. They differ in the degree to which they are amenable to control. Iranian policy makers are alert to the major domestic economic challenges they face, and thus have revised many development strategies and proposed numerous new programs to meet them. The need to revise Iran's agricultural strategy has been recognized, and agricultural development efforts are being expanded and strengthened. Programs have been outlined to expand the transportation system, to increase employment, and to enlarge the supply of trained managers. While all of these areas are important, the eventual success of the

TABLE 10.5

Financial Surplus, 1975-90
(billions of rials)

Year	Exports	Imports	Net Factor Payments	External Gap	Productive Investment	Surplus Deficiency (-)	Cumulative	Cumulative 8 Percent, Annually Compounded
1975	1981.6	982.3	359.5	639.9	859.8	762.3	762.3	762.3
1976	2225.4	1100.9	399.1	725.4	954.2	872.1	1634.4	1695.4
1977	2617.9	1233.8	463.0	921.1	1102.9	1052.0	2686.4	2883.0
1978	2832.1	1382.7	497.9	951.4	1206.5	1127.7	3814.1	4241.4
1979	3100.8	1549.6	541.7	1009.6	1329.3	1229.8	5043.9	5810.5
1980	3439.7	1736.6	596.8	1106.3	1454.7	1388.2	6432.1	7663.5
1981	3415.7	1946.3	592.9	876.5	1596.7	1226.1	7658.2	9502.7
1982	3464.2	2181.2	600.8	682.1	1752.6	1110.8	8769.0	11373.7
1983	3408.7	2444.5	591.8	372.4	1926.7	890.2	9659.2	13173.8
1984	3398.5	2739.6	590.1	68.8	2119.9	688.5	10347.7	14916.2
1985	2915.9	3070.3	511.6	-666.0	2335.0	69.3	10417.0	16178.8
1986	2510.6	3441.0	445.6	-1375.9	2574.3	-509.3	9907.7	16963.8
1987	2141.6	3856.4	385.5	-2100.3	2840.7	-1084.6	8823.1	17236.3
1988	1942.4	4132.2	357.1	-2546.9	3137.3	-1552.0	7271.1	17063.2
1989	1800.6	4238.3	329.9	-2767.6	3467.8	-1997.1	5274.0	16431.2
1990	1679.9	4242.2	310.3	-2872.6	3836.3	-2466.7	2807.3	15278.9

Source: Compiled by the author from Tables 10.2 and 10.3.

Iranian economy will finally depend on the development of industrial exports.

Even as late as 1975, Iran's nonoil exports still consisted mainly of traditional products, that is, fruits and nuts, rather than industrial goods. Clearly the development of manufactures for export is necessary for implementing a successful export promotion policy. In this regard Iran has a long and difficult task ahead. Even as late as 1970 the Bank Markazi Iran reported that

> despite the considerable prosperity of various domestic industries in recent years, many of these industries are still in the assembly phase and their value added in international prices is rather low. Therefore, due to the high cost of production, the prices of some industrial goods cannot compete with those of similar products abroad.[3]

Until the early 1970s only a slight increase occurred in industry's share of GNP, rising to about 14.5 percent of nonoil GNP by the end of the 1960s. The main causes of the sector's relatively slow development were chiefly due to a lack of technology, know-how, management, and credit facilities. Recently, however, industry has been accelerating its output at an average annual rate of 15.6 percent during the period from 1965 to 1970, and steeper rises of 16 percent in 1971, 18.5 percent in 1972, and over 20 percent in 1973-76. Structural changes are reflected in the development of the durable consumer and capital goods sectors producing such goods as motors, metals, tires, and chemicals. The petrochemical industry is making big strides within the framework of the recent development plans, particularly in sulfur, ammonia, plastics, detergents, and caustic soda.

While in the past ten years impressive strides have been made to provide a broad industrial infrastructure—virtually from scratch—the country still has a very long path to tread before achieving any degree of industrial self-sufficiency, let alone export capacity. Indeed, it is becoming increasingly apparent that infrastructure constraints, coupled with the inevitable delays in project implementation, will prolong the process of import replacement. At the same time, the tremendous surge in consumption, much greater than foreseen at the beginning of the oil boom, has resulted in much of the sector's output being absorbed by local demand, leaving little significant export capacity.

This is also likely to be the case with the infant steel industry, perhaps less with petrochemicals, and certainly so in the automotive sector, machine tools, and construction materials, which, beginning with the Fourth Five-Year Plan, have been the main pillars of the industrialization program. In 1975, industrial production rose by an average of 23 percent, while consumption rose even higher. The gap between demand and supply has become evident in the black market prices paid for such items as bricks and cement. Local manufacturers cannot produce fast enough to meet demand.

In the automotive industry, 87,000 units were produced and sold in 1975 (often with a black market markup to avoid three to five month waiting lists), and another 65,000 were imported. In 1976, even with production expected to be over 120,000 units, at least 35,000 units are likely to be imported.

The same pattern is occurring in steel. In two years (1974-75) consumption has increased from 2.2 million tons to 4.5 million tons, and in 1976 it increased to nearly 5.5 million tons. At best, domestic production will double by 1977, to around 1.9 million tons. Based on the current rate of expansion, however, there will be no new capacity until the early 1980s. This output will be absorbed immediately by the domestic market.

The same is true of certain types of petrochemicals. Domestic demand for fertilizers is increasing by 25 percent a year even though growth in the agricultural sector is much slower than Fifth Plan targets. At present rates of domestic consumption, the Plan target of 1.7 million ton fertilizer capacity by 1977-78 would just be adequate to supply the local market. Clearly Iranian industry's main concern over the next five to seven years must be to catch up with domestic demand so that a surplus will be available for export.

Again, the problem of domestic inflation cannot be overemphasized. The high cost of labor will be an increasingly important factor in determining both the nature of industrial investment and the competitiveness of Iranian products in international markets. The surge in public and private spending since the beginning of the oil boom has resulted in rapidly increasing wages and salaries—both being pushed up by the scarcity of skilled and semi-skilled labor. Wage costs on the average went up 35 to 45 percent in 1975. In the larger concerns a profit-sharing bonus equivalent to up to three months wages was also paid out. In 1976, wage increases averaged between 25 and 30 percent.

Complicating the problem of expanding industrial exports is the low productivity of Iranian labor, which of course makes the recent wage increases even more unacceptable. For instance, it has been calculated that it takes 45 man-hours to assemble the General Motors Chevrolet in Iran, while in West Germany the same car is produced in 25 man-hours. Unless there is a relatively quick increase in productivity, it is hard to see how many of the new industries will ever survive without high customs tariffs.

A DEVELOPMENT STRATEGY FOR IRAN   159

Of course, the factors mitigating against the establishment of a strong export-oriented industrial base by the 1990s could be influenced by Iran's greatest asset, the availability of cheap energy. Yet, unless the cost and productivity problems that Iranian industry now faces can be overcome, the advantage of cheap energy cannot be taken for granted.

CONCLUSIONS

While the benefits of oil to the country are clear, there are a number of risks that must be anticipated if the country is to achieve its ambitious goals. The most obvious are that, since an oil-dependent growth process requires an ever-increasing level of oil revenues in order to sustain its growth momentum, the country must be prepared for the time when the oil revenues begin to taper off and decline;[4] the fiscal authorities who have looked on oil as an easily accessible source of revenue must not be lulled into a false sense of security that would retard the smooth and gradual development of a tax base sufficiently broad to meet the country's requirements in such areas as education and defense, and that an easy source of access to foreign exchange now must not encourage production to meet only local demand. Export targets should be designed with an eye to developing a wide number of internationally competitive industrial products and services. There are few doubts that the long-term development of the Iranian economy is eventually dependent on the building of a nonoil export sector capable of meeting its future import requirements. Present availabilities of foreign exchange should not cloud the planners' foresight with respect to future possibilities and future requirements.

If these pitfalls can be avoided, Iran's long-range outlook should be promising. There will be short-term interruptions in the momentum of the development drive. Iran has become increasingly dependent upon uncontrollable forces in the international environment, but the nation is better prepared than ever before, with resources, experience, trained personnel, and self-confidence to meet future challenges. In the new international environment, it will be difficult to maintain a 12 percent annual growth rate. However, 8 to 10 percent annual growth rates appear to be reasonable and should carry Iran along the development road at a pace that many other nations would envy.

NOTES

1. A number of oil revenue forecasts have been made for the period under consideration. The ones surveyed for the forecasts in

Chapter 10 were: Charles Blitzer et al., "A Dynamic Model of OPEC Trade and Production," Journal of Development Economics (December 1975), pp. 319-35; B. A. Kalymon, "Economic Incentives in OPEC Oil Pricing Policy," Journal of Development Economics (December 1975), pp. 337-63; J. Alexander Caldwell, "The Evolution of the OPEC Current Account Surplus: Recent Trends, Likely Developments, and Major Policy Implications," Journal of Energy and Development (Spring 1976), pp. 297-305; Teruyasu Murakami, "Policy Simulation for Crude Oil Production of OPEC Countries," Policy Sciences (March 1976), pp. 93-111; and Merith Celasum and Frank Pinto, Energy Prospects in OECD Countries and Possible Demand for OPEC Oil Exports to 1980 (Washington, D.C.: IBRD, 1975). A critical evaluation of some of the leading models is given in Dietrich Fischer et al., "The Prospects for OPEC: A Critical Survey of Models of the World Oil Market," Journal of Development Economics (December 1975), pp. 363-86.

2. The original Plan Organization forecasts are given in Iran, Plan and Budget Organization, Planometric Bureau, A Twenty-Year Macro-Economic Perspective for Iran, 1351-1371 (Tehran: Plan and Budget Organization, 1974). Several modifications were introduced to update the forecasts in light of oil price increases and OPEC negotiations culminating in December 1976.

3. Bank Markazi Iran, Annual Report and Balance Sheet, 1351, p. 45.

4. The mechanics are described in Firouz Vakil, Determining Iran's Financial Surplus, 1352-1371 (Tehran: Institute of International, Political, and Economic Studies, 1975). See also Jahangir Amuzegar and M. Ali Fekrat, Iran: Economic Development Under Dualistic Conditions (Chicago: University of Chicago Press, 1971) for an excellent discussion of the consequences a reduction or deceleration in the rate of increase of oil revenues would have on the Iranian economy in its current state of development.

APPENDIX A
IRAN IN THE
ADELMAN-MORRIS STUDY

Irma Adelman and Cynthia Taft Morris examined data from 73 noncommunist underdeveloped countries, after classifying these countries into three groups (high potential, intermediate potential, and low potential) according to their past records of economic growth.[1] Through discriminant analysis, four (out of 29) indicators were selected that together accounted for 97 percent of the distinguishable variance between the three groups of countries.[2] After normalizing the estimated equation so that its variance in each group is unity, the following result was obtained:

$$D_1' = 127F + 65K + 108M + 72 \tag{1}$$

where F is financial development, K transport improvement, M modernization in outlook and acceptance of economic development on the part of the population at large, and L the commitment of leadership to development.[3] In terms of the overall contribution to the discriminating power of the function, the order of importance of the variables is given by ranking the magnitudes of their coefficients.

Adelman and Morris then omitted all countries that had originally been classified on the basis of their past economic growth according to the results of Equation 1 and reran the discriminant analysis. This produced the following result:

$$D_2' = 95F + 139M + 88L + 70A$$

where A is improvement in agricultural productivity.[4] This equation accounts for over 97 percent of the overall observed variance.

The probability of Iran's membership in the intermediate potential group is 0.91, with a score of 105.[5] The mean scores for the three groups are 174, 113, and 53 for the high, intermediate, and low groups, respectively. In contrast to Iran, Venezuela was given a 1.00 probability of being in the high potential group, and had a score of 198. On the other hand, Ecuador, Iraq, Algeria were placed in the low potential group.[6]

An important point to note is that the data used for this study refer, in general, to the 1336-41 (1957-62) period, when the country was entering and experiencing a recession phase in its development. Nevertheless, there had been fairly rapid development in the fields of banking and road building, the commitment to development was relatively strong among the country's leaders, and the population had not become disillusioned with the development program. Because of these developments Iran was classified as among

> countries that have demonstrated a marked improvement in the effectiveness of their financial institutions as indicated by qualitative information on saving and lending activities, and in most instances, by either (1) an increase of more than 5 percentage points in the ratio of time and demand deposits to GNP or (2) a more than five-fold increase in the real value of private domestic liabilities to the banking system.[7]

With respect to agricultural productivity, Iran was classified as a B country (on a scale of A, B, C, and D) because it is a country

> in which there has been moderate improvement in agricultural productivity since 1950. Among these countries are a number in which cultivatable land has been expanded through the application of modern irrigation methods or multicropping techniques.[8]

On the degree of modernization in outlook, however, Iran received the lowest rating (C, on a scale of A, B, and C) because it was a country "in which the outlook of the educated urban sector was partially but not significantly modernized and in which programs of modernization, if they existed, had gained relatively little support among either the urban or rural population."[9]

Finally, Iran appears as one of a number of countries

> in which some government leaders evidenced a definite commitment to economic development (during the period 1957-62) as indicated by the practice of some form of national development planning. However, it was typical of the countries of this category that the activities of agencies involved in central guidance of the economy were poorly coordinated and that the government attempts to alter institutional arrangements unfavorable to economic growth were infrequent or poorly sustained.[10]

One might simply add that had the data referred to the late 1960s, instead of the early years of that decade, Iran's score would have been considerably lower than the 105 achieved in the Adelman-Morris study.

NOTES

1. Irma Adelman and Cynthia Taft Morris, "Performance Criteria for Evaluating Economic Development Potential: An Operational Approach," <u>Quarterly Journal of Economics</u> (May 1968), pp. 260-80.

2. For a detailed description of the theory and application of discriminant analysis, see Jacob Cohen and Patricia Cohen, <u>Applied Multiple Regression/Correlation Analysis for the Behavioral Sciences</u> (Hillsdale, N.J.: Lawrence Erlbaum Associates, 1975), pp. 433-36.

3. Adelman and Morris, <u>Performance Criteria</u>, p. 269.

4. Ibid., p. 277.

5. Ibid., p. 278.

6. Ibid.

7. Irma Adelman and Cynthia Taft Morris, <u>Society, Politics, and Economic Development—A Quantative Approach</u> (Baltimore: Johns Hopkins University Press, 1967), p. 108.

8. Adelman and Morris, <u>Society, Politics and Economic Development</u>, p. 108.

9. Ibid., p. 51.

10. Ibid., p. 80.

APPENDIX B
PATTERNS OF
INCOME DISTRIBUTION

In addition to those patterns outlined in Chapter 4, several other characteristics of Iran's income distribution are of interest.[1] First, there is a definite inverse relationship between the proportion of households in a given expenditure bracket with no literate member and household expenditure. While 82 percent of households in the lowest expenditure class were without a literate person in the early 1970s, the same was true of only 6 percent of the households in the highest expenditure bracket. The policy implications are clear. Iran will need to orient its educational program to lower income groups if the country is to be successful in reducing the degree of income inequality among households. At present, the distribution of educational attainment of households is severely skewed, but with recent efforts to widen the educational base in both urban and rural areas, income distribution is expected to become somewhat more equal in the future.

Another clear pattern is that there is a significantly higher unemployment rate for the 20 percent of households in the bottom income group compared with the 80 percent in the upper income group. Also, a larger proportion of households in urban areas (11.8 percent) had no employed person than in rural areas (6.8 percent).

Several other characteristics of households shed light on the country's income inequalities. First, while the majority of household heads in the low-expenditure classes are employed in the agricultural and construction sectors, household heads in the high-expenditure classes are generally employed in the service sector. Second, the heads of most households in the low-expenditure classes are wage and salary earners, a pattern more prevalent in urban than in rural areas. About 24 percent of household heads in rural areas, and about 33 percent in urban areas, are wage and salary earners.

To summarize, available data indicate that several clear relationships exist between employment, educational attainment, and the occupation of household members and the distribution of income in Iran. It is possible that other variables, such as the rate of industrialization, differential productivity growth between the modern and the transitional sectors, the magnitude and pattern of government expenditure, the rate of inflation, the sex and age composition of the population, and the rate of rural-urban migration, have significant effects on the size distribution of incomes in Iran.

APPENDIX B

Regional variations in household expenditures are also quite marked in Iran and shed additional light on the underlying determinants of the existing patterns of income distribution. The share of the bottom 10 percent of households in both the Central and Fars regions is 1.76 percent, which is lower than the country's average. The shares of the top 10 percent of households in these two regions were 37.11 percent and 38.3 percent, compared with 34.2 percent in the country as a whole. The share of the bottom 10 percent of households in the other regions ranged between 2.0 and 3.62 percent.

Regional variations in the upper end of the household expenditure distribution in Iran are much greater than in the lower end. The share of the top 10 percent of households in the country's 14 regions ranges between 26.17 percent and 38.48 percent. The shares of the top 10 percent of households in Sistin-Baluchestan, Fars, West Azerbaijan, and Central Ostan Provinces are 38.48, 38.30, 37.20, and 37.11, respectively, which are considerably higher than the percentage for the country as a whole.

For most of the 14 regions, inequality is greater in urban than in rural areas. For regions with a more developed rural sector, the inequality is greater in rural than in urban areas. It should be noted, however, that the relation between average household expenditure (a proxy for per capita income) and inequality in a given region is not a simple one. In fact, Gilan, with an average household expenditure second only to that of Central Ostan Province, has a more even income distribution (as measured by a Gini coefficient) than that in the provinces of Khorasan or Fars.

The ratio of rural to urban household expenditure is also significant in explaining interregional variations in income inequality. Those regions with a lower ratio of urban to rural household expenditure have a more equal expenditure distribution. For instance, in spite of the fact that the average household expenditure in West Azerbaijan is slightly larger than in Fars (7,492 rials per month, as against 7,326 rials per month), the inequality is greater in Fars than in West Azerbaijan mainly because the ratio of urban to rural household expenditure is higher in Fars (1.96) than in West Azerbaijan (1.12).

NOTE

1. For a more detailed analysis of the changes in Iran's income distribution, see M. H. Pesaran, "Income Distribution and Its Major Determinants in Iran," in <u>Iran: Past, Present and Future—The Persepolis Symposium</u>, ed. Jane Jacqz (New York: Aspen Institute for Humanistic Studies, 1976), pp. 267-87.

APPENDIX C
INDEXATION
OF CRUDE
OIL PRICES

Indexation of crude oil prices by the OPEC countries was first discussed in early 1962. At that time, the OPEC countries were examining a number of economic aspects of the international petroleum industry, including the formation of prices and price-support mechanisms. Indexation was suggested as a useful tool towards maintaining the purchasing power of their oil revenues in the event that they should assert control over pricing. Details of the plan were not worked out, but it was suggested that once OPEC had selected a base for its crude oil pricing, further movements would be determined by indexation; the UN World Export Price Index of Manufactured Goods was specifically mentioned as one of the indexes that might be used as a basis for the pricing of oil exports.

In the early and mid-1960s, however, inflation was not a major problem: the UN index of manufactured goods prices were increasing at only one or two points per year, and had actually fallen on several occasions. The idea of indexation was therefore not developed and, so long as OPEC did not in fact assert control over prices, remained only a theoretical possibility. When OPEC first attempted price setting in 1965, the approach chosen was not indexation, but market sharing or pro-rationing. This method concentrated on halting the slow but steady decline in oil prices, rather than on introducing a higher price and using indexation to maintain the purchasing power of revenues derived at that price.

When prices were dramatically raised at the end of 1973 and in 1974, their increases were not the outcome of a predetermined and consistent policy, but resulted mainly from attempts to cut the operating companies' profits.

In fact, since OPEC effectively took control of prices in October 1973 it has not had a well-defined, long-term pricing policy, but instead has proceeded with a series of ad hoc measures culminating in a series of temporary price freezes.

OPEC thinking on pricing policy has been based largely on setting prices based on some sort of parity with alternative sources of energy. Indexation is, however, not inconsistent, nor is it precluded by, this approach to pricing.

OPEC's first justification of the price increases to about $10.00 per barrel at the beginning of 1974 (a level the market had amply demonstrated it was willing to pay, at least in the short term) was that oil prices were now on a par with the cost of alternative sources

APPENDIX C

of energy produced or producible in quantity by some of the major industrial countries. The cost of these alternatives was also seen by OPEC leaders as possibly forming the basis for future pricing.

There are a number of disadvantages in basing oil prices on the cost of alternative sources of energy. Obviously, each alternative has a different cost structure, and it is not clear which alternative would be best for comparison. Secondly, a number of alternatives have not been developed on a commercial scale, so there is little or no actual basis for estimating their cost. Finally, while it is theoretically possible for OPEC members intent on maximizing revenue to set a price for oil that would effectively make development of higher-cost sources uneconomical, in practice a number of important OPEC countries, such as Kuwait, are more concerned with conservation of resources than maximizing revenue. In practice, the price established by OPEC at the beginning of 1974 (about $10.00 per barrel) was generally thought by the member countries to approximate the cost of such alternatives as shale oil, tar sands, and coal gasification. This price level was then used as an ex post facto justification of the price level chosen.

Within this context of price setting, indexation of oil prices can be an effective basis upon which to modify prices.

The great attraction of indexation is, of course, the protection it would provide the OPEC countries against inflation. It also puts the blame for future oil price increases squarely on the United States, Japan, and the Western European countries—exporters of manufactured goods. It is often argued by the Shah that if the industrial countries cannot control their domestic inflation (which is reflected in the prices of the goods they export), then they must expect oil exporters to protect themselves. The point stressed by the Shah and other leaders of OPEC is that inflation should not be a one-way street, permitting industrialized countries to acquire their raw materials at progressively lower prices, in real terms.

The practical problems involved in indexation are, however, technically complex. Because of the differing import patterns of the OPEC countries, indexation of oil prices could not be tied precisely to any one index, thereby compensating each OPEC country for the increase in world prices. As a result, some fairly simple expedient would have to be adopted to compensate for inflation in an approximate manner. The obvious indexes are the IMF Export Price Index for Industrial Countries and the UN Index of Export Prices of Manufactured Goods.

In negotiating the adoption of any import index as the basis for setting OPEC prices, Iran should press for a method whereby an over-all index is built up based on OPEC imports by type of commodity and country of origin.

All the possibilities for indexation listed above suffer from considerable time lags. In practice it would probably be necessary to allow for a lag of at least two quarters, and more likely three. Practical difficulties also arise because the rates of import inflation experienced by Iran and each of the other OPEC members will differ. Hence, some member countries would be overcompensated, and some undercompensated, by the use of a single index.

A slightly more refined way of indexing oil prices would use the overall export price indexes of the main industrial exporting countries, weighted by the value of these exports to the OPEC countries. This ignores the composition of the exports by the type of commodity, however. In practice the different import patterns of the various OPEC countries would result in a significant divergence of Iran's import index from that of the OPEC countries as a whole.

If Iran and the other OPEC countries retain control over oil prices it will be necessary to formulate a long-term pricing policy. For the present, indexation is one of several possibilities, and has considerable attraction for the organization. Indeed, if some alternative arrangements do not emerge from the ongoing producer-consumer dialogue on energy, raw materials, and development, it is difficult to see how OPEC can avoid some form of indexation, and suitable methods for measuring inflation would need to be agreed upon. It is in Iran's best interest to begin analysis on its own best position concerning such factors as the base price, base currency (for example, the dollars or the SDRs), and base period.

APPENDIX D
STABILITY OF
THE IRANIAN ECONOMY

INTRODUCTION

Because the Iranian economy appears to have a relatively low propensity to increase its expenditures in the short run, it is likely that the country will have difficulty in absorbing all of its increased oil revenues, at least through the 1970s. The tendency of the economy to increase its expenditures on investment and consumption (both public and private) is here examined over the 1959-74 period, at current prices.

The estimated equations are:

$$C_t^p = 4.0567 + 0.1451\ Y_t + 0.8459\ C_{t-1}^p \qquad r^2 = 0.9989 \qquad (2)$$
$$(13.62) \qquad (102.1)$$

$$C_t^g = 31.1743 + 0.1688\ Y_t + 0.3393\ C_{t-1}^g \qquad r^2 = 0.9972 \qquad (3)$$
$$(12.1) \qquad (63.7)$$

$$I_t^m = 6.5702 + 0.0282\ Y_t + 0.9110\ I_{t-1}^m \qquad r^2 = 0.9912 \qquad (4)$$
$$(3.8) \qquad (36.5)$$

$$I_t^c = -8.8897 + 0.0569\ Y_t + 0.7879\ I_{t-1}^c \qquad r^2 = 0.9957 \qquad (5)$$
$$(6.5) \qquad (52.2)$$

where: C_t^p equals private consumption in year t; Y_t equals gross national product in year t; C_{t-1}^p equals private consumption in the previous year; I_t^m equals investment in machinery in year t; I_{t-1}^m equals investment in machinery in the previous year; I_t^c equals investment in construction in year t; I_{t-1}^c equals investment in construction in the previous year; and r^2 is the goodness of fit, and the "t" statistic in parenthesis. All of the equations are significant at the 0.01 level.

LONG- AND SHORT-RUN PROPENSITIES

Equation 2 expresses private consumption expenditures as a function of GNP and private consumption expenditures in the previous year. This formulation implies that past consumption, as well as present GNP, affects present consumption. Private consumption, therefore, conforms to a variant of the consumption permanent income hypothesis.[1] Equation 2 allows for estimates of both the short- and long-run marginal propensity to consume.

Let

$$C_t^{p*} = a + bY_t$$

be the long-run equilibrium consumption function. The parameter 2 is the long-run marginal propensity to consume. Implicit in this definition is the assumption that consumers, given an increase in income, will require several years to fully readjust their consumption behavior.

Assume the following partial adjustment mechanism:

$$(C_t^p - C_{t-1}^p) = (C_t^{p*} - C_{t-1}^p)$$

where C_t^p is actual observed consumption in time period t. Substituting the equation for C_t^{p*} into the above equation gives:

$$C_t^p - C_{t-1}^p = x(a + bY_t - C_{t-1}^p)$$

or

$$C_t^p = xa + xbY_t + (1 - x) C_{t-1}^p$$

Estimates of the parameters in this equation give the short-run marginal propensity to consume (xb) and the long-run marginal propensity to consume (b). The estimated coefficients for private consumption were: x = 0.1541, xb = 0.1451, and (1 - x) = 0.8459. The short-run marginal propensity to consume (mpc) is therefore 0.1451, and the long run mpc is 0.9416.

If GNP were to increase by one million rials, personal consumption would increase by 145,100 rials in the same year. Eventually, consumers would adjust their consumption behavior to their highest income level, so that in the long run consumption would increase by 941,600 rials.

For government consumption C_t^g the key parameters are: x = 0.6607, xb = 0.1688, and (1 - x) = 0.3393, indicating a short-run government mpc of 0.1688, and a long-run mpc of 0.2555.

For investment in machinery I_t^m the key parameters are: x = 0.0890, xb = 0.0282, and (1 - x) = 0.9110. The short-run investment function is 0.0282, and the long-run propensity to invest in machinery equals 0.3169.

APPENDIX D

For investment in construction I_t^c the key parameters are: $x = 0.2121$, $xb = 0.0569$, and $(1 - x) = 0.7879$. The short-run function is 0.0569, and the long-run function 0.2683.

If

$$M_t = -26.0375 + 0.1483\ Y_t + 0.5006\ M_{t-1} \qquad r^2 = 0.9938 \qquad (6)$$
$$(4.6)(37.7)$$

then the key parameters for imports M_t are: $x = 0.4994$, $xb = 0.1483$, and $(1 - x) = 0.5006$. The short-run marginal propensity to import is 0.1483, and the long-run propensity is 0.2970.

Conclusions

Thus, for the major macrorelationships—equations 2 through 6—the long-run propensities are significantly higher than the short-run relationships.

Clearly, one can conclude that a high degree of stability exists in the Iranian economy. Expenditures over time tend to adjust to values higher than exhibited in the short run. A sudden jump in oil revenues (and thus Y_t), therefore, may not be effectively absorbed in productive expenditures in the short run.

The country should seriously consider placing these funds in investments abroad until it has adjusted to the higher levels of income.

CONSTANT PRICES

In constant 1959 prices the consumption, investment and import relationships are as follows:

$$C_t^p = 60.6210 + 0.4913\ Y_t + 0.0629\ C_{t-1}^p \qquad r^2 = 0.9896 \qquad (7)$$
$$(2.2)(29.2)$$

$$C_t^g = 23.2674 + 0.0904\ Y_t + 0.8480\ C_{t-1}^g \qquad r^2 = 0.9876 \qquad (8)$$
$$(1.2)(26.8)$$

$$I_t^m = -14.3544 + 0.0560\ Y_t + 0.6673 \qquad r^2 = 0.9488 \qquad (9)$$
$$(3.4)(12.5)$$

$$I_t^T = -28.8322 + 0.2583\ Y_t + 0.0144\ I_{t-1}^T \qquad r^2 = 0.9772 \qquad (10)$$
$$(4.1)(19.2)$$

$$M_t = -28.4007 + 0.1557\ Y_t + 0.4999\ M_{t-1} \qquad r^2 = .9884 \qquad (11)$$
$$(3.9) \qquad\qquad (27.4)$$

where I_t^T equals total investment ($I_t^c + I_t^m$).

For private consumption the key parameters are: $x = 0.9371$, $xb = 0.4913$, and $(1 - x) = 0.0629$. The short-run marginal propensity to consume is 0.4913, and the long-run propensity is 0.5243.

For government consumption the key parameters are: $x = 0.1520$, $xb = 0.0904$, and $(1 - x) = 0.8480$. The short-run marginal propensity to consume is 0.0904, and the long-run marginal propensity is 0.5947. It should be noted, however, that the government consumption is not statistically significant at the 0.01 level in terms of GNP.

For investment in machinery the key parameters are: $x = 0.3327$, $xb = 0.0560$, and $(1 - x) = 0.6673$. The short-run marginal propensity to invest in machinery is 0.0560, while the long-run propensity is 0.1683.

For total investment the key parameters are: $x = 0.9856$, $xb = 0.2583$, and $(1 - x) = 0.0144$. The short-run marginal propensity to invest is 0.2583, while the long-run marginal propensity is 0.2621.

For imports the key parameters are: $x = 0.5001$, $xb = 0.1557$, and $(1 - x) = 0.4999$. The short-run marginal propensity to import is 0.1557, while the long-run propensity is 0.3113.

Conclusions

These estimates confirm the conclusion reached above, that is, that the Iranian economy is quite stable in the long run, but does not increase expenditures rapidly in the short run.

NOTE

1. See Thomas Mayer, Permanent Income, Wealth, and Consumption (Berkeley: University of California Press, 1972) for a thorough analysis of the short- and long-run expenditure functions. An excellent description of some of the statistical problems of estimating these functions is given in Ahmad Shahshahani Madani, "An Econometric Model of Development for an Oil-Based Economy: The Case of Iran" (Ph.D. dissertation, University of Colorado, Boulder, 1976).

APPENDIX E
PROBLEMS OF
MONETARY CONTROL

In the wake of the rise in oil revenues, budgetary expenditures in Iran were greatly expanded for both current needs and development purposes. Total central government spending increased to nearly $19 billion in 1974, compared with about $5 billion in 1972, the fiscal year before the increase in oil prices began. As a result, the rate of increase in current government expenditures, including defense outlays, between 1973 and 1974 was more than 325 percent, and that of fixed capital, almost 300 percent.

Iran's money supply and quasi money increased by 57 percent in 1974, compared with an annual average increase of 32 percent over the preceding two years (see Table E.1). The factors affecting the growth in domestic liquidity are clearly the result of the increased oil revenues. As the consolidated accounts of the banking system indicate, the accumulation of net foreign assets by the banks appears as the primary determinant of expansion (offset by any buildup in net public sector deposits resulting from budgetary surpluses).

The consolidated accounts of the banking system, while yielding insights into the country's monetary mechanism, are somewhat limited in providing a full explanation of the precise manner in which the country's money supply expands and contracts. The main shortcoming of these accounts is that the main factor underlying the rise in net foreign assets—the receipts of oil revenues by the government— has no immediate monetary effect (as is true for the other oil-exporting countries).[1] These revenues simply are counterbalanced in the consolidated accounts by an equivalent rise in government deposits.

Fortunately, an examination of the balance of payments and public sector budget is capable of isolating the effect of budget operations on changes in domestic liquidity. This is done analytically by defining the growth of money and quasimoney essentially as a function of public sector net domestic expenditures. When examined from this perspective the private sector is seen to have contributed little to the expansion of Iran's domestic money supply. In fact, the monetary impact of private sector economic activity was contradictory on a net basis, as the private sector balance-of-payments deficit exceeded the growth of credit to that sector (see Table E.2).

Initially, Iran was able to avoid inflation as both public and private sector imports expanded rapidly in 1974, alleviating the buildup in domestic demand pressures. Direct public sector foreign

TABLE E.1

Factors Responsible for Changes in the
Money Supply, 1972-75
(billions of dollars)

	1972	1973	1974	1975
Changes in money and quasi money	+1.36	+1.71	+4.36	+4.92
Public sector net domestic expenditures	+1.61	+2.74	+8.70	+8.88
Monetary impact of private sector	+0.17	+0.01	-1.13	-2.03
Changes in claims on private sector (increase +)	+1.12	+1.86	+3.10	+5.53
Private sector lending to central government (increases -)	-0.07	-0.11	-0.02	—
Private sector balance of payments (deficit -)	-0.88	-1.74	-4.21	-7.56
Changes in net unclassified bank liabilities	-0.27	-0.67	-1.64	-1.38
Discrepancy	-0.15	-0.37	-1.57	-0.55

Source: Computed from Bank Markazi Iran data.

exchange outlays for imports, supplemented by official capital outflows, contributed to limiting public sector net domestic expenditures. Public sector payments abroad for imported goods and services rose from nearly $3 billion in 1973 to about $7 billion in 1974. Government foreign aid, loans, investments, and accelerated debt repayments resulted in an additional outflow of more than $2 billion.

The surge in public expenditures during the last quarter of 1974 resulted in a sharp buildup in domestic liquidity and the intensification of inflationary pressures. Initially, the government responded by introducing an administrated price control program. With this program, the upward movement in prices was suppressed. Clearly, these measures by themselves could not moderate the underlying excess demand pressures in the economy, and the government was forced to restrain its expenditures.

The government's decision to slow the growth of its budget outlays was partially imposed by stagnating oil sector revenues; although oil prices increased by about $1 per barrel during 1975, world demand for oil continued to decline and Iranian petroleum exports fell by over 10 percent for the year as a whole. Central government budget outlays for 1975 were held close to original estimates and rose by about 20 percent, considerably below the extraordinary rate of increase in the previous year. However, the absolute increase still amounted to over $4 billion.

In summary, the very rapid rise in oil revenues over the period since 1973 has contributed to a very rapid growth rate and the beginnings of a double digit inflation. Given the inability of the economy to transform all of its oil revenues into productive capacity in a short period of time, it is clear that the country will continue to suffer from inflationary pressures as long as its oil revenues continue to create a condition of capital surplus and excessive liquidity. The proper management of oil revenues is, therefore, critical to the

TABLE E.2

Foreign Exchange Receipts and Payments, 1972-75
(billions of dollars)

	1972	1973	1974	1975
A. Receipts from the oil sector	2.60	4.83	18.67	19.05
B. Other Goods and Services*	-2.70	-4.71	10.06	-16.26
Exports	0.47	0.64	0.69	0.65
Imports	-2.99	-4.96	-10.64	-16.04
Private sector	-1.57	-2.70	-5.02	-7.62
Public sector	-1.42	-2.26	-5.62	-8.42
Services*	-0.18	-0.39	-0.11	-0.87
C. Total (A + B)	-0.10	0.12	8.61	2.79
D. Nonmonetary capital	0.59	0.93	-1.98	-3.13
Official loans and credits*	0.52	0.76	-2.20	-2.88
Private capital*	0.07	0.17	0.22	-0.25
E. Errors and omissions*	–	0.10	-0.47	-0.24
F. Total (C + D + E)	0.49	1.15	6.16	-0.58
G. Monetary movements (increase in assets -)	-0.49	-1.15	-6.16	0.58

* = net.

Source: Computed from Bank Markazi Iran, <u>Annual Report and Balance Sheet</u>, various issues.

long-run development of the country, since these represent real resources that can be saved until such time as the economy's absorptive capacity will permit their efficient local utilization. Both the determination of the time path of absorptive capacity and the design of a foreign investment policy are matters that will affect the country's growth, inflation, and balance-of-payments considerations over the short, medium, and long run.

The ultimate aim of securing a financial surplus from oil exports is to develop the domestic economy, both from a social and economic vantage point. Consequently the placement of funds abroad is justified, due simply to the inability of the domestic economy to absorb these funds productively in the short run.

Seen in this light, Iranian policy makers must make a clear distinction between those funds destined for internal use and those destined for foreign investments in line with absorptive capacity, so as to avoid excessive inflationary pressures in the initial years, and to smooth Iran's growth path over the longer term.

Iran and the other oil economies have had particular problems in adapting their government budgets to the inflow of oil revenues, particularly since these expenditures have been associated with domestic inflation. The problem becomes more difficult in the absence of prior programming.

NOTE

1. For a comparison of Iran and Saudi Arabia, see Henry E. Jakobiak and M. Taher Dajani, "Oil Income and Financial Policies of Iran and Saudi Arabia," <u>Finance and Development</u> (December 1976), pp. 12-15. The analysis of the Iranian situation presented here is based on the approach adopted by Jakobiak and Dajani.

APPENDIX F
A MACROECONOMIC
MODEL OF IRAN

INTRODUCTION

The macroeconomic model developed for Iran is designed to obtain a quantitative insight into the nature and magnitudes of the mechanisms at work in the Iranian economy, and to be the basis for several forecasts of the country's major economic aggregates under assumptions of varying rates of oil revenues and domestic inflation.

The econometric relationships in Table F.1 have been computed on the basis of annual data for the period 1962 to 1974 in current prices for investment, consumption, credit, imports, exports, oil revenues, money supply, and the GNP deflator. Admittedly, this procedure has the disadvantage that the parameters thus estimated have been influenced by former development plans whose orientation was somewhat different from the Fifth Five-Year Plan (1973-77).

The author agrees with Firouz Vakil[1] that an economic and social entity, such as Iran, is very complex and that as such it is very difficult to describe it via models capable of reflecting all the interactions of all the relevant social and economic variables. One is left, therefore, with two choices: build models that are approximations of reality, or analyze each situation on a partial equilibrium basis, that is, holding all other variables constant. The advantage of the former method is that it enables one to examine effects of a change in one variable, such as government expenditure, on all other variables in the system, and, in turn, to examine the effect of their changes on government expenditures at a later point in time. This method provides a simultaneous solution on a general equilibrium basis. The advantage of the latter method is that it gives a more precise depiction of certain problems. Its disadvantage, however, is that it is not amenable to long-range forecasting (other variables cannot realistically be kept constant as one examines changes in a single economic variable).

For purposes of analyzing macroeconomic alternatives for Iran over the next 15 years, the first method was, therefore, selected. This method enables construction of econometric models capable of projecting, through computerization and common sense, all the key macroeconomic variables. In this form the model enables one to evaluate alternative policy actions.

TABLE F.1

Macroeconomic Model, 1962-74
(billions of rials)

1. $C_t^p = 115.1534 - 0.0934 C_{t-1}^p - 0.2717\, CRG_{t-1} + 1.2442\, CRP_{t-1} + 0.3205 Y_{t-1}$ $r^2 = 0.99$
   $\quad\quad\quad\quad (112.7)\quad\quad\quad (8.2)\quad\quad\quad\quad (12.4)\quad\quad\quad\quad (4.4)$

2. $C_t^g = -29.3995 + 0.4325\, CRG_{t-1} + 0.0633\, OR_t + 0.3223\, OR_{t-1} + 0.1443 Y_{t-1}$ $r^2 = 0.99$
   $\quad\quad\quad\quad (105.5)\quad\quad\quad (23.9)\quad\quad\quad (5.0)\quad\quad\quad\quad (2.4)$

3. $C_t^T = C_t^p + C_t^g$

4. $I_t^C = -1.7080 - 0.3935 I_{t-1}^C + 0.2926\, CRP_t + 0.4328 I_t^M + 0.0759 Y_{t-1}$ $r^2 = 0.99$
   $\quad\quad\quad (316.2)\quad\quad (13.9)\quad\quad\quad\quad (2.6)\quad\quad\quad (2.0)$

5. $I_t^M = -18.7886 + 0.4749 I_{t-1}^M - 0.3329 I_{t-1}^C + 0.1548\, CRP_{t-1} + 0.0898 Y_{t-1}$ $r^2 = 0.99$
   $\quad\quad\quad\quad (43.6)\quad\quad\quad (11.5)\quad\quad\quad\quad (3.5)\quad\quad\quad\quad (2.7)$

6. $I_t^T = I_t^M + I_t^C$

7. $S_t = Y_t - C_t^T$

8. $GAPD_t = S_t - I_t^T$

9. $M_t = -4.2791 + 0.1733\, OR_t + 0.6112\, OR_{t-1} + 0.7645 M_{t-1}$ $r^2 = 0.99$
   $\quad\quad\quad (143.0)\quad\quad\quad (22.9)\quad\quad\quad\quad (15.9)$

10. $NFP_t = 36.8517 + 0.1628 E_t$ $r^2 = 0.91$
    $\quad\quad\quad\quad (10.6)$

11. $E^t = E_O (1 + r)$

12. $GAPE_t = M_t + NFP_t - E_t$

13. $CRG_t = -11.6190 + 0.6635\, CRG_{t-1} + 0.3119 MS_t$ $r^2 = .99$
    $\quad\quad\quad\quad (89.9)\quad\quad\quad\quad (8.8)$

14. $CRP_t = -14.6456 + 0.0296\, CRP_{t-1} + 0.5356 MS_t + 0.8224 MS_{t-1} - 0.3826\, CRG_t$ $r^2 = 0.99$
    $\quad\quad\quad\quad (247.3)\ (19.1)\quad\quad\quad (6.2)\quad\quad\quad\quad (2.5)$

15. $CRT_t^T = CRG_t + CRP_t$

16. $MS_t = -5.4949 + 0.9908 MS_{t-1} + 0.6825\, OR_{t-1}$ $r^2 = 0.99$
    $\quad\quad\quad\quad (100.6)\quad\quad\quad\quad (15.4)$

17. $OR_t = OR_o(1+x)^t$

18. $rY_t^C = rY_o^C(1+z)^t$

19. $Y_t = -1.3381 + 1.0943 Y_t^C + 1.23336 GNPD_t$
    $\qquad\qquad\ (64.3)\qquad\qquad (15.2)\qquad\qquad r^2 = 0.99$

Variables	Values
Endogenous	
C_t^p = private consumption	1127.7 (1974)
C_t^g = government consumption	586.2 (1974)
I_t^M = investment in machinery	203.8 (1974)
I_t^C = investment in construction	335.2 (1974)
Y_t = gross national product	2975.1 (1974)
MS_t = money supply	830.1 (1974)
CRP_t = credits of the banking system to the private sector	698.3 (1974)
CRG_t = credits of the banking system to the public sector	445.9 (1974)
M_t = imports	816.4 (1974)
NFP_t = net factor payments	299.5 (1974)
$GNPD_t$ = gross national product deflator	133.1 (1974)
Exogenous	
C_{t-1}^p = private consumption	818.5 (1973)
CRG_{t-1} = credits of the banking system to the public sector	298.4 (1973)
Y_{t-1} = gross national product	1742.5 (1973)
CRP_{t-1} = credits of the banking system to the private sector	489.1 (1973)
OR_t = oil revenues	1297.4 (1974)
OR_{t-1} = oil revenues	477.5 (1973)
I_{t-1}^C = investment in construction	223.2 (1973)
M_{t-1} = imports	859.0 (1973)
MS_{t-1} = money supply	515.8 (1973)
rY_t^C = rate of growth GNP constant 1972 prices	43.0 (1974)

Source: Compiled by the author.

STATISTICAL TECHNIQUE

Estimation of the ten behavioral equations was performed with ordinary least squares regression techniques. Because consistent sets of data are only available for the period 1962-75, it was not possible to use simultaneous estimation techniques, such as two-stage least squares. The number of time series observations (13), in some cases reduced by the inclusion of lagged variables (to 12), precluded the use of more sophisticated techniques.

The complete estimated model is shown in Table F.1. All macroeconomic variables are measured in billions of rials in current prices except for GNPD, which is an index number with 1972 equal to 100.0.

All the results were quite satisfactory, considering both the very high values of the coefficients of determination (r^2) and the size of the t statistic for each coefficient (in parenthesis below the coefficient). The regression package used (Hewlett-Packard 9815A) did not give the Durbin-Watson statistic. It did, however, provide a table of residuals. Using this table it was possible to check for the extent of serial correlation (by examining the sign changes in the residuals). Thus, any regression which had four or more sign changes in the residual was deemed relatively free of serial correlation: most of the estimated behavioral equations exhibited four to six sign changes.[2]

Admittedly, the model has been formulated at a highly aggregated level, and it is hoped that as more data become available (particularly an up-to-date and detailed input-output table), an elaborate model involving sectoral breakdown at a reasonably disaggregated level can be developed.

Within the given limitations the model is, nevertheless, useful in many ways: it furnishes estimates of important structural parameters of the Iranian economy; in quantifying economic forces in the economy, the model throws into sharper focus a number of mechanisms at work in the economy that were previously discussed in a qualitative sense; and, in treating the functioning of the economy as a system of simultaneous relations that bind the major variables together, the model provides a framework within which the interdependence and interactions of these variables can be schematically traced.

The reduced form of analysis (see Table F.2, which was derived by solving the equations in Table F.1 simultaneously) restates the dilemma of development policy in Iran. The country is still quite dependent on oil revenues for its imports and must import in order to realize investment, a necessary condition if high levels of income growth are to be sustained.

TABLE F.2

Impact-Multiplier Matrix Derived from the Macroeconomic Model, 1974

Endogenous Variables	Exogenous Variables									
	C^p_{t-1}	I^m_{t-1}	I^c_{t-1}	M_{t-1}	Y_{t-1}	CRP_{t-1}	CRG_{t-1}	OR_{t-1}	OR_t	E_t
C^p_t	-0.934	0.000	0.000	0.000	3.205	12.442	-2.717	0.000	0.000	0.000
C^g_t	0.000	0.000	0.000	0.000	1.443	0.000	4.325	3.223	0.633	0.000
C^T_t	-0.934	0.000	0.000	0.000	4.648	12.442	1.608	3.223	0.633	0.000
I^m_t	0.000	4.749	-3.329	0.000	0.898	1.548	0.000	0.000	0.000	0.000
I^c_t	0.000	2.055	-5.376	0.000	1.148	0.757	-0.743	0.818	0.000	0.000
I^T_t	0.000	6.804	-8.705	0.000	2.046	2.304	-0.743	0.818	0.000	0.000
CRG_t	0.000	0.000	0.000	0.000	0.000	0.000	6.635	2.095	0.000	0.000
CRP_t	0.000	0.000	0.000	0.000	0.000	0.296	-2.538	2.796	0.000	0.000
MS_t	0.000	0.000	0.000	0.000	0.000	0.000	4.097	6.717	0.000	0.000
$GNPD_t$	0.000	0.000	0.000	0.000	0.000	0.000	0.000	0.443	0.000	0.000
M_t	0.000	0.000	0.000	7.645	0.000	0.000	0.000	6.112	1.733	0.000
Y_t	-0.934	6.804	-8.705	7.645	6.693	14.746	0.865	-2.071	-1.100	8.372

Note: The impact of a ten unit change in an exogenous or predetermined variable on any endogenous variable can be found by locating the number corresponding to the row and column of selected endogenas and given variables (for example, the effect of a rials/10 increase in oil revenues will increase imports by 1.733).

Source: Compiled by the author.

TABLE F.3

Domestic and External Gaps, 1975-82

(billions of rials)

	1975	1976	1977	1978	1979	1980	1981	1982
Gross national product	3338.2	3814.2	4358.1	4979.6	5689.7	6501.1	7428.1	8487.4
Consumption, ex ante	2290.4	3364.1	3753.7	4102.3	4499.5	4931.5	5408.2	5900.7
Consumption, ex post	1826.5	2151.4	2487.3	2940.3	3514.4	4194.2	5140.8	6218.1
Investment in machinery	337.5	419.9	509.4	580.4	657.4	739.7	833.4	939.1
Investment in construction	521.6	545.4	618.5	670.7	741.0	814.3	899.8	995.2
Total investment	859.0	965.2	1127.9	1251.2	1395.4	1554.1	1733.2	1934.3
Savings, ex ante	547.8	450.1	604.5	877.3	1190.2	1569.6	2019.9	2586.6
Savings, ex post	1511.7	1662.8	1870.8	2039.3	2175.3	2306.9	2287.3	2269.3
Exports	2019.8	2244.0	2493.1	2769.8	3010.8	3272.7	3367.6	3485.5
Imports, ex post	1011.5	1144.3	1307.4	1493.9	1706.9	1950.3	2228.4	2546.2
Imports, ex ante	1669.5	1927.8	2166.6	2435.3	2729.8	3031.3	3345.1	3614.5
Net factor payments	365.7	402.2	442.7	487.8	527.0	569.7	585.1	604.3
External gap, ex post	652.7	697.6	742.9	788.1	776.9	752.8	554.1	335.0
Domestic gap, ex ante	-311.2	-515.1	-523.4	-373.9	-208.2	15.5	286.7	939.1
External gap, ex ante	-15.4	-86.0	-116.2	-153.3	-246.0	-328.3	-562.6	-733.3
Domestic gap, ex post	652.7	697.6	742.9	788.1	776.9	752.8	554.1	335.0

<u>Note</u>: Assumptions: 2 percent of inflation, high oil revenues, 12 percent annual increase of real GNP.

<u>Source</u>: Compiled by the author.

TABLE F.4

Domestic and External Gaps, 1983-90
(billions of rials)

	1983	1984	1985	1986	1987	1988	1989	1990
Gross national product	9697.6	11080.5	12660.6	14466.0	16528.9	18885.9	21579.0	24656.1
Consumption, ex ante	6466.7	7133.7	7835.0	8618.8	9479.1	10454.2	11560.3	12815.8
Consumption, ex post	7314.7	8761.5	10433.4	12446.4	14748.7	17381.6	20392.4	23834.8
Investment in machinery	1059.5	1196.3	1352.1	1529.4	1731.2	1961.1	2222.9	2521.2
Investment in construction	1103.5	1225.8	1364.2	1521.0	1698.6	1899.9	2128.4	2387.9
Total investment	2163.0	2422.1	2716.4	3050.4	3429.8	3861.0	4351.3	4909.1
Savings, ex ante	3230.9	3946.9	4825.6	5847.2	7049.8	8431.7	10018.7	11840.3
Savings, ex post	2382.9	2319.0	2227.2	2019.6	1780.2	1504.3	1186.6	821.3
Exports	3781.8	3891.3	3996.5	3996.5	3996.5	3996.5	3996.5	3996.5
Imports, ex post	2909.3	3324.2	3798.2	4339.8	4958.7	5665.8	6473.7	7207.2
Imports, ex ante	3946.1	4368.6	4747.7	5157.3	5572.2	6046.4	6588.2	7207.2
Net factor payments	652.5	670.4	687.5	687.5	687.5	687.5	687.5	687.5
External gap, ex post	219.9	-103.1	-489.2	-1030.8	-1649.6	-2356.7	-3164.7	-3898.2
Domestic gap, ex ante	1067.9	1524.8	2109.2	2796.8	3620.0	4570.7	5667.4	6931.2
External gap, ex ante	-816.7	-1147.7	-1438.7	-1848.3	-2263.2	-2737.4	-3279.2	-3898.2
Domestic gap, ex post	219.9	-103.1	-489.2	-1030.8	-1649.6	-2356.7	-3164.7	-3898.2

<u>Note</u>: Assumptions same as in Table F.3.
<u>Source</u>: Compiled by the author.

TABLE F.5

Domestic and External Gaps, 1975–82
(billions of rials)

	1975	1976	1977	1978	1979	1980	1981	1982
Gross national product	3274.3	3669.5	4112.4	4608.8	5165.2	5788.7	6487.4	7270.5
Consumption, ex ante	2788.7	3328.3	3694.9	4006.0	4331.9	4702.8	5106.7	5467.8
Consumption, ex post	1774.5	1989.3	2167.5	2538.4	2922.6	3332.1	4118.2	4939.6
Investment in machinery	337.5	414.3	496.7	557.5	621.5	687.7	761.5	843.0
Investment in construction	522.3	539.9	606.2	648.9	707.9	766.9	835.2	909.5
Total investment	859.8	954.2	1102.9	1206.5	1329.3	1454.7	1596.7	1752.5
Savings, ex ante	485.5	341.1	417.6	602.8	833.3	1085.9	1380.7	1802.7
Savings, ex post	1499.8	1680.2	1944.9	2070.4	2242.6	2456.6	2369.2	2330.9
Exports	1981.8	2226.2	2523.4	2727.5	2985.8	3315.1	3291.6	3340.3
Imports, ex post	982.3	1100.9	1233.7	1382.7	1549.6	1736.6	1946.2	2181.2
Imports, ex ante	1664.9	1894.1	2129.1	2387.0	2622.8	2904.9	3190.9	3347.0
Net factor payments	359.5	399.3	447.7	480.9	522.9	576.6	572.9	580.7
External gap, ex post	640.0	726.0	842.0	863.9	913.3	1001.9	772.5	578.4
Domestic gap, ex ante	-374.3	-613.1	-685.3	-603.7	-496.0	-368.8	-216.0	50.2
External gap, ex ante	-42.6	-67.2	-53.4	-140.4	-159.9	-166.4	-472.2	-587.4
Domestic gap, ex post	359.5	726.0	842.0	863.9	913.3	1001.9	772.5	578.4

Note: Assumptions: 2 percent rate of inflation, low oil revenues, real GNP increases at 10 percent.
Source: Compiled by the author.

TABLE F.6

Domestic and External Gaps, 1983–90

(billions of rials)

	1983	1984	1985	1986	1987	1988	1989	1990
Gross national product	8148.1	9131.7	10234.0	11469.3	12853.8	14405.4	16144.2	18093.0
Consumption, ex ante	5879.9	6313.5	6781.3	7184.6	7685.9	8270.2	8969.9	9767.4
Consumption, ex post								
Investment in machinery	934.1	1035.6	1148.9	1275.3	1416.4	1573.9	1749.8	1946.1
Investment in construction	992.5	1084.2	1185.9	1298.8	1424.1	1563.3	1717.9	1889.9
Total investment	1926.6	2119.8	2334.9	2574.2	2840.5	3137.2	3467.7	3836.0
Savings, ex ante	2268.2	2818.2	3452.7	4284.7	5167.9	6135.2	7174.2	8325.6
Savings, ex post								
Exports	3285.2	3276.3	2723.9	2328.9	1970.8	1777.8	1640.5	1522.9
Imports, ex post	2444.4	2739.5	3070.2	3440.8	3856.1	4036.6	4072.8	4025.6
Imports, ex ante	3541.8	3718.1	3873.1	3834.2	3900.0	4036.6	4072.8	4025.6
Net factor payments	571.7	570.2	480.3	415.9	357.7	326.3	303.9	284.8
External gap, ex post	269.1	−33.4	−826.6	−1527.8	−2243.0	−2585.1	−2736.2	−2787.5
Domestic gap, ex ante	341.6	698.4	1117.8	1710.5	2327.4	2998.0	3706.5	4489.6
External gap, ex ante	−828.3	−1012.0	−1629.5	−1921.2	−2286.9	−2585.1	−2736.2	−2787.5
Domestic gap, ex post	269.1	−33.4	−826.6	−1527.8	−2243.0	−2585.1	−2736.2	−2787.5

<u>Note:</u> Assumptions same as in Table F.5.
<u>Source:</u> Compiled by the author.

TABLE F.7

External Gap, 1975–90—High Oil Revenues
(billions of rials)

Year	GNP 12 Percent, Inflation		GNP 10 Percent, Inflation		GNP 8 Percent, Inflation	
	2 Percent	5 Percent	2 Percent	5 Percent	2 Percent	5 Percent	10 Percent
1975	652.7	620.2	671.8	639.4	691.0	658.6	604.5
1976	697.6	622.2	714.0	667.1	783.5	711.1	584.9
1977	742.9	611.7	816.6	690.3	887.5	766.0	545.3
1978	788.1	585.0	899.4	705.5	1004.3	823.3	479.7
1979	776.9	482.0	934.2	660.9	1079.7	826.8	325.5
1980	752.8	341.8	966.4	592.8	1160.3	821.1	118.6
1981	554.1	-2.8	836.2	339.4	1087.3	644.9	-312.4
1982	335.0	-404.4	699.9	52.7	1018.4	453.3	-824.9
1983	219.9	-746.5	684.7	-145.3	1082.3	371.5	-1308.9
1984	-103.1	-1350.7	481.4	-569.9	971.9	887.7	-2093.5
1985	-489.2	-2083.9	238.7	-1079.9	837.6	-248.8	-3055.2
1986	-1030.8	-3052.4	-131.9	-1172.1	593.3	-232.0	-4312.0
1987	-1649.6	-4195.0	-547.3	-2573.4	324.9	-1280.9	-5817.1
1988	-2356.7	-5542.7	-1012.9	-3501.1	30.0	-1904.3	-7619.5
1989	-3164.7	-7132.4	-1534.6	-4575.2	-294.0	-2612.4	-9777.8
1990	-4087.8	-9007.7	-2119.3	-5818.7	650.1	-3416.7	-12362.3

Source: Compiled by the author, based on forecasts using Table F.1.

TABLE F.8

External Gap, 1975-90—Low Oil Revenues
(billions of rials)

Year	GNP 12 Percent, Inflation 2 Percent	GNP 10 Percent, Inflation		GNP 8 Percent, Inflation	
		2 Percent	5 Percent	2 Percent	5 Percent
1975	620.9	640.0	607.6	659.2	626.8
1976	682.6	726.0	652.2	768.6	696.1
1977	768.3	842.0	715.7	912.9	791.4
1978	752.7	863.9	672.1	968.8	787.8
1979	755.9	913.3	640.0	1058.8	805.9
1980	788.2	1002.0	628.3	1195.8	856.6
1981	490.4	772.6	275.8	1023.6	581.2
1982	213.4	578.5	-68.7	896.9	331.6
1983	-195.8	269.1	-560.9	666.7	44.3
1984	-618.1	-33.4	-1084.8	457.0	-426.3
1985	-1554.6	-826.6	-2145.1	-227.7	-1314.2
1986	-2426.9	-1527.9	-3168.0	-802.7	-2128.2
1987	-3345.5	-2243.0	-4269.0	-1370.8	-2976.9
1988	-4214.2	-2870.1	-5358.3	-1827.2	-3761.9
1989	-5137.1	-3506.7	-6547.2	-2266.2	-4585.0
1990	-6158.7	-4189.8	-7889.0	-2720.7	-5487.8

Source: Compiled by the author, based on forecasts using Table F.1.

TABLE F.9

Financial Surplus, 1975-90
(billions of rials)

Year	Exports	Imports	Net Factor Payments	External Gap	Productive Investment	Surplus, Deficiency (-)	Cumulative	Cumulative 8 Percent Annually Compounded
1975	2019.8	1001.5	365.7	652.7	859.0	795.1	795.1	795.1
1976	2244.0	1144.3	402.2	697.6	965.2	876.6	1671.7	1735.3
1977	2493.1	1307.4	442.7	742.9	1127.9	922.5	2594.2	2796.6
1978	2769.8	1493.9	487.8	788.1	1251.2	1030.8	3625.0	4051.2
1979	3010.8	1706.9	527.0	776.9	1398.4	1085.4	4710.4	5460.7
1980	3272.7	1950.3	569.7	752.8	1554.1	1148.9	5859.3	7046.4
1981	3367.6	2228.4	585.1	554.1	1733.2	1049.3	6908.6	8859.4
1982	3485.5	2546.2	604.3	335.0	1934.3	946.9	7855.5	10374.8
1983	3781.8	2909.3	652.5	219.9	2163.0	966.3	8821.8	12171.1
1984	3891.3	3324.2	670.4	-103.1	2422.1	798.8	9620.6	13943.6
1985	3966.5	3798.2	687.5	-489.2	2716.4	592.6	10213.2	15651.7
1986	3996.5	4344.8	687.5	-1030.8	3050.4	258.6	10471.8	17183.1
1987	3996.5	4958.7	687.5	-1649.6	3429.8	-120.8	10351.0	18437.0
1988	3996.5	5665.8	687.5	-2356.7	3861.0	-552.0	9799.0	19359.9
1989	3996.5	6473.7	687.5	-3164.7	4351.3	-1042.3	8756.7	18317.6
1990	3996.5	7207.2	687.5	-3898.2	4909.1	-1600.1	7156.6	18182.9

Source: Computed from Tables F.3 and F.4.

TABLE F.10

Financial Surplus, 1975-90
(billions of rials)

Year	Exports	Imports	Net Factor Payments	External Gap	Productive Investment	Surplus, Deficit (-)	Cumulative	Cumulative 8 Percent Annually Compounded
1975	1981.8	982.3	359.5	359.5	859.8	762.5	762.5	762.5
1976	2226.2	1100.9	399.3	726.0	954.2	872.7	1635.2	1696.2
1977	2523.4	1233.7	447.7	842.0	1102.9	972.8	2608.0	2804.7
1978	2727.5	1382.7	480.9	863.9	1206.5	1040.1	3648.1	4069.2
1979	2985.8	1549.6	522.9	913.3	1329.3	1133.6	4781.7	5528.3
1980	3315.1	1736.6	576.6	1001.9	1454.7	1283.8	6065.5	7254.4
1981	3291.6	1946.2	572.9	772.5	1596.7	1122.0	7187.5	8956.7
1982	3340.3	2181.2	580.7	578.4	1752.5	971.1	8158.6	10644.4
1983	3285.2	2444.1	571.7	269.1	1926.6	786.9	8945.5	12282.8
1984	3276.3	2739.5	570.2	-33.4	2119.8	586.3	9531.8	13851.7
1985	2723.9	3070.2	480.3	-826.6	2334.9	-91.3	9440.5	14868.6
1986	2389.9	3440.8	415.9	-1527.8	2574.2	-600.2	8840.3	15457.8
1987	1970.8	3856.1	357.7	-2243.0	2840.5	-1227.4	7612.9	15467.1
1988	1777.8	4036.6	326.3	-2585.1	3137.2	-1685.7	5927.2	15018.7
1989	1640.5	4072.8	303.9	-2736.2	3467.7	-2131.1	3796.1	14089.1
1990	1522.9	4025.6	284.8	-2787.5	3836.0	-2597.9	1198.2	12618.3

Source: Compiled from Tables F.5 and F.6.

While the Iranian economy has undergone important changes in the last decade or so, the reduced form of the macromodel indicates that the country remains heavily dependent on foreign trade. Thus its development continues to be highly sensitive to changes in external markets. However, the public sector investment programs, together with a fairly successful industrialization policy, have been effective in maintaining economic stability and in promoting growth. The initiation of development programs, with their positive impact upon the economy, has given the country a fair amount of internal maneuverability.

A number of simulations of the economy, for comparison with the values for the leading macroaggregates presented in Chapter 10 (Tables 10.2-10.5) are presented in Tables F.3-F.10.

NOTES

1. Firouz Vakil, "An Econometric Model for Iran," Bank Markazi Iran, Bulletin (1972), pp. 115-20; Firouz Vakil, "An Econometric Model for Iran: Estimated Structural Equations," Bank Markazi Iran, Bulletin (1973), pp. 633-55.

2. This procedure was considered sufficient for the purposes of forecasting. For an examination of the statistical problems in using time series data and a model of the Iranian economy similar to Firouz Vakil's, see Ahmad Shahshahani Madani and J. Malcolm Dowling, Jr., "An Econometric Model Forecast of Iran, 1975-1985," Journal of Energy and Development (spring 1976), pp. 148-62.

BIBLIOGRAPHY

Adelman, Irma, and Morris, Cynthia Taft. "Performance Criteria for Evaluating Economic Development Potential: An Operational Approach." Quarterly Journal of Economics (May 1968), pp. 260-80.

_____. Society, Politics, and Economic Development—A Quantitative Approach. Baltimore: Johns Hopkins University Press, 1967.

Adelman, Morris A. The World Petroleum Market. Baltimore: Johns Hopkins University Press, 1972.

Ahmad, Yusuf J. Oil Revenues in the Gulf. Paris: OECD, Development Center, 1974.

Akins, James. "The Oil Crisis: This Time the Wolf Is Here." Foreign Affairs (April 1973), pp. 462-90.

Alnasrawi, Abbas. Financing Economic Development in Iraq. New York: Praeger, 1967.

Al-Otaiba, Mana Saeed. OPEC and the Petroleum Industry. New York: Halsted, 1975.

Aminzadeh, F. "Human Resources Development: Problems and Prospects." In Iran: Past, Present and Future—The Persepolis Symposium, edited by Jane Jacqz. New York: Aspen Institute for Humanistic Studies, 1976.

Amuzegar, Jahangir. "Capital Formation and Development Finance." In Iran Faces the Seventies, edited by Ehsan Yar-Shater. New York: Praeger, 1971.

_____. "Ideology and Economic Growth in the Middle East." Middle East Journal (winter 1974), pp. 1-9.

Amuzegar, Jahangir, and Fekrat, M. Ali. Iran: Economic Development Under Dualistic Conditions. Chicago: University of Chicago Press, 1971.

Aresvik, Oddvar. *The Agricultural Development of Iran*. New York: Praeger, 1976.

Avramovic, Dragoslav. "Industrialization of Iran: The Records, the Problems and the Prospects." *Tahqiqat-e Eqtesidi* (spring 1970), pp. 1-13.

Badre, Albert Y. "Economic Development of Iraq." In *Economic Development and Population Growth in the Middle East*, edited by Charles A. Cooper and Sidney S. Alexander. New York: Elsevier, 1972.

Bagley, F. R. C. "A Bright Future After Oil: Dams and Agro-Industry in Khuzestan." *Middle East Journal* (winter 1976), pp. 25-35.

Baldwin, George. *Planning and Development in Iran*. Baltimore: Johns Hopkins University Press, 1967.

_____. "The Iranian Brain Drain." In *Iran Faces the Seventies*. New York: Praeger, 1971.

Bank Markazi Iran. *Annual Report and Balance Sheet*, various issues.

_____. *Annual Survey of Household Expenditures*, various issues.

_____. *Bulletin*, various issues.

Bartsch, William. "The Industrial Labor Force of Iran: Problems of Recruitment, Training and Productivity." *Middle East Journal* (winter 1971), pp. 15-30.

Benedick, Richard. *Industrial Finance in Iran*. Boston: Harvard University, Graduate School of Business Administration, 1964.

Benoit, Emile. *Defense and Economic Growth in Developing Countries*. Lexington, Mass.: D. C. Heath, 1973.

Bhanoji, Rao, V. V., ed. *Inflation and Growth*. Singapore: Stamford College Press, 1974.

Bharier, Julian. *Economic Development in Iran, 1900-1970*. London: Oxford University Press, 1971.

BIBLIOGRAPHY

Blitzer, C., et al. "A Dynamic Model of OPEC Trade and Production." Journal of Development Economics (December 1975), pp. 319-35.

Bruno, Michael. "Economic Development Problems of Israel, 1970-1980." In Economic Development and Population Growth in the Middle East, edited by Charles A. Cooper and Sidney S. Alexander. New York: Elsevier, 1972.

Caldwell, J. Alexander. "The Evolution of the OPEC Current Account Surplus: Recent Trends, Likely Developments, and Major Policy Implications." Journal of Energy and Development (spring 1976), pp. 297-305.

Celasum, Merith, and Pinto, Frank. Energy Prospects in OECD Countries and Possible Demand for OPEC Oil Exports to 1980. Washington, D.C.: IBRD, 1975.

Chenery, H. B. "Reconstructing the World Economy." Foreign Affairs (January 1975), pp. 242-63.

____, et al. Redistribution with Growth. London: Oxford University Press, 1974.

Clawson, Marion, et al. The Agricultural Potential of the Middle East. New York: Elsevier, 1971.

Cohen, Jacob, and Cohen, Patricia. Applied Multiple Regression/Correlation Analysis for the Behavioral Sciences. Hillsdale, N.J.: Lawrence Erlbaum Associates, 1975.

Cooper, Charles A., and Alexander, Sidney S., eds. Economic Development and Population Growth in the Middle East (New York: Elsevier, 1972.

Echeverria, R., et al. Current Economic Position and Prospects of Ecuador. Washington, D.C.: IBRD, 1973.

Eckbo, Paul Leo. The Future of World Oil. Cambridge, Mass.: Ballinger, 1976.

Eckstein, Otto. "Investment Criteria for Economic Development and the Theory of Intemporal Welfare Economics." Quarterly Journal of Economics (February 1957).

The Economist Intelligence Unit. Quarterly Economic Review–Iran, no. 2 (1976).

_____. Quarterly Economic Review–Iran, no. 4 (1974).

_____. Quarterly Economic Review of Iraq, no. 2 (1976).

_____. Quarterly Economic Review of Iraq, 4th Quarter 1976.

_____. Quarterly Economic Review, Venezuela, no. 1 (1976).

_____. Quarterly Economic Review Special, no. 18. Oil Production, Revenues and Economic Development. London, 1974.

Ensor, Richard. "Brother, Can You Spare a Dollar? Well, the Fondo Has Billions, but. . . ." Euromoney (December 1976), pp. 13-21.

Euromoney, May 1975.

Fallon, Padraic. "The Man Most Courted by the Leaders Keeps Venezuela on the Path of Sobriety." Euromoney (December 1976), pp. 22-23.

Fekrat, M. Ali. "Economic Growth and Development in Iran." In Iran: Past, Present and Future–The Persepolis Symposium, edited by Jane Jacqz. New York: Aspen Institute for Humanistic Studies, 1976.

Fesharaki, Fereidun. Development of the Iranian Oil Industry: International and Domestic Aspects. New York: Praeger, 1976.

Financial Times, July 30, 1975.

Firoozi, Ferydoon. "Demographic Review: Iranian Censuses 1956 and 1966–A Comparative Review." Middle East Journal (spring 1970), pp. 220-28.

Fischer, Dietrich, et al. "The Prospects for OPEC: A Critical Survey of Models of the World Oil Market." Journal of Development Economics (December 1975), pp. 363-86.

Fisher, W. B., ed. The Cambridge History of Iran. Vol. 1. The Land of Iran. Cambridge: Cambridge University Press, 1968.

BIBLIOGRAPHY

Fitzgerald, Frances. "Giving the Shah Everything He Wants." Harpers 249, no. 1494 (November 1974).

Friedman, Irving S. Inflation: A Worldwide Disaster. Boston: Houghton Mifflin, 1973.

Friedman, Milton. "Monetary Policy for a Developing Society." In Bank Markazi Iran, Bulletin (March-April 1971), pp. 267-86.

Friedman, Milton, and Schwartz, Anna. A Monetary History of the United States, 1867-1960. Princeton: Princeton University Press, 1963.

Fry, Maxwell J. Finance and Development Planning in Turkey. Leiden, Neth.: Brill, 1972.

_____. The Afghan Economy: Money, Finance and the Critical Constraints to Economic Development. Leiden, Neth.: Brill, 1974.

Gebelein, C. A. "Effect of Conservation on Oil Prices: Analysis of Misconceptions." Journal of Energy and Development, no. 1 (autumn 1975), pp. 53-69.

Ghiles, Francis. "Bankers Have Reasons that Algeria Will Ignore at Its Peril." Euromoney (August 1976), p. 49.

Gibson, Charles. Foreign Trade in the Economic Development of Small Nations: The Case of Ecuador. New York: Praeger, 1971.

Gouverneur, J. "Hirschman on Labor Productivity Differentials: An Empirical Analysis." Bulletin of the Oxford University Institute of Economics and Statistics (November 1970), pp. 259-65.

Graham, Robert. "When the Dreaming Had to Stop." Financial Times (February 26, 1976), p. 18.

Hamilton, Adrian. "End of Old Assumptions on Oil Prices." Financial Times (September 29, 1975), p. 25.

Hart, A., and Kennen, P. Money, Debt and Economic Activity. Englewood Cliffs, N.J.: Prentice-Hall, 1961.

Hassan, Mostafa F. Economic Growth and Employment Problems in Venezuela: An Analysis of an Oil Based Economy. New York: Praeger, 1975.

Hershlag, A. Y. The Economic Structure of the Middle East. Leiden, Neth.: Brill, 1975.

Hirschman, Albert O. The Strategy of Economic Development. New Haven: Yale University Press, 1961.

Inter-American Development Bank. Economic and Social Progress in Latin America. Washington, D.C.: Inter-American Development Bank, 1974.

International Labor Office. Employment and Income Policies for Iran. Geneva: International Labor Office, 1973.

International Monetary Fund. International Financial Statistics (October 1976).

_____. International Financial Statistics (December 1976).

_____. IMF Survey (January 7, 1974).

_____. IMF Survey (February 17, 1975).

Iran, Ministry of Interior. The First Census of Iran. Tehran: Ministry of Interior, 1956.

Iran, Plan and Budget Organization, Planometrics Bureau. A Twenty-Year Macro-Economic Perspective for Iran, 1351-1371. Tehran: Plan and Budget Organization, 1974.

_____. Iran's Fifth Development Plan, 1973-1978, Revised—A Summary. Tehran: Plan and Budget Organization, 1975.

Iranian Statistical Center. National Census of Population and Housing. Tehran: Iranian Statistical Center, 1968.

_____. "Past Population Trends and Future Forecast of Iran Population up to 1991." Mimeographed. Tehran: Iranian Statistical Center, 1971.

Iraq. The National Development Plan, 1970-74. Baghdad: Planning Board and Ministry of Planning, 1971.

Iraq, Ministry of Education. Education in the Republic of Iraq. Baghdad: Ministry of Education, 1973.

Irvin, G. W. Roads and Redistribution: Social Costs and Benefits of Labor Intensive Road Construction in Iran. Geneva: International Labor Office, 1975.

Ispahani, Ahmed Saboonchi. "The Optimization of Economic Resources for Economic Growth in Iran." Ph.D. dissertation, University of Southern California, 1966.

Jacqz, Jane, ed. Iran: Past, Present and Future—The Persepolis Symposium. New York: Aspen Institute for Humanistic Studies, 1976.

Jakobiak, Henry E., and Dajani, M. Taher. "Oil Income and Financial Policies of Iran and Saudi Arabia." Finance and Development (December 1976), pp. 12-15.

Jalal, F. The Role of the Government in the Industrialization of Iraq, 1950-65. London: Frank Cass, 1972.

Kader, Ahmad Abdul. "The Role of the Oil Export Sector in the Economic Development of Iraq." Ph. D. dissertation, University of West Virginia, Morgantown, 1974.

Kalymon, B. A. "Economic Incentives in OPEC Oil Pricing Policy." Journal of Development Economics (December 1975), pp. 337-63.

Kaneda, H. "Agriculture." Mimeographed. Tehran: International Labor Organization, 1973.

Kanovsky, E. Economic Development of Iraq. Tel Aviv: Tel Aviv University, David Horowitz Institute for the Research of Developing Countries, 1974.

Kayhan (international edition). May 3, 1975.

_____. December 18, 1976.

Kendall, Sarita. "Ecuador: Oil and Development." Bank of England and South America Review (May 1975), pp. 316-22.

Khan, Mohsin. "Experiments with a Monetary Model for the Venezuelan Economy." Staff Papers, International Monetary Fund (November 1974), pp. 389-413.

Khatkhate, Deena, et al. "A Money Multiplier Model for a Developing Country: The Venezuelan Case." Staff Papers, International Monetary Fund (November 1975), pp. 740-57.

Lambton, A. K. S. Landlord and Peasant in Persia. London: Oxford University Press, 1969.

Laumas, Prem. "A Note of Friedman's Law of Economic Growth." Weltwirtschaftliches Archiv (1975), pp. 116-20.

LeBaron, Allen, et al. Long Term Projections of Supply and Demand for Selected Agricultural Products in Iran. Logan: Utah State University Press, 1970.

Lima, Gregory, et al. The Revolutionizing of Iran. Tehran: International Communicators Iran, 1973.

Lioi, V. Corbo. Inflation in Developing Countries: An Econometric Study of Chilean Inflation. Amsterdam: North-Holland, 1974.

Looney, Robert E. The Economic Development of Iran: A Recent Survey with Projections to 1981. New York: Praeger, 1973.

_____. Income Distribution Policies and Economic Growth in Semi-industrialized Countries: A Comparative Study of Iran, Mexico, Brazil, and South Korea. New York: Praeger, 1975.

_____. Income Distribution Policies and Economic Growth in Semi-industrialized Countries. New York: Praeger, 1975.

_____. "Iran: Rise of a World Power." Countermeasures, no. 2 (May 1975), pp. 10-16.

Machlup, Fritz. Essays on Economic Semantics. Englewood Cliffs, N.J.: Prentice-Hall, 1963.

_____. "The International Transmission of Inflation." Euromoney (July 1975), pp. 241-45.

Madani, Ahmad Shahshahani. "An Econometric Model of Development for an Oil-Based Economy: The Case of Iran." Ph.D. dissertation, University of Colorado, Boulder, 1976.

Madani, Ahmad Shahshahani, and Dowling, J. Malcolm, Jr. "An Econometric Model Forecast of Iran, 1975-1985." Journal of Energy and Development (spring 1976), pp. 148-62.

BIBLIOGRAPHY

Majidi, Abdolmajid. "Social Change in the Modern World." Iran: Past, Present and Future–The Persepolis Symposium, edited by Jane Jacqz. New York: Aspen Institute for Humanistic Studies, 1976.

Mallakh, Ragaei El. "Industrialization in the Arab World: Obstacles and Prospects." In Arab Oil, edited by Naiem A. Sherbiny and Mark A. Tessler. New York: Praeger, 1976.

Mayer, Thomas. Permanent Income, Wealth, and Consumption. Berkeley: University of California Press, 1972.

Middle East Annual Review. London: Middle East Review Co., 1975.

Mikesell, Raymond F. U.S. Private and Government Investment Abroad. Eugene: University of Oregon Books, 1962.

Murakami, Teruyasu. "Policy Simulation for Crude Oil Production of OPEC Countries." Policy Sciences (March 1976), pp. 93-111.

Naraghi, E. "Regional Studies in Iran." In Multidisciplinary Aspects of Regional Development. Paris: OECD, 1969.

Nirumand, Bahman. Iran: The New Imperialism in Action. New York: Monthly Review Press, 1969.

Nott, Davis. "Venezuela: The Apportionment of Oil Wealth." Bank of England and South America Review (May 1975), pp. 196-99.

Oil and Gas Journal, various issues.

Penrose, Edith. The Growth of Firms, Middle East Oil and Other Essays. London: Frank Cass, 1971.

Perez, Carlos Andres. "Special Message." Mimeographed. Caracas, April 29, 1974.

Pesaran, M. H. "Banking and Credit Control in Iran." Euromoney (May 1975), pp. 51-52.

_____. "Income Distribution and Its Major Determinants in Iran." In Iran: Past, Present and Future–The Persepolis Symposium, edited by Jane Jacqz. New York: Aspen Institute for Humanistic Studies, 1976.

_____. World Economic Prospects and the Iranian Economy. Tehran: Institute for International Political and Economic Studies, 1976.

Platt, Kenneth B. "Land Reform in Iran." In Land Reform in Iran, Iraq, Pakistan, Turkey and Indonesia. Agency for International Development. Washington, D.C.: Department of State, 1970.

Richardson, Harry W. "Regional Planning in Iran." Growth and Change (July 1975), pp. 16-19.

Rifai, Taki. The Pricing of Crude Oil: Economic and Strategic Guidelines for an International Energy Policy. New York: Praeger, 1975.

Rischer, Gunter. "The Tehran Stock Exchange." Euromoney (May 1975), pp. 32-36.

Salazar-Carrillo, Jorge. Oil in the Economic Development of Venezuela. New York: Praeger, 1976.

Samuelson, Paul. "Interest Rate Determinations and Oversimplifying Parables: A Summing Up." In Essays in Modern Capital Theory, M. Brown, et al. Amsterdam: North-Holland, 1976.

Schliephake, Konrad. "Regional Development and Oil Strategy: The Case of Algeria." Intereconomics, no. 7 (1975), pp. 202-06.

Sherbiny, Naiem A., and Tessler, Mark, eds. Arab Oil: Impact on the Arab Countries and Global Implications. New York: Praeger, 1976.

Shoja, Reza Doroudian. "Econometric Models for the Fourth Plan." Tahqiqat-e Eqtesadi (1968), pp. 432-51.

"Snags of Indexing Oil Prices." Financial Times (February 14, 1975), p. 4.

Stevens, Willy J. Capital Absorptive Capacity in Developing Countries. Leiden: A. W. Sijthoff, 1971.

Stickley, S. Thomas, and Najafi, Bahaoldin. "The Effectiveness of Farm Corporations in Iran." Tahqiqat-e Eqtesadi (winter 1971), p. 24.

BIBLIOGRAPHY

"A Survey of Iran." The Economist (August 28, 1976), pp. 1-44.

Swamy, S. Indian Economic Planning: An Alternative Approach. Delhi: Vikas, 1971.

Tofigh, Firouz. "Development of Iran: A Statistical Note." In Iran: Past, Present and Future—The Persepolis Symposium, edited by Jane Jacqz. New York: Aspen Institute for Humanistic Studies, 1976.

"Trading with OPEC." Financial Times (April 29, 1976), pp. 15-19.

Tugwell, Franklin. The Politics of Oil in Venezuela. Palo Alto, Calif.: Stanford University Press, 1975.

United Nations Economic Commission for Asia and the Far East. Economic Survey of Asia and the Far East, 1970. Bangkok: 1971.

_____. "Iran." Interregional Trade Projections, Effective Protection and Income Distribution, Vol. 2, Effective Protection (Bangkok: 1972), pp. 62-74.

Vakil, Firouz. "An Econometric Model for Iran." Bank Markazi Iran, Bulletin 9 (1972), pp. 115-20.

_____. "An Econometric Model for Iran: Estimated Structural Equations," Bank Markazi Iran, Bulletin (1973), pp. 633-55.

_____. Determining Iran's Financial Surplus, 1352-1371. Tehran: Institute for International, Political, and Economic Studies, 1975.

_____. "Iran's Basic Macroeconomic Problems: A 20-Year Horizon." In Iran: Past, Present and Future—The Persepolis Symposium, edited by Jane W. Jacqz. New York: Aspen Institute for Humanistic Studies, 1976.

Vatikiotis, P. J. "The Politics of the Fertile Crescent." In Political Dynamics in the Middle East, edited by Paul Y. Hammond and Sidney S. Alexander. New York: Elsevier, 1972.

Vicker, V. Ray. "Caveat Vendor—Merchants in Iran Face Citizen Army of Price Policeman." Wall Street Journal, October 5, 1976.

Wallich, Henry. "Is There a Capital Shortage?" Challenge (September-October 1975), pp. 30-43.

"Why OPEC's Rocket Will Lose Its Thrust," First National City Bank Monthly Review (June 1975).

Weisskopf, Thomas. "An Econometric Test of Alternative Constraints on the Growth of Underdeveloped Countries." Review of Economics and Statistics (February 1972), pp. 67-78.

Zahedani, Abdolhossain. "Iran: Evaluation of Agricultural Development Strategy, 1962-1972." Ph.D. dissertation, University of California, Davis, 1974.

Zonis, Marvin. The Political Elite of Iran. Princeton: Princeton University Press, 1971.

INDEX

Abu Musa, 89
ADBI (see, Agricultural Development Bank)
Adelman, Morris, 63
Afghanistan, 86-87, 89
Agricultural Development Bank (ADBI), 78-79, 80; regional development branches, 80
Ahwaz, 33, 79
Akins, James, 63
Algeria, 3, 7, 9, 11, 12, 60, 118, 125-30, 142, 143; industrialization through oil, 125, 127; regional development, 125, 127-28, 142; shift to lighter, labor-intensive industries, 125-27, 128; SONATRACH, 128
American Petroleum Institute (API), 62
Ankara, 31
Arab-Israeli conflict, 89
Arzew, 128
Ashland Oil Company, 90
Australia, 91, 92
Ayramehr Steel Company, 33
Azerbaijan, 12

Bafq, 33
Bagly, F. R. C., 81
Baluchistan, 12
Bandar Pahlavi, 30-31
Bandar Shahpur, 30
Bank Markazi Iran, 99, 100, 104, 105, 106, 111, 157
Bank of America, 79
Bejaia, 127
Boeing, 88

British Petroleum, 64
Bushehr, 129

California, 79
Canada, 60, 92
capital formation, 70-71, 114
Caribbean Development Bank, 132
Caspian Sea, 30-31
CENTO (communications) system, 31
Central American Integration Bank, 132
Central Ostan (province), 128-29
Central Province, 48
Central Treaty Organization (CENTO), 31
Chase Manhattan Bank, 79, 90
Citicorp International Development, 79
communist countries, 60
Compagnie Française des Pétroles, 64
Cotts, Mitchell, 79

Deer, John, 79
Dez River, 30
Dhofar, 89
Diamond A Cattle Ranch, 79

Ecuador, 3, 7, 9, 11, 12, 21, 50, 60, 118, 136-40, 141, 142; Fondo de Inversiones de Venezuela (FONADE), 139; GDP, 139; inflation, effects of, 137-40; National Development Bank, 139; National Plan for Transformation and Development, 140; National Planning and Economic Coordination

Board, 140; National Pre-Investment Funds, 139-40; National Statistical Institute, 137; oil revenues, effects of, 137; overseas investments, 137, 142
Engel's Law, 27
Ethiopia, 79
Eurocurrency, 4, 133
Eurodollar market, 133
Euromarket, 6
European Economic Community (EEC), 92
Exxon, 64

Fars, 48
Finance Corporation of the Andean Pact Countries, 132
<u>Financial Times</u>, 143
France, 5, 87, 125

General Dynamics, 88
Gini coefficient, 47
Great Britain, 5, 87, 88
green revolution, 76

Hawaiian Agronomics, 79
Hirschman, Albert O., 30

IMF (<u>see</u>, International Monetary Fund)
India, 89
Indonesia, 11, 15, 60, 71
inflation, world, 1, 60-61, 97-98, 106, 135, 137, 141, 151
Inter-American Development Bank, 132
International Labor Organization (ILO), 43; industrial training center (Turin, Italy), 43
International Monetary Fund (IMF), 5, 87, 132, 137

Iran, 11, 60; administrative and entrepreneurial corps, 17, 21-22, 125; agriculture, 2, 12, 24, 26, 58, 123-24, 155 [commercial-farming failures, 78-80; insufficient production, 75-78; land reform, 73-75, 77-78; problems in developing, 72-81]; Agriculture, Ministry of, 73, 75, 76, 77, 78, 80, 81; balance of payments, 4-6, 12; capital formation, 70-71, 114; communications, 31; Cooperatives and Rural Affairs, Ministry of, 80; credit, 99-100, 104, 105-06, 111, 114; Economic Affairs and Finances, Ministry of, 114; economic growth, 1-3, 5, 9, 14-34, 50, 58, 124 [government, role of, 15, 27-34; indicators of, 17-18; oil, role of, 18-20; sources of, 15-18]; economic planning, 5-6, 7, 8, 15, 19-34; economy, international importance of, 1-2; Economy, Ministry of, 129; education and training, 21-23, 27, 28, 31, 32, 34, 41, 42, 43, 44-45, 48, 74, 124; Eighth Plan, 62; employment [foreign labor, 42-43, 44; problems of, 38-41, 42-45, 80; skilled manpower, shortage of, 41, 42-43, 44, 85; unskilled labor, oversupply of, 38-39, 43, 44; women in labor force, 40]; expenditure distribution, 12, 44-45, 46-51, 114, 129; external borrowing, 4-6, 7, 8; Fifth Plan (1973-77), 5-6, 7, 8, 23-27, 38, 41, 43, 62, 65, 71, 73, 76, 80, 81, 129, 158 [objectives of, 23; objectives of revised plan, 26, 42; priorities of revised plan, 26-27; upward revision of, 24-27]; First Seven-Year Plan (1949-55), 20; foreign investment, 15, 24, 27, 34, 124, 142,

154-55; foreign trade, 54-63, 65-67 [exports, 59, 66-67, 68, 124; imports, 54-59, 66, 68, 75-76, 81, 97-98, 151; nonoil exports, need for, 154, 155-59; OPEC price rises, influence of, 61-63; tariffs, 54, 56, 68, 158]; Fourth Plan (1968-72), 4, 15, 21, 22, 24, 75, 129, 130, 157; future domestic economic problems, 155-59; future national policy, implications for, 148-55; GNP, 15, 19, 21, 30, 58, 59, 66, 88, 92, 98, 106, 111, 124, 151, 154, 157; government enterprises, success of, 32-33; government spending, 6-7, 84, 85-89, 100, 105; income distribution, 12, 44-45, 46-51, 114, 129; indigenous (agricultural) sector, 18-19, 21; industrialization, 27-28, 31, 58, 71-72, 124, 157-58; inflation, 1, 5, 7, 8, 12, 45, 78, 92-94, 97-115, 142, 151, 155 [demand pull, 99-106; forces inducing, 97, 158; and foreign borrowing, 151; government attacks upon, 106-11, 118, 136; incomes, suggested policy on, 111-14; from increased import prices, 97-98; need to control, 151; repressed, 110-11]; infrastructure, investments in, 15, 30-31, 33, 157; Justice, Department of, 108; labor, 19, 23, 26, 28, 38, 158; Labor, Ministry of, 42, 44, 45 [Vocational Training Board, 43]; Labor Act of 1959, 51; lessons from experiences of other oil producers, 123-25, 128-30, 136, 140, 142-43; modern (industrial) sector, 18-19, 20, 21, 27, 124; national output, 1;

natural gas, 33, 65, 66, 67, 68, 85; natural resources, 2, 15, 59; Natural Resources, Ministry of, 77; oil, 2, 4, 5-9, 12, 15, 18-20, 21, 24, 26, 27, 28, 33, 34-35, 40, 58, 59, 60-66, 67, 68; oil revenues [areas for utilization, 83; for discretionary spending, 86-87; and domestic consumption, 84-86; foreign aid, 87; and inflation, 92-94, 95, 97, 99-115, 142, 151, 155; investing of, foreign or domestic, 89-92, 154-55; money supply determined by, 100, 105, 114-15; for national security, 87-89, 99; and reserves, projections of, 63-65, 66, 70, 123, 149-51]; OPEC and, 6, 7-8, 9, 11, 61-63, 148, 149, 151; population growth, 23-24, 38; press coverage, 2, 7; price control, 108-09, 110, 111-14; private sector, 4, 6, 17-18, 20, 21, 24, 32, 33, 104, 108, 111, 125, 130; regional development policy, 129-30; Roads, Ministry of, 129; Second Seven-Year Plan, 20; Seventh Plan (1983-87), 38, 51, 62; Shah, 7, 8, 15, 17, 32-33, 44, 73-74, 86, 87, 89, 147-48; Sixth Plan (1978-82), 33, 44, 62, 77; steel industry, 32-33, 58, 157, 158; Third Plan (1963-67), 20-21; transportation, 21, 30-31, 32, 33, 58, 115, 155; wages, 45-46, 158; wealth, uneven distribution of, 12; welfare system, 51-52, 129 [Social Security Organization, 51]; White Revolution, 15, 17, 123
Iran America, 79
Iran California, 79
Iran International, 79
Iran Shellcott, 79

Iranian Oil Participants (the Consortium), 61, 63, 65; (see also, Western Consortium)
Iraq, 3, 7, 9, 11, 12, 21, 41-42, 50, 60, 64, 89, 118-25, 142, 143; and Arab socialism, 118-19; Ba'ath Party, 119; cash shortage in, 122; contrasts with Iran, 123-25; diversified economy, desire for, 122, 142; economic development, factors inhibiting, 119-21; economic development, potential for, 119; economic planning, faulty, 121-22; GNP, 122; oil production and revenue less than Iran's, 123; Planning, Ministry of, 121
Iraq Petroleum Company (IPC), 119
Ircon, 64
Isfahan, 17, 33
Israel, 21

Japan, 11, 15, 60, 91, 92

Karachi, 31
Karaj, 43
Kerman, 33
Khorramshahr, 30
Khuzestan, 7; commercial-farming experiments in, 78-80, 81; oil fields in, 64-65
Korea, 49
Kurdish war, 119
Kuwait, 9, 21, 60, 62, 63

Latin America, 132
Lebanon, 21
Libya, 9, 60

McDonnell Douglas, 88
Majiles (Parliament), 24
Middle East, 17, 21, 60, 63, 64, 87, 117, 125, 147
Military Industries Organization, 88

Mitsui, 79
Mobil, 64
multinational companies, 1

National Iranian Oil Company (NIOC), 4, 64, 65
National Iranian Steel Industries Company (NISCO), 33
natural gas, 33, 65, 66, 67, 68 85; liquefaction of, in Algeria, 125; steel mills using, 33
New York State, 90
New Zealand, 92
Nigeria, 11, 60, 71
NISCO (see, National Iranian Steel Industries Company)
NISIC (see, State National Iranian Steel Industries Company)
North Rumaila oil field, 123

oil, 4, 5-13; Doha, meeting at, 6; employment in industry, 40; exporting nations, groupings of, 9-11; Iraqi concentration on, 122; Kuwait agreement, 4; role of, in Iranian development, 18-20; skilled manpower need in industry, 41; sociological peculiarities of countries producing, 37-38; Tehran agreement, 4, 148; trade and production patterns in, 60; (see also, OPEC)
Oil Daily, 63
Oman, 89
OPEC, 6, 7, 9, 11, 60, 71, 132, 148, 149, 151; Doha, meeting at, 6; members of, 60; price increases by, 60-61, 62; price reductions by, 62-63; (see also, oil)
Organization of Petroleum Exporting Countries (see, OPEC)
Pakistan, 31, 87, 89
Parliament (see, Majiles)

INDEX

Persepolis, 87
Persian Gulf, 30, 31, 89
Petroleum (see, oil)
Plan Organization, 20, 21, 61, 149, 155

Qatar, 9
Quito, 137

Rastakhiz (Resurgence) Party, 108
real bills doctrine, 104-05
"Reality Beneath the Dogma, The," 143
recession, world, 1
Reza Shah, 32-33, 73
Royal Dutch Shell, 79

Safiabad, experimental agricultural station at, 79
Sahara Desert, 127
Saudi Arabia, 4, 6, 9, 11-12, 60, 62, 63, 64, 85, 89
SDRs, 5
Setif, 128
Sheli, 129
Shell (Oil Co.), 64
Sistin-Baluchestan, 129
Skikda, 128
Soviet Union, 33, 88, 89
Standard Oil of California, 64
State National Iranian Steel Industries Company (NISIC), 33

Tabriz, 17
Taiwan, 49
Tehran, 4, 12, 17, 30, 43, 45, 128, 129, 130
Tehran University, Institute for Social Studies and Research, 40

Texaco, 64
Thum Islands, 89
tous-azimuts theory, 88
Transworld, 79
Turkey, 21, 31

United Arab Emirates, 6, 9, 60
United States, 11, 33, 60, 88, 90, 92, 98, 104, 133

Venezuela, 3, 7, 9, 11, 12, 50, 60, 92, 118, 130-36, 137, 140, 141, 142; Agricultural and Livestock Bank, 131-32; Agricultural Development Bank, 132; Agricultural Fund, 131; antiinflation measures, 133-36; GDP, 136; GNP, 135; Income Tax Law, 132; Industrial Bank, 132; Industrial Development Fund, 131, 132; Organic Act of the National Treasury, 131; overseas investments, 130, 131, 132, 133, 136, 142; using increased oil revenues, 130-33; Venezuelan Development Corporation, 132; Venezuelan Investment Fund (VIF), 131, 132-33, 136, 139, 140, 154, 155
VIF (see, Venezuela: Venezuelan Investment Fund)
Volga-Don Canal, 31

West Germany, 98, 158
Western Consortium, 4, 64, 65
Western Europe, 11, 32, 60, 66, 90, 91
World Bank, 4, 6, 87, 132
World War II, 32, 33, 130

Zaboos, Sultan, 89

ABOUT THE AUTHOR

ROBERT E. LOONEY is an assistant professor of economics at the University of California at Santa Clara. He has been a faculty member of the University of California at Davis, development economist at the Stanford Research Institute, and senior economist for Louis Berger International. He has served as an economic adviser to the governments of Iran, Panama, and Mexico.

Dr. Looney has published numerous articles in professional journals and is the author of The Economic Development of Iran: A Recent Survey with Projections to 1981 (Praeger 1973); Income Distribution Policies and Economic Growth in Semiindustrialized Countries: A Comparative Study of Iran, Mexico, Brazil, and South Korea (Praeger 1975); and The Economic Development of Panama: The Impact of World Inflation on an Open Economy (Praeger 1976).

Dr. Looney earned his B.S. and Ph.D. degrees from the University of California at Davis.

RELATED TITLES
Published by
Praeger Special Studies

THE AGRICULTURAL DEVELOPMENT OF IRAN
      Oddvar Aresvik

CAPITAL INVESTMENT IN THE MIDDLE EAST:
The Use of Surplus Funds for Regional Development
      Ragaei El Mallakh,
      Mihssen Kadhim, Barry Poulson
      with assistance from
      Fred R. Glahe, Carl McGuire

*DEVELOPMENT WITHOUT DEPENDENCE
      Pierre Uri
      foreword by William P. Bundy

THE ECONOMIC DEVELOPMENT OF PANAMA:
The Impact of World Inflation on an Open Economy
      Robert E. Looney

THE KUWAIT FUND AND THE POLITICAL
ECONOMY OF ARAB REGIONAL DEVELOPMENT
      Soliman Demir

MIDDLE EAST ECONOMIES IN THE 1970s:
A Comparative Approach
      Hossein Askari
      John Thomas Cummings

OIL AND REGIONAL DEVELOPMENT: Examples
from Algeria and Tunisia
      Konrad Schliephake
      translated by Merrill D. Lyew

THE SAUDI ARABIAN ECONOMY
      Ramon Knauerhase

*Also available as a PSS Student Edition.